ADVANCE PRAISE

"Reading *Imagine a Door* is like taking a course in book publishing with field trips into the writing process and a writing life itself. Author Laura Stanfill is our warm and generous teacher and guide who answers our questions with knowledgeable insight, real-life examples, and sincere caring about the art and the artist. She does more than provide information—so much great information—but shares her own experience and that of writers she's worked with over her years as a student of writing, acclaimed novelist, and successful publisher of a small press. Start here, and keep going."

—Judy Reeves, author of *A Writer's Book of Days*

"Laura Stanfill does what the best, most inspirational publishers do: she identifies gaps on the shelf and fills them with things that are inspiring and make so much sense that they are obvious in hindsight. Stanfill holds tremendous wisdom and empathy, holding our hands and delivering each author to locate a door that nobody ever noticed. She helps everyone to feel seen."

—Joe Biel, author of *A People's Guide to Publishing*

"*Imagine a Door* is the book I needed when I first embarked on my publishing path as a writer. Part mental health book, part publishing industry primer, *Imagine a Door* offers readers a gentle method for setting realistic and sustainable goals for their writing practice and publishing endeavors. In these pages, Stanfill re-establishes the writer and their unique wants, needs, and aspirations as the center of the publishing journey. *Imagine a Door* is a toolkit, a lifeline, for writers treading water in the vast ocean of the publishing industry landscape."

—Christina Vega, publisher at Blue Cactus Press
and author of *Decay*, *Vega*, and *Maps*

PRAISE FOR *SINGING LESSONS FOR THE STYLISH CANARY*

"Lyrical."

—*Shelf Awareness*

"Delicately gilded writing."

—*Publishers Weekly*

"Enchanting."

—*The Oregonian*

"A charming debut."

—*Buzzfeed*

"Enrapturing."

—*Foreword Reviews*

"Reads like a fairytale."

—*Oenobooks*

"Utterly beguiling."

—*Cleaver Magazine*

"Highly recommended."

—*Independent Book Review*

"A fine and fun listen."

—*Audiofile*

"Captivating and memorable."

—*Small Press Picks*

"Resplendent and transcendent."
—Gigi Little, bookseller, Powell's Books

"Un veritable plaisir."
—James Crossley, bookseller, Leviathan Books

IMAGINE A DOOR

IMAGINE A DOOR

A writer's guide to unlocking your story, choosing a publishing path, and honoring the creative journey

LAURA STANFILL

FOREST AVENUE PRESS
Portland, Oregon

Project funded with a $5000 grant from the Regional Arts and Culture Council

Library of Congress Cataloging-in-Publication Data is on file with the publisher.

Distributed by Publishers Group West
Printed in the US

Forest Avenue Press LLC
P.O. Box 80134
Portland, OR 97280
forestavenuepress.com

1 2 3 4 5 6 7 8 9

For Liz Prato

CONTENTS

QUERYING / 369

FOREWORD

Beth Kephart

Imagine a door, Laura Stanfill says. Close your eyes, she suggests. And dream.

A door into a world of your own making. Through the light that holds the shadows of the past. Toward a moment in glimmering future time when something you have imagined, something you have made, something you have with perseverance polished and finessed, feels whole and right in your heart and hands.

Because isn't that what writers *do*?

Isn't that who we *are*?

Imaginers. And dreamers.

I don't know when I first allowed myself to imagine a life built with words. The nine-year-old who watercolored her pages before she scribbled her stories all across them (clumsy words riding waves of buckled fibers) was not thinking: *Writer*.

The high school version of me—mistress of purple prose, sister of a quite fine limerick maker—would never have dared to surface such a thought. *Writer?* Are you kidding?

The college freshwoman who, red faced, stuffed her scraps and stacks of new poetry beneath her bed in a major hurry when she discovered them to be the source of another's guffaw was most assuredly not thinking *Writer.* She was thinking, *Better get yourself a law degree. Better get that law degree quick.*

I didn't run in literary circles. I had no literary friends. The only undergraduate English class I ever took left me feeling shamed, naïve, and broken. All I ever knew was that I really did like words. I liked them a lot. I was happy among them—stringing them along, stacking them tall, leaning my weight up against them.

Words didn't just let me be me. They discovered new possibilities in me. I sat with them. I let them.

I wonder now what my life might have been, back in those prehistoric days (oh time, how it passes, how it gallops), had I had a friend like Laura Stanfill.

Someone who knows what writing is. [It's an idea, it's a sound, it's a chase, it's a pause.]

Someone who knows how to unlock the writerly potential in others, and also in herself. [What if we begin here? What if we shift perspective? What if we make room for something else? Do we need the past tense? Can this remain in the present?]

Someone who won't be fooled—by a contract, by a distribution plan, by social media buzz, by a review (or by lack of reviews), by a ghosting or an effusing or a promise made, then broken, then remade. (But a remade promise is never quite the same.)

Someone who understands that sometimes we need poetry and sometimes we need spreadsheets and at precisely no time should we allow ourselves to be defined as simply one thing (the dream) or the other (the mathematical facts).

Someone who makes both time and space for many ones—the time and space that gives dimension to the dream.

Someone whose very wardrobe—images of books in the folds of her fabric, hats bespeaking character (and characters) on her head—speaks volumes upon volumes, in every hue under the sun.

I wish I'd known Laura, all those years, back then. But you don't have to do that wishing, because here in the pages to come she is: funny, encouraging, honest, insightful, a little mad at publishing and a lot in love with publishing, and standing up, always and profoundly, for all that she believes.

Laura's book unfurls with a poem. It then shakes out a toothy key. It cracks open one lock after another, making way and making room so that you might imagine yourself through your very own pleasingly idiosyncratic door.

Your door might be a garden gate.

Your door might be a portal.

Your door might be bright red or lavender-pink, built of twined twigs or polished copper, way up on the eighteenth floor of a skyscraper or down among the happy moles in the earth.

Whatever and wherever your door is, you no longer have to open it alone. Laura is here with her kindness and wisdom.

Laura has a thousand keys. What you hear is the sound of them clicking.

IMAGINE A DOOR

YOU TURN THE HANDLE AND find yourself in a—

Kitchen
Courtyard
Underground cave
Jungle
Corporate boardroom
Bedroom
Cockpit
Dark alley
School

You hear—

A car alarm
Branches moving in the wind
Water droplets
An unfamiliar bird call

A droning,
monotone
presentation

Snoring
Steady, high-pitched beeps
Nothing
A yelling adult

You feel—

Worried; your car, *again*?
Soothed
Excited—is there a hidden hot spring?
Delighted and curious
Impatient
Annoyed
Confused—hello?
Hesitation
A thrill of disobedience

You decide—

That none of these scenarios are financially viable.

That none of these directions are going to earn you an agent or a six-figure publishing deal or even a small-advance agreement with a reputable small press.

That you, obviously, in the ecstatically creative throes of imagining a door, have conjured exactly *nothing* of value, because wherever your story leads, it's not going to get you enough social media followers to prove you have an audience to an agent who cares about metrics.

Besides, you've probably chosen the wrong protagonist.

You still haven't figured out how to make dialogue seem realistic without being boring.

You have dinner to conjure.

The imagined door slams shut. The story pieces fall and shatter.

You walk away, the paragraph dangling midsentence, the chapter unfinished.

AT SOME POINT WRITERS WHO dream of book deals shift away from the sheer pleasure of writing and wondering—of capturing moments or imagining scenes or tinkering with language—toward commodification. Delight and playfulness cede their place to worry.

Is this good enough to get me an agent or a book deal?

Are there books out there like mine? (Is mine different *enough*? Or is it too different for anyone to care?)

Do I have enough followers?

Does my story matter to anyone but me?

What if I've gone far over/under the expected word count for my genre?

How do I decide what to do with the manuscript?

What's better?

What's best?

IN A RESULTS-DRIVEN, CAPITALIST SOCIETY, writing has become inextricably linked with selling.

Over and over, writers working on book-length manuscripts maroon ourselves on islands of discontent and doubt. Through the first draft and second and third. Through the pitch process. Through critique sessions that don't go deep enough or ones that go too deep without the balance of praise to temper the bitterness. Through silence from agents who are too busy to say no and contest entries that say IN PROGRESS for more than a year. Through all the retreats and classes and conferences—and all the dollars spent, all the notes taken—that *still* don't yield a book deal.

Where is the guidebook for allowing the process to unfold despite a lack of quantifiable results? Why can't we harness confidence in our own ability to find our way through the mess instead of pinning hopes on a donkey that isn't even turned our direction?

Whatever happened to giving ourselves the time and space to contemplate?

To thinking quietly?

To being present with ourselves not because it's part of creating a brand or looking good online but because we enjoy the process of writing.

I love working with editors and peer reviewers. They see so much I don't. But sometimes I need to remind myself that revisions also come from within—from acknowledging there's something more to find. Something that's not quite on the page yet. We find solace and surprises and beauty when we let our minds work on a story problem.

It's listening to ourselves that disappears when we tune in to everyone else's voices. And that's tough for us creative types, especially those of us who are neurodivergent. We fill all our free time with noise these days—scrolling on our phones, responding to beeps and vibrations, clicking on the next dozen newsletters that flood our inbox. We are both content producers and content receivers—interacting at fast speeds or closing our browser and feeling left behind when we log back on, even if it has only been a few hours. The idea of the writer in the cabin in the woods, alone with capital-*I* Ideas, is hopelessly quaint. It has been replaced by desperation scrolling for proof that others are doing better than you.

Even many of the lucky ones—those who find enthusiastic publishers for their book-length manuscripts—struggle with misaligned expectations and confusion, not to mention the emotional toll of shouting about their work in the hope of more sales. In the hope that people still care (even though you're on your third month of sharing pictures of your book on shelves, on ironed tablecloths, on a beach in paradise). You spent, perhaps, three years on this book. Or a decade. Or two decades. And already you feel sick of yourself, but you're too busy to find a quiet mind space to write new work and besides, isn't this what authors do? Lean into the social media current? Make themselves look successful while bracing to cry over the next royalty report?

GO AHEAD AND CONJURE THAT door again. Is it locked? Where's the key? What might be on the other side? What if there's a lion? A ghost? A lost toddler? A hospital bed in the middle of an otherwise ordinary living room?

How does it feel to let the sparks catch?

To let yourself wonder?

This part—the investigation of story—is the only piece of publishing that we *can* control.

You can take a simple scenario someplace fresh. Your lived experience, personality, scars and triumphs, imagination, and particular way of using words will lead to a new story. And only you can decide to spend time in this alternate world of your own creation instead of immersing yourself in someone else's TV show or book, or your social media feed.

That's the magic of writing. We get to be alone with ourselves. We can write to understand our paths, to know others, to exorcise old hurts and hauntings, and for the sheer joy of spending time with our stories, our hopes and worries, ourselves.

PUBLISHING IS A BUSINESS. WITH contracts and advances (sometimes) and consumers and profit and loss statements and, if you earn a contract with a distributed press, sales reps who might talk booksellers into carrying your book.

To get there, to the commercial side of things (which can be soul crushing), first you have to learn to protect the magic. To create safe boundaries within which your brain can play.

You have to imagine the door.

ABOUT THIS BOOK

I BECAME A PUBLISHER IN 2012 so I could learn how the industry works and share the information with writers on the outside. If I were on a hero's quest, this book would be my journey home, carrying what I've learned.

This—*gestures wildly at the following chapters*—is for you.

As a former journalist, I chose to do all my own reporting for *Imagine a Door* instead of relying on existing sources. These interviews were conducted by me, most of them between 2016 and 2023, by phone, in person, or via email. They have not appeared in print or online with the following exceptions: I interviewed Selden Edwards for my Seven Questions blog series in 2012. Rene Denfeld's quote on rejection and Tina Connolly's book promotion dream were first shared on social media; they graciously agreed to let me include their words here. Ari Honarvar's interview was conducted for my essay "Publishing a Book Is Hard on Your Mental Health," which appeared in *Catapult* in April 2022.

I'm grateful to the many experts who shared their perspectives for this project. I appreciate their time and their trust. Mistakes and omissions are my own.

The quotes I started collecting in 2016 are among the jewels in this finished book; they show how the industry has remained constant in some ways and changed in others. They also ground me as the writer, reminding me that I didn't dash off this project. I spent those in-between years publishing and being published, actively pushing against my own negative self-talk. Squeezing my doubts into smaller boxes. They're still there—dully knocking around in my skull—but I've been able to replace some of them with kinder words.

You write books, I remind myself. *And you have something to say.*

I spend a lot of my time on the other side of the door these days—responding to submissions, pitching reviewers, and all the other industry tunnels and mountains that most writers don't get to access directly.

Through my role in the literary community, I have held space for countless stories of author jealousy, folded publishers, messed-up communication, lost agents, and devastating career setbacks. As a book publisher, I have brought more than twenty novels, short story collections, and memoirs into being. And as a (finally!) published novelist, my debut now rests in readers' hands without me standing over them whispering, *Be kind. That's fifteen years of my life.* I've also let go of several novels that I believed in, which felt at the time like giving up on myself.

Starting in high school, already sure of my career path, I devoured books on craft and the writing life, wanting to unlock the door for myself. None of them prepared me for the emotional truth of publishing. They made it seem easy.

Do this, those books said, *and you will get published.*

Do this, I thought, *and you will be a published novelist by age twenty-five.*

Or thirty-five.

Or forty-five.

I worked hard on my craft, attending conferences, reading storms of stories and how-to articles, subscribing to *Poets & Writers,* and each of those anticipated milestones rolled by.

Forty-six turned out to be my lucky number—still decades earlier than some.

I know how it feels from both sides of the desk. Not from an add-water-and-succeed point of view but through all those decades of quiet slogging. Of saying no to invitations because I wanted to work through a scene. Of waiting to be discovered. Of self-doubt when I submitted a manuscript—my best work yet!—and heard crickets.

From this place, in the middle of my publishing journey, I hold out these pages to you. I hope they recalibrate your sense of success and help you feel less lonely.

BEGIN

CHOOSE YOUR WORD

IF YOU'RE READING THIS PAGE, you might already consider yourself a writer, author, poet, novelist, essayist, playwright, storyteller, or journalist.

Or, when a well-meaning person asks, "Are you an author?" you might shake your head no. Or, conversely, when a friend asks what you're up to, you panic about how to answer. Do you mention your new space-set novella? Your daily poetry practice? Even if you love the person, it's hard to make such declarations if you don't know what to call yourself.

Here's my thinking: if you're doing the work practicing the craft, even (*especially*!) if it's not on a regular schedule or with a confirmed publication plan, it counts. However you do it—longhand in a spiral notebook, keys pounded on a laptop or typewriter, a few lines of shorthand dashed off on a napkin—it's all writing. Which means you get to pick a word if you want one.

You've earned it. I promise.

Publication is one possible result of doing the work of writing. Perhaps it's the point, for some of us, but it's not the only reason to write. The more you can remind yourself of this in the drafting stages, the better shored up your ego will be when it comes time for submission.

Besides, there are other ways to share your creative output. You can participate in open mics or share your pages with a writing group. You can write essay-like social media posts. You can recite a story over dinner. You can make your work slide deck brilliant or ace a class assignment that only the teacher will see.

Sometimes, when we rush full tilt with all our hopes toward the promise of publication, we forget about all those other reasons for writing and all those ways of sharing our stories. We begin to measure ourselves by acceptance or rejection.

Yes or *no*.

Wanted or *unwanted*.

Good or *bad*.

Pretty harsh, isn't it?

We writers, when we don't have creative projects taking up our brain space, can put our imaginations toward less productive tasks—negative self-talk, worrying about things we can't control, getting stuck in a self-doubt spin, and otherwise making ourselves miserable.

And sometimes, when we do get published, instead of celebrating the moment we get obsessed with counting likes and shares and sales, wondering—worrying—if we've fallen short. If others are doing better. If the person who published us likes the number of views, hits, or purchases that result from choosing us over someone else's work.

I say *us* and *we* because I spent the first few decades of my writing life not getting published and imagining all kinds of reasons for why I wasn't good enough. When really I was doing the work obsessively, learning a ton about myself in the process and sharpening my craft. Those are all wins I ignored, fixating instead on the end result: rejections.

I took each no, each time, as being about the quality of my work. I believed the gatekeepers could tell I was talentless, a fraud, a *hack*. No way they would ever open their doors to me! I shelved those first novels, but I kept writing anyway. It didn't occur to me until I became a publisher that the mainstream New York publishers only want certain types of work, books that fit into narrow categories or appeal to specific demographics. Or that those rejections had nothing to do with my ability. They were simply measuring the distance between the stories I love telling and what they thought they could sell.

Calling yourself a *writer* (or an *author* or a *poet*) helps realign the process to focus on the drafting. The creating. The art of it.

You don't have to finish—and you definitely don't have to publish—for your efforts to count.

ARI HONARVAR, AN IMMIGRATION ACTIVIST and the author of *A Girl Called Rumi,* actively engages with success metrics by resisting them. She told me she doesn't judge her creative work by the number of copies sold. "Receiving all the praise and notes from readers is absolutely beautiful and life-art-affirming," she told me. "People's response to my work with refugees and individuals is also incredible. But it occurs to me that I don't measure myself with the accolades, admiration, and reader response either. My self-worth corresponds to whether I'm doing right by my relationships, with myself, others, nature, and the unknown—am I a worthy lover of life? I'm the only one who can answer this and if I'm not holding back love and effort as I proceed in life, the answer is a resounding yes."

Are you a worthy lover of life? Ari asks.

We can pose this question to ourselves as often as we need to.

I still love to write, we might tell ourselves when a rejection comes in.

I love this book I wrote, we might add when an awards list comes out and our title isn't on it.

My writer friend deserves this success, we must insist, when jealousy creeps in.

I'VE SEEN *AUTHOR* DEFINED AS someone who has a signed book contract, someone who makes money from writing, and/or someone who has been published. *Writers,* these guides suggest, are the rest of us. Depending on the person trying to establish the hierarchy, *how published* you are might matter too. Like, a full-length book would count: congrats, you're an author! But an essay in a small-circulation journal might not.

But I say all of it counts. If you're writing, that's as legitimate a practice as anyone else's. Hierarchical definitions pit us against each other. They make some of us doing the work of writing feel smaller or lesser. They also are intended to shore up outdated societal structures—ones that have historically promoted racist and ableist thinking.

The distance between a person working on the second draft of a novel and a person with three published essay collections isn't wide. What separates them (us) is time spent writing, understanding of the industry, and luck. Especially if you're stuck in the middle—working on a project you believe in but far from having a finished draft. Being in that middle-ness, inhabiting that liminal space of creation, definitely means you've earned a word.

I happen to love being called a writer because the word matches the activity; it's connected to the *act* of making. The pleasure of sitting with my characters. It's not a word that tilts toward publication, which comes with its own special terrors. The only time I use *author* to refer to myself is when I need to mention a specific work in a bio. *Author,* to me, feels like putting on a hat, preparing to step onstage. *Writer* is me at my desk, puzzling. But you can use whatever you'd like.

Or maybe you don't want a word.

You might say, *I like to write,* and that's enough. Just try not to let your anxiety cause you to question others' choices. If you hear a friend calling herself an author, and you want to quibble because she only had one essay published in a small journal six years ago, ask yourself why it matters to you. It really shouldn't.

It's her choice.

What you call yourself is *yours*.

When Nonwriters Ask Questions

You see a former neighbor at the store and mention you're writing a book.

You're at your high school reunion and the former football captain pops the question: What are you up to these days? You smile and use your writer-identity word. *I'm a(n)* ___________________.

You are standing in the rain with another parent at school pickup and you mention that you had a good writing day.

It feels good—strong!—to claim your word. To own your identity based on what you're spending time and energy on. Until . . .

What have you written? says the neighbor.

Anything I might have read? says the friend you bump into at the grocery store.

Where can I buy your book? says the coworker.

Uh . . . might be your first thought.

And your second.

How come curiosity can seem intentionally mean? might be your third thought.

People who aren't writers don't know how wide a gulf there is between doing the work and getting a piece published. They're completely different activities: writing and submitting. And submitting doesn't necessarily lead to acceptance.

I don't have anything published yet tends to shut down the conversation. People turn away with a knowing nod, like, *Oh. You aren't a real writer.* Or at least it's easy to interpret their nods like that when you're new to telling people.

Then again, over the years when I've shared that I was five or ten years into writing a novel, people made jokes about me being slow. Which didn't feel good either.

So what can you say? You don't have to educate people about the literary world or try to explain that it takes a lot of writing to get a project ready for submission, and you're not at that stage yet. But you can if you want—and if you are real friends with the person asking, it might be worth the trouble of explaining. That way, next time you see them, they can ask a more specific question that's easier to answer.

I've also found steering the conversation toward process has helped limit the awkwardness and keep me feeling good about my work.

What have you written? could lead to what you're working on right now. It's close enough to *What are you writing?* to gently adjust the questioner's focus.

Anything I might have read? could lead to sharing that you've just submitted a piece to a famous magazine or journal and you're waiting to hear back. Or that you're in the process of working on a piece for submission. If you have a piece published, that's great! Share the name of that magazine or journal and either that'll sate the person's curiosity or if they genuinely care, they might even look up your work.

Where can I buy your book? is a little trickier. You can respond with your hopes, like *Someday, at the local bookstore.* Or that you plan to meet some agents at a conference next summer. Or if you have any pieces in journals, mention one of those. Or you can be totally PR-proactive and say, *If you sign up for my newsletter or follow me on social media, you'll be the first to know when I get a book deal!*

The key to surviving these awkward asks, which are often well intentioned, is to not feel bad about yourself if your writing path doesn't match up with the question being asked. People *love* to know writers; often that's where their curiosity comes from. They probably aren't plotting to make you feel bad.

If you plan answers ahead of time, you can gently divert the conversation to process or your hopes for your work.

PRACTICE MAKES PROGRESS

THINKING ABOUT A NEW PROJECT, especially a book-length one, can be thrilling and terrifying. There are so many unknowns. But there's also endless possibility.

You can do this!

It's your time!

But then you *do* start. You jot down a phrase or an idea. And it looks . . . small.

(*Can* you do this?)

Your first paragraph looks . . . far from perfect.

Very far from publishable.

And you have so many more words to go before you have a full draft to revise!

It will take so much more time, talent, energy, and self-belief to spin a manuscript from this fragment.

And maybe—now that you're looking again at these first sentences—this first fragment doesn't work. Maybe it's all so much straw that will never, ever spin into gold.

BOOMING VOICE:
Of course it's a false start!
Who just sits down and
has brilliance pouring out?

YOU, WHISPERING: *The writers portrayed in movies. The best-selling series writers. The authors who give interviews about how anyone can write a book if they sit down and do it.*

BOOMING VOICE:
Maybe it's easy for the real writers,
and you're just a fraud!
FRAUD! FRAUD!

Suddenly your wish to write feels dimmed.
(FRAUD!)

You have opened yourself to the risk of creating something fresh and new and *yours* and found a tunnel of worries instead. Maybe you shouldn't even be pondering something creative when you are out of kale and hand soap, and you really ought to sit down and pay bills, and what about moving your laundry to the dryer because you can't forget about it (again)? Not to mention you need a good night's sleep to function at work tomorrow.

Laundry will move your life forward. It will make a difference to future you. Writing will just use up time, and you'll still have that pile of dirty clothes to contend with when you stop.

Does this sound familiar? The quotidian battle between the concrete and the ephemeral? We all have lists of to-dos, personal and professional, and unless you make it a priority, writing can seem less urgent. Even inessential. But it's such a powerful tool to put words on the page. To express yourself. There's something so refreshing about sitting still and letting your brain work. I don't meditate, and my yoga practice is spotty, but I think we can make a case for writing as a mindfulness practice. Afterward, when I emerge from a session of writing or editing, I feel like I've traveled someplace. I suddenly notice the light pooling on the living room floor. The smell of coffee. The reassuring, floofy bulk of my dog pressing against my hip. I always feel better after writing, unless the writing leads to worrying about publishing, and then I feel worse.

If you can't set your task lists aside, put writing on one of them. Cross it out when you're done. *Go you!* Or set a timer. Do a writing sprint for ten minutes.

WRITING SPRINT: Set the timer, get your keyboard or your pen ready, and 3-2-1, GO! Write without stopping. The exercise isn't meant to create perfect work; it's a way to explore characters or scenes.

Then you can carry on with the rest of your day. Or choose a handful of tasks to complete *before* you write. Enough to make you feel like you've gotten something done but not so much that you're unable to focus on writing.

Dreaming of a bookstore reading? You won't get there if you don't start here, if you don't make time for writing or thinking about your story. The work you want to do, the work you someday want to put into the world, it happens here and now. Even if it's only a few spare minutes. If you're waiting in the car for your kid's soccer practice to end and you start scribbling on the back of a receipt, *here* might not be ideal and *now* lasts until cleats are thrown into the backseat, but it's something.

You can feel good now for writing, for fitting it in.

You can write more later.

You can revise later too.

There's time for all that.

All you have to do now is begin. Practice. Play. Create. Erase. Play some more.

I STARTED LEARNING THE SPORT of roller derby in my midforties, right around the same time I began self-identifying as disabled. I had no business going fast on wheels. But skating made me so happy, and I became determined to get stronger.

Roller derby and writing have repetition in common. You don't gear up and get on the track, learn a skill, and then walk off the track, never to skate again. You keep gearing up. You keep getting better, faster, and more confident.

Sports teams call this *practice*. But when we sit down to write, as individuals with heads full of story, sometimes we forget that it takes a lot of commitment and repetition to get good at a skill. A lot of the time we spend thinking about our stories is practice.

Every once in a while, if you're in the zone or the grooviest groove, words flow out in final form. More typically, there's a lot of throat clearing, subject investigation, and messy draft material. Revision is where we clean up, adjust our choices, and move swaths of text around. But you can't get to that point if you don't show up to practice.

One of my roller derby coaches said once you learn how to do a good plow stop, you'll never stop working on plow stops. It's a skill that takes practice.

We learn new techniques all the time when we write and revise. It's all practice. Always. Those skills might be new to us or iterations of the same skills we've been practicing for years. They might be experiments that fail or exist only to push back on a certain teaching that feels constricting.

We are all still understanding the nuances of point of view.

We are all chipping away at dialogue, playing with how to say a lot in a few words.

We are all figuring out settings and the beats of a scene.

Every piece of writing teaches us about ourselves.

There's no such thing as practicing art until it's perfect. You can work on it until the piece goes into the world, and then you can't tinker with it anymore. You have to let go and dig in to something new.

CHRIS MCDONALD, THE EXECUTIVE DIRECTOR of the nonprofit Write Around Portland, helps writers, well, write. To get their stories out. He told me:

> We have to redefine success when it comes to writing. So many writers become writers because they've encountered mind-bending, life-altering books. They want to do that, too, and they believe that the only route to success is by getting the most eyes on their work. But in most other art forms (including modern poetry), the artist, too, gets to benefit from the art form. The artist is (somewhat) freed from the notion that millions of others must understand what they're trying to say. The painter, potter, or dancer gets to put something out in the world and enjoy it not for its revenue but for the community it fosters and the ideas it adds to a (sometimes small, sometimes quite small) cultural conversation.

Writing, Chris believes, should be like that too. "It can glow brightly in a dark corner, and its light shines with the same intensity regardless of the number of eyes looking at it. The question is—can we as writers divorce ourselves from notions of fame? Why do we feel that writing is only good when it can be sold? Are you limited, squished, squeezed by notions of 'readability' or 'relatability'? How many bold, gorgeous, weird, memorable, frustrating, heartbreaking works are sitting inside writers' heads because they're not 'marketable'?"

Our heart projects, the ones that we're drawn to again and again, often feel terribly risky. With these stories, we're writing without a map, without an *x*-marks-the-spot destination. Nobody has said what we want to say exactly in the way we envision saying it. The process of unlocking these sentences, of trying new forms and formats, can be the glow that Chris talks about. Why not set aside thoughts of publishing and recognize there's a lot of power there, in the act of writing? In closing the gap between our hoped-for outcome (a manuscript) and what exists on the laptop screen: one chapter, perhaps, or eight chapters. An imperfect work in progress.

We use hours and weeks and days we could be dedicating to other pursuits in search of this intangible finish line, knowing that once we reach it, we will have to start again from the beginning to revise. This takes time but it also takes courage. And if you tap into courage by imagining what will happen after you've done the work, maybe that will help your motivation, but it might also set you up for disappointment. Why not instead engage in the process for what it is?

Chris said:

> Let's ease that pressure of the big, heavy dream of being a "best-selling author," because the truth is that that group becomes narrower and narrower every year and because the big publishers aren't going to take a risk on something different (and we desperately need different right now and always) and because even if you achieved that heavy dream, it wouldn't actually solve all of your problems . . . no matter what your mom says.

What if you spent your whole life writing amazing work and only a few people got to read it? Was that life worth it? Unfortunately, your dreams of being a respected Author with a capital *A* might never come to fruition, no matter how hard you work or how good your work is. But fortunately, you can live an amazing writing life right now and forever, and success gets to look how you want it to look, and you get to laugh and chat with your writer friends about writerly things in tucked-away corners without ever having to contort yourself and your writing into something they're not. Doesn't that sound better?

CALLING WRITING SESSIONS *PRACTICE* HELPS me stir up story bits instead of doubts. It works like giving your writer identity a name, only backward, as *practice* takes the pressure off. It unidentifies the work by decoupling it from its potential future identity (as a novel, as a poem). There's no plan or door in sight when you *practice*. You can follow the weird and wondrous path your brain wants to take. You can lean into the spark. You can surprise yourself.

Writing lets you access hidden spaces, memories you've locked away, sensory experiences and connections that linger. So don't waste your imagination on worrying about the future of your words. Instead, put your brain in wondering gear and harness that energy in your work. Write until you're hungry. Until your chronic pain flares. Until a child calls for you. Until your timer beeps. Until you lift your head from the page, think, *Now what?* and rejoin the real world.

Let the process of writing be its own journey. For the sake of art. For the joy of play. For the catharsis of releasing trauma or setting down a memory that feels too heavy to keep carrying alone.

TIME MANAGEMENT

MANY HOW-TO ARTICLES ABOUT CREATING a successful writing practice suggest carving out a specific block of time to write every day. *If you don't sit at your desk at the same time every day,* this advice warns (wagging its finger), *you won't ever be a real author.*

But regular writing hours can be impossible for people who work long hours, for those of us who are primary caregivers of children and/or aging parents, and writers with disabilities. Among others.

Making routine time for art elevates the privileged and gnaws away at the rest of us, leaving room for imposter syndrome and self-doubt. Many of us cannot afford to have a regular block of quiet, uninterrupted hours, let alone when our brains are at their most functional and creative. We need to save our best hours for life tasks and those that for sure will earn us money. (Creative writing, unless you've sold your nonfiction proposal for a sizable advance or have a multibook contract, is usually a *write now, maybe you'll earn money later* arrangement.)

Even the most organized writer, who has the executive function skills and the permission of time to create a routine, may not be able to keep that constancy in times of grief or emergency.

I have limited hours where my body feels good and my brain is fogless; autoimmune symptoms are unpredictable. Sometimes I can summon words; other times I need to rest. Sometimes my brain is clear, and I want to write, but my fingers are swollen and it hurts to type. If routines are your jam and they keep you motivated and focused, great! But it's not essential. There are lots of barriers to access for writing and publishing, so it's okay to let go of this idea of a stringent practice schedule. However you work on your pages, whenever and wherever, pat yourself on the back. It all counts.

I asked Wendy Chin-Tanner, author of the debut novel *King of the Armadillos* (Flatiron) and two poetry collections, to share her advice on setting up a creative practice. She urges writers to think about what works best for us:

> The way I get my writing done won't necessarily be the way you or anyone else might get theirs done. But I do think that if you're going to write with any level of consistency, peace, and satisfaction, then you're going to have to work with yourself. I used to be all about fixing my "bad habits" and trying to conform to what successful writers prescribed, but the truth is, incremental change is far more achievable, not to mention sustainable, than dramatic change. All you really have to do is learn what kind of environment best suits your creative process, which, let's get real, consists mostly of finding a way to put in the hours, and then learn how to get out of your own way.

Wendy's words resonate deeply with me. When my children were young, I tried to insist on a daily schedule to ground me in the practice of art during this physically intense time of being needed by small humans. Waking up a few hours before the kids seemed like a good habit to establish; doing creative work kept me tethered to my long-term professional goals. It made me happy.

And occasionally it worked. More often, though, life intervened. My kids didn't sleep through the night. Often I jolted upright with my alarm anyway, going about the motions of my writing routine while too exhausted to create on demand. Or one of the children would wake up before my alarm, ruining my schedule. Frustration roared through my veins on those mornings. I just wanted a small slice of the day for myself! *Is that too much to ask?* I wondered.

I just wanted this one thing for myself, I remember thinking on those mornings when a child woke up and I couldn't access my writing life. Then I'd feel terrible for feeling terrible, because I love my children and it's pretty great to play cribbage together before school. Insisting on a routine that depended on other people made me feel bad about myself—as a writer, as a parent. I had the self-discipline to set the alarm, but I didn't have the flexible circumstances to get enough sleep and wake to a quiet house. My failed attempts at a writing routine became another block in my process, a hurdle to overcome instead of a doorway to story. It's hard enough to write when there are dishes waiting and a rejection, fresh and stinging, in your inbox. If you allow experts to trick you into believing that you're doing it wrong, that's just another hurdle to overcome.

Maybe this insistence on writing routines is like the expert advice in the baby books, I decided eventually. Those books scare the hell out of families whose children don't conform to the perfect, healthy, neurotypical behaviors in the text. Only some families are represented, leaving all the others out.

I replaced my attempts at a routine with carrying my story around in my head, thinking of my characters while feeding my children, driving to preschool, or walking in the park. When I had the emotional bandwidth and the mental clarity, I engaged with my writing, even if I didn't have a notebook or a laptop within arm's reach. I could still figure pieces out. Move the characters around the mental chessboard. On the days when I felt groggy from lack of sleep, or catching another kid cold, I gave myself the grace of patience. I didn't force the process. I took naps when I needed them.

To my delight, as soon as I stopped getting in my own way, I could consider what was getting in my characters' way. And slowly, very slowly, a story emerged. The more I wrote, the more mothers appeared on the page. Tending, crying, trying. Doing their best.

And that's the novel that sold.

Trick Yourself

HERE ARE A FEW OF the techniques I've used to override my shame (*your kitchen's a mess; you should be mopping!*) and fear (*who are* you *to dare to tell?*) when I sit down to write. Especially in the early stages of a project, where I'm not deep enough yet for my practice to be self-sustaining, I rely on these mental sleights of hand.

- Focus on your ultimate goal. A bookstore event? Your sibling checking your book out from the library? It doesn't have to be publishing related, but it could be. Kindle your patience with your learning process by holding this dream close. You will get there if you keep practicing.
- Take care of yourself. This can mean

preparing to write with a cozy blanket, snacks, and a warm beverage. I've sometimes let myself work on a creative project until my tea runs out and then I get back to real-world tasks. Sometimes writers promise themselves a treat after writing. That doesn't work for me; I start worrying about whether I've done *enough* to earn a break. But it works for lots of people.

- Find a friend. Schedule a full writing session or a few fifteen-minute sprints with another writer, in person or online. Once you settle in, fingers on keys or pen on paper, you'll find a rhythm and forget the other person is there.
- Set a timer. For those of us easily distracted, neurodivergent caregiver types who find their attention wandering elsewhere, short bursts can be an effective way to break into a scene or a character's mindset. Try five minutes! Then break and come back to it another time. I like using the Time Timer for sprints; it's a visual timer, showing the remaining time in color blocks, and it doesn't startle me the way a beeping alarm does.
- When you feel exhausted by your own work or lagging attention, write toward an exciting scene. I usually have something I am desperate to write, a kernel of an exciting idea that I can't wait to get to. I make myself earn those pages without jumping ahead. Pretty soon, either I get to the juicy bits or—better yet—I find myself obsessing over the material

of the moment as my focus gets sharper. What's between now and that special scene becomes exciting.

- What works for you? Make a list here:

THE SECRET

THE DIFFERENCE BETWEEN WRITERS AND people who someday *want* to write is time spent doing the work.

That's it.

Want to be a published writer? You have to write. That's the secret. Now you know.

If you've started writing, even if you have no idea what you're doing, you're already on the path.

Rosanne Parry, author of the *New York Times* best-selling middle grade novel *A Wolf Called Wander*, began writing when her daughter Colette was a week old. Two dear friends brought casseroles to her house and chatted about how busy they were. Rosanne was deep into parenting her older children and taking care of a new baby—an incredibly physical, all-hours intensity, which was much different from her friends' concept of *busy*.

"The insight afterwards was, if I'm going to wait for some not-busy time of my life to start writing, it's never going to happen," Rosanne said. "There's never going to be a not-busy time of my life. That was very inspiring. I had no idea if I could finish but I thought if I don't start, if I don't try, I'll never know."

If you don't start.

If you don't try.

You won't know what you can do.

Rosanne went on to write her first book, *Heart of a Shepherd,* which came out in 2009. Four more middle grade novels followed before her breakout hit, *A Wolf Called Wander,* was published by Greenwillow in 2019. (And that very baby grew up to work in book publishing.)

We can't anticipate what happens after we write. Putting words down on paper is the one thing we can control. Investing in our ideas takes time and a pen or pencil or laptop or typewriter. When we get ahead of ourselves and begin researching agents or presses that might be a good fit for our ideas, we're creating expectations for our work in place of doing the work.

Wendy Chin-Tanner's *King of the Armadillos* started as a nonfiction project based on her father's childhood experience of being quarantined in Carville, Louisiana, at a federal home for people with Hansen's Disease. At the time Wendy had published a few essays and *Turn* (Sibling Rivalry), her debut poetry collection. "Initially, I thought I'd try to write the book as creative nonfiction with the intention of leaning on my experience in academic writing," Wendy said, "but I quickly realized that in order to tell the story I wanted and needed to tell, I was going to have to teach myself how to write a novel."

She began with what she knew: the topic, the historical period, and the places (Carville and New York). With her father's support and help, Wendy earned access to hundreds of pages of archival records, photographs, and documents. "This abundance of material was both amazing and totally overwhelming," she said. "The weight of the responsibility I felt around doing justice to that material was also extremely heavy. For a while, I felt kind of frozen, unsure of how to navigate the process, afraid of mishandling the topic, and confused about how to enter the narrative."

I have frozen like this at multiple points in every project. Usually it's because I am at a crossroads between drafts, I am making a major adjustment to the scope of my idea, or I am working through a life change. When my developmental edits came back for this book—with warm and loving feedback and a clear road map for revising—I fell into a panicky despair. The notes on structure and content made me excited to get back to work, and I trusted my editor's insights would lead me closer to the book I had intended to write, but fear clouded my judgment for weeks.

I couldn't write because I couldn't get past the worry.

You're not up for this task.

Nobody's given you permission to write a book like this.

What if someone disagrees?

What if you make someone mad?

You are too small. You are nothing.

Of course everyone will disagree.

If they even read it.

Putting these thoughts down on the page, acknowledging the spin of panic that set in between drafts, helps me see the harshness of my self-talk. *The inner critic,* teachers often call it. But I don't have any distance from mine; it's all me, pushing myself around. Worrying that I'm going to let people down. I started interviewing agents, editors, and publishers for an early version of this book in 2016. It didn't have a voice; I hid my experiences behind the quotes from experts. After a few years of working on it, I quit. I felt like I wasn't qualified to land a book project of this magnitude.

You are too small. You are nothing.

Thinking I wasn't good enough to pull these *real* experts' thoughts together, I let everyone down. Especially myself.

I did get to work on a different manuscript, though, and that's exactly what Wendy did when she felt overwhelmed with her Carville research. She set *King of the Armadillos* aside and wrote her second poetry collection, *Anyone Will Tell You,* also published by Sibling Rivalry. That creative process helped her find her way back to the novel.

"When it was time for *King of the Armadillos,* I had to follow the path of least resistance by going back to what I already knew how to do—drafting a bunch of poems, finding the threads that connected them, and arranging them into narrative arcs that would cohere into a book," Wendy said. "So as not to spook my feral cat of a muse and coax it to stay, I started with little vignettes that I treated as prose poems without worrying about where they might belong in the story."

You don't have to know everything to begin. That's what revision is for.

"There's no harm that can come from starting to write," Laini Taylor, author of the Strange the Dreamer duology, told an audience at the Oregon Country Fair in 2024. "When you free yourself from expectation, that's when the good stuff happens."

You just need an idea.

The passion to go for it.

And the resilience to keep going.

READ WITH ABANDON

THROUGH MY TWENTIES AND THIRTIES, I approached reading like a homework assignment. I used critical thinking skills to engage with texts, just like my high school teachers and college professors taught me. Reading with intent exercised my writer muscles and helped me feel more professional when I sat down to write. I considered adjectives to use in my reviews while midchapter. I thought a lot about character development, pacing, and backstory. And I asked myself craft questions:

How does varying sentence length impact the reader?

Where do dialogue descriptors help me keep track of who's speaking and what the stakes are? Where do they slow things down?

Which words are loud on the page, obnoxious in their eruditeness? Do they serve a purpose, or is the writer showing off? And if the writer is showing off, is it in service of the story? Does it work as an intentional technique?

How does an author get away with two third-person, past-tense points of view alongside one first-person, present-tense POV?

Are you even allowed to do that?

Can *I* do that?

When I began querying agents, reading became a primary way to study the publishing landscape. I stopped choosing books for content and picked them for commercial research.

If this agent represents this author, maybe she'll like my book too.

Who is writing in my city, and what kind of work are they producing?

Is there a book description formula that will help my query letter stand out? How many sentences does a best-selling book in my genre use to hook readers? What happens in each of the sentences?

I also made notes about the names of small presses earning good press coverage, those with consistently excellent cover designs, and agents and editors who had signed authors in my community. That's how I made my querying lists—and that dedicated study of the industry through reading earned me my first agent.

LITERARY AGENT: A publishing professional who represents authors and queries publishers on their behalf. Many agents do an immense amount of editorial work with their clients before submitting manuscripts and proposals. Agents don't ask for up-front fees; they earn a cut of earnings (15 percent is standard) from the books they sell. Either the publisher sends all the money to the agent, who then sends the author's share along, or it's becoming more common for agents to ask for two payments from

> publishers: their cut, sent directly to the agency, and the author's share, sent directly to the author. That's more work for the publisher, but it's less cumbersome for the agency, and it gets authors paid faster.

There's no better way to understand publishing than by reading. During my agent hunt, with every book I checked out from the library or purchased at a local bookstore, I felt a twinge of virtuousness. I cared! I was putting a coin (or fifteen dollars) into the literary slot machine and maybe someday I'd earn it back! I wanted to spend quality time considering someone's art, but I was also quite literally paying my dues, buying books so the authors could see another sales notch on their royalty balance sheets. (I love the library, and I've always been a book buyer. You can love both!)

At some point, though, it was supposed to be my turn. I craved seeing my debut novel on the shelf, but my first agent couldn't sell it. She dismissed me as a client when I turned in my second novel because it was 2008 and the US was going through a terrible recession. Publishing layoffs were making the news. My agent said I had written a better book than the previous one, but she wouldn't be able to sell it either.

I had learned so much reading with intent, but the process tamped down the wonder and joy that drew me to fiction in the first place. There I was, still reading with intent and turning up at book launches, with no agent and nothing to show for my effort except for a full bookshelf. I knew the landscape—I had paid my dues in learning who was publishing what—and my writing kept getting better. I learned how to use my penchant for whimsy in service of the story. I even figured out some things about plot, which has always been hard for me. None of this made me feel any better when reckoning with another round of rejections or seeing a friend's book on the shelf near where mine was supposed to go.

Somewhere along the line in pursuit of my goals, I had stopped being passionate about dragons and selkies and fairy tale retellings. I quit mooning around midstory, relishing a favorite sentence. I began to hoard descriptive words to recommend books to friends instead of gushing, *It's soooooo good!* The work of being a writer felt like it included writing savvy, upbeat reviews to help other writers get more eyes on their books. I got so wrapped up in reading to learn and to promote other authors that I forgot to read for *fun*. My press even tilted away from the magical and wondrous for a while as I held myself back from my true taste in pursuit of seeming literary and sophisticated.

Here's a reminder: you can read however you want! Revel in the emotions and the surprise and the pleasure and the magic. Let yourself fall into someone else's imagined *moment*. Sweep into a passionate life you haven't lived. Submerge in someone's deep grief. Analyze how the bend of a sentence changes the emotional tenor of the scene. Talk to a friend about where a shift in point of view in a best-selling fantasy left you frustrated. Applaud publicly with a review, a recommendation to a friend, or a social media photo of the cover when a book works!

The reading-as-studying years made me the writer I am, helped me find my place as a small press publisher, and turned me into an author booster. But reading for pleasure has brought me back to myself. It's coddled me in times of transition. And slowly it's helped me release some of the hard, bitter thoughts about the industry that sit curing in the dark room under my ribcage. When I take those ugly truth curls out and dust them off and look at them, sometimes I even feel a little better.

CASE STUDY #1: Thrillers and Mysteries

DANA HAYNES IS A POPULAR thriller author, mystery author, and journalist; his books include *Crashers* (Minotaur) and *St. Nicholas Salvage & Wrecking* (Blackstone). Under the pen name James Byrne, he also writes the Dez Limerick series for Minotaur.

Dana drafts in longhand because he is a journalist and learned to take notes on paper. It also slows his brain down. "I get a chance to pause and think before each sentence," he said. "When I'm typing, I tend to write like a Gatling gun, and the quality (ahem) shows."

The process also allows him to activate the creative part of his brain. "The process of typing that morning's writing, into my laptop, allows me to analyze the story afresh every day," Dana told me.

He uses a steno pad to keep track of his pacing. "I can get 350 words on a page (give or take). If I get through a page without moving forward either my plot or my character development, or crafting the mechanism to set up a nice 'reveal,' then I'm going too slow and need to pick up the pace."

When I asked him specifically about this method for writing in the mystery and thriller genres, he said, "I don't know anyone who teaches 'mystery or thriller pacing' in a way that's universally useful. Pacing is so hard to define, and it differs from writer to writer. If you find a metric that works for you, use it!"

If you want to write in a specific genre, the first step is to study that genre. Read widely. Tap into social media conversations. Take classes, attend readings at local bookstores, and learn from authors working in those genres. Many authors do interviews and write essays about process as part of spreading the word about their new books; these are great sources of information that you can apply to your own genre projects. I don't know a lot about YA pacing or the structure of romances, but lots of people work in these areas and share their insights in their newsletters, their online interviews, and their conference appearances.

Dana explained that thrillers are a subset of the mystery genre, which is where he started his book-writing career. "The primary difference," he added, "lies in time's arrow: A straight-up mystery, or whodunit, is about solving a crime or terrible event in the past. A thriller often focuses on stopping a crime or terrible event in the future. This isn't perfect. A lot of mysteries segue into thrillers in act III—that is, something bad happens in act I; the heroine tries to solve this past event in act II; and act III is a race to stop the bad guy from doing XYZ. So I'd generally say that thrillers look toward the future event throughout."

A thriller needs two forms of tension, he said: time and danger. "In a thriller, a worthy protagonist needs a worthy antagonist or antagonistic force. You need the ping-pong of it."

CLOCK: This term is frequently used to reference how time can be used to amp up the stakes in storytelling. Something has to happen before time runs out.

Here's more from Dana:

> These factors—time and danger—work in all subgenres:
>
> - Legal thriller: Can I beat the brilliant criminal before the jury renders its verdict?
> - Psychological thrillers: Am I gorilla-shit crazy? And if not, can I convince the authorities that this threat is real in time to stop it?
> - Medical thrillers: Can I find a cure for this virulent disease before it wipes out Shreveport?

If you're a budding fantasy author, or want to work on an experimental memoir, then study successful books in those genres like they're homework. What propels the narrative? How is it structured? What similarities do you see between books in the same genre? Compare a book in your genre to an example in a different genre. What can you learn?

PINPOINT YOUR WHY

IF YOU AREN'T SURE OF your genre, there are fewer signposts in the early months of drafting. Which leads to this important question: How do you find your material if you're not sure what you want to write about? If you don't want to create a portal in your kitchen? If you want to write memoir but worry about who might get hurt? If you have a million story starts and can't commit to one?

Ask yourself why writing is important to you. I did this as a brainstorming exercise and came up with the following:

There's always another story I want to tell.

My teachers told me I was a good writer.

My language skills are my most marketable ones.

I haven't seen my lived experience in a book before.

I need to process something slowly, on the page, without anyone telling me how to feel or think, because I'm too quick to believe other people over my own instincts.

I perseverate over conversations and events and sometimes I can't move on. Writing fiction helps me transfer that power of imagination into creating art instead of revisiting real-life moments I can't change.

This simple question opens up all kinds of brain doors. There are no wrong answers in this kind of exercise; even the most unrealistic, unexpected *why* is valuable because it tells you something about your intent. And if you go into drafting a book-length work with intent, you can lean on that for direction. Understanding the reasons you write will also help way down the road as you sift through publishing options and decide what fits your goals.

Sit with your *why* in quiet moments and loud ones, while at the grocery store, while taking the bus to work, right before you fall asleep, while watching a movie. The answer is likely buried under layers, which are tucked neatly behind other layers, and if you look for it while going about your day, you might find something unexpected. Something that reveals a path forward, over the threshold of your doubt.

MY AUTHENTIC SELF, BEING NEURODIVERGENT, is kind of all over the place, so my passion for writing has a tangled root system instead of one clear taproot. In my earliest school days, teacher praise was a major motivator. I grew up taking cues from everyone else, sure my way of seeing the world was wrong and berating myself when I missed a social cue or couldn't keep my desk organized. Teachers telling me that I did excel at something helped me brace against my negative self-talk. I might have a messy desk, but at least I could *write*. I thrived on praise. Those words made me feel better about myself when my frustration about my deficits surged.

When drafting my first two novels, though, I bought into a false story: I was too boring to be a real writer. I didn't have deep scars; I didn't have anything to say. As a child I lived a safe, happy life with a stable family, a sweet dog, and the privileges of white skin and secure housing. I had access to food and clothes that mostly came from the mall. I even had an allowance! I wasn't addicted to substances, nor were my friends or family members. I didn't self-harm or know anyone who did. I didn't have any scary health diagnoses or an unexpected pregnancy. Surely nothing had *happened* to me that could count as inspiration. It all felt so shallow. So plain. So ordinary.

Obviously, I borrowed ideas of what makes a writer from pop culture and from my own imaginings. Your trauma can be your work's taproot, but so can loving a river or being curious about the migration pattern of swifts. Besides, the normal-boring-whatever story I told about myself actually was a shell. Much more coursed beneath the surface. I just didn't have the tools or the words to understand those currents. Every winter in high school, I came down with debilitating exhaustion, brain fog, and other mysterious symptoms. I lost weight and muscle. I didn't have the strength to walk from the bed to the bathroom and back; I crawled on all fours. I think my mom worried she'd find me dead one winter, like a nineteenth-century heroine, keeled over from a case of the vapors. My physical condition haunted her. She mail-ordered liquid vitamins to help restore me. I was too sick and exhausted to care about dying. I slept and watched movies my mom borrowed from Curry Home Video in Bloomfield, which had a handwritten ledger to keep track of inventory.

In normal times I had trouble walking because of extra-long knee ligaments. They locked together when I played sports or romped around with my dog. Not having diagnoses, though, meant those things weren't really part of my story. I never used the word *disabled*. If someone had suggested it, I might have nodded silently, then crawled into the closet and cried myself to sleep. And I didn't want to talk about any of the other unusual parts of my life, like how I attended mechanical music conventions with my parents, spending hours listening to hand-cranked street organs, slideshow travelogues on European cathedrals, and presentations on restoring the elusive self-playing violin machine.

In other words, I ignored the rich, strange, wondrous experiences of my life as *not interesting enough*. Without diagnoses, I didn't feel like I could explain my health issues or claim neurodivergence. Without choosing mechanical music—being the tagalong in my parents' adventures—I didn't have a story to tell about that either.

My first few novels—the one that earned me an agent and the second that lost me that agent—were well written, but they fell flat as stories. Like I've done my whole life, I tried to fit my ideas and characters into a frame that New York editors would find acceptable. One novel didn't have any plot at all. In the next I refused to dig in to what scared me, instead swiping an anecdote a friend mentioned in passing and turning that into the climax. I opted to kill a character in that second book—plot!—then proceeded to turn the novel into a series of clues about how she died.

I didn't pull either off, but looking back now, I can see both books are about a neurodivergent person trying to hide their oddness from neurotypical peers. In the second novel my protagonist models her conversation styles and interests and attire after her roommates. In fixating on learning their behaviors with such ferocious insistence, she stands apart even more and creates conflicts she doesn't understand. She's on the spectrum and has no idea because *I* had no idea as her creator.

Those novels—built from studying others' work and listening to advice and spending hours at the keyboard—didn't sell because instead of leaning into my imagination, I tried to blot out everything that makes me, well, *me*. Bits of my personality kept popping up through the storyline like perennials that just keep reseeding themselves even though you never planted them in the first place. But I kept trying to tamp them down, hide them. And the results didn't work as books. I wasn't clear enough on my *why*.

I lost years of my writing life to practicing being someone else on the page.

I built a carapace of words.

I didn't think I had anything worth saying.

I had no idea what New York wanted, but I tried to make books for them anyway. It's not like I had access to the conference rooms where acquisitions meetings were held. I wish I could grip my younger self's shoulders and say, *Quit making yourself small. Your stories matter. Be as loud and weird in them as you want.*

I wish someone had said to me, *Be as brave in what you say as how you say it.*

JUHEA KIM, AUTHOR OF THE novels *Beasts of a Little Land* and *City of Night Birds*, has an intentional relationship to the *why* of her work.

She starts every writing session by revisiting her mission statement. "After years of writing without any validation, I had to ask myself whether such struggle was worth it," she said. "Then I created my personal mission statement for the first time: to use my talent for writing to save nature and reduce animal suffering. I realized at that moment that I would continue even if I never publish a book, because whether I write an essay, article, or even a blog post, it would be in service of a greater purpose. I stopped measuring my success based on the visible markers and more on whether I fulfilled my mission in any shape or form. Ironically, this became the turning point for my writing career when I experienced many breakthroughs. To this day, I take a walk every morning in my neighborhood and reflect on my mission statement before starting work. Whether I'm miserable because of some perceived failure or restless because of unexpected good fortune, my mission keeps me grounded, calm, and ready to return to the most important matter of all."

Writing is a way of insisting your voice gets heard.

I love how Juhea uses a mission to keep herself focused on the importance of her commitment to writing. Having written, we expect results. But not everything we put on paper will automatically reach an audience. So we have to find other ways to assess our progress. Page count. Word count. Daily practices or monthly practices. Measuring our work against our mission statement. *Am I doing what I set out to do?*

What if this concept makes you anxious? Maybe you have no idea what you want to write about—the idea of writing a statement sounds efficient and lovely, but you don't have a specific intention in mind. Or maybe you're resistant because you aren't sure how to thread your big belief system through a story without grandstanding. Or maybe you have parts of yourself locked away, hidden from your conscious brain. Whether or not you have a mission you can write down on paper, there's probably a theme or intent threading through your work. You might not be ready to put it into words. You might never put it into words. But investigating it is a useful tool when you're trying to pin down your why.

I have always written neurodivergent characters—not intentionally but because that's how I think. When editors turned my newspaper novel away because my protagonist seemed immature, I felt crushed. I knew how her mind worked because *my* mind worked like that too.

What about people like me? I wondered. *Am I the only one who feels like this?*

Now I realize if I had labeled my protagonist as autistic, the story might have made more sense to neurotypical readers. I had set out to write a novel about identity within a group of "normal" people; I just didn't have the words for it.

If you get stuck, if you're not ready for a mission statement, ask yourself that question.

Am I the only one who feels like this?

Then ask: *Feels like what?*

THE WHY OF OUR WORK isn't static. It changes as we change.

I love reading books by the same author, seeing how they have embroidered themes and passions into new creations. In my twenties I always kept my eyes open for references to bears, wrestling, prep school, and car accidents in John Irving's work. In my thirties I scoured Julia Glass's novels for insights into family relationships, grief, and the way she gets loneliness on the page.

Even when we gravitate to certain themes or objects in our work, how we approach them changes as we change and grow. Humans aren't static; books reflect the author's identity at the time they were writing. One of the great joys—and reliefs—of having my debut novel out is being able to consider it independently from my life. The text and the characters stopped growing and changing when we arrived at the deadline for the final proof, but I am still changing and aging. And I have more stories to tell.

After her mother died, Nastashia Minto—author of the poetry collection *Naked: The Rhythm and Groove of It. The Depth and Length to It.* (Eldredge Books)—started approaching her work from a new perspective. "At first, I was afraid," she said. "My own voice told me it wouldn't be received because it was 'too deep,' 'too emotional,' and 'too heavy.' Then I begin to hear all the external voices from my past say, 'This is too much,' 'Stick with one theme,' or 'It's all over the place.' I heard all of this as a child, teenager, college student, and even as an adult. I was never confident in my creations, because I was always told they were too much or my emotions were too much."

Nastashia decided to lean into this *too-muchness* with her second collection, *A Body Tangled in Time: A Tapestry of Self-Love and Shadow Work*, also published by Eldredge Books. "I knew I couldn't live life in a half-ass way anymore," Nastashia said about processing her mother's passing. "So, in this collection, I poured my entire self into it, which comes with many twists and turns. I decided to allow myself to live authentically in my vastness."

It's important for us to identify what boundaries and barriers we're putting around our work—where we are leaning away from our instincts instead of toward them.

To live, as Nastashia says, *authentically in our vastness*.

What's *Your* Why?

If the exercise feels relevant to your process, consider crafting a mission statement like Juhea does.

What do you want to say to the world? Why?

If you have no idea or aren't in an emotionally steady enough place where using words to write a mission statement will help, consider using paint, newspaper articles, a mood board, a few favorite objects, or even a few photos from an old album or your phone's camera roll. Your mission doesn't have to be made of words.

If you get stuck, think about these questions:

- How are you showing up in the world right now? How is it similar or different from your eight-year-old self?
- Can you look at an old photograph of yourself and appreciate what you hadn't yet survived? Conjuring grace and love for that former self might lead you to a deeper understanding of the reasons behind your work.
- What makes you happy?
- What mortified you as a teenager?
- What do you want to *say* but you're afraid of an audience hearing?
- Imagine your manuscript as a microphone. You can use it to entertain. You can use it for change. You can try to make people feel less alone. What appeals to you? There's no wrong answer.
- List ten things you are drawn to right now—they can be colors, textures, objects, ideas, sounds, songs, really anything. What does your list say about you in this moment? How can you relate that list to your work in progress? If you like the idea, mark on your calendar to make another list in three months without looking at the first one. What's similar or different? Did the change in seasons impact your choices? How can you apply this self-knowledge to your work in progress?

Write that. And that. Or that.

THE FIFTY-FIRST PAGE TEST

In 2016 Jamie Yourdon and Michael Shou-Yung Shum, two Forest Avenue Press authors, connected at a writing conference in Los Angeles.

AWP: The Association of Writers & Writing Programs is an organization that hosts an annual spring conference with panels and a bookfair. The location changes every year. Many presses and authors go every year to teach, learn, and make connections.

During his conversation with Michael, Jamie rattled off a series of failures in his writing career—eight books in twelve years, represented by two different agents. None of them got picked up by an editor. The first novel Jamie sold was through the slush pile to a small press publisher: me.

Froelich's Ladder is a madcap fabulist tale about two brothers and a giant ladder. Right away, I loved its big-heartedness, its humor, and its imaginative arcs. "When Michael asked what differentiated *Froelich's Ladder* from my previous seven manuscripts," Jamie said, "I shared with him something my ex-wife had said. 'No one but you could've written this book,' she told me. 'Even if you gave them fifty pages, they couldn't write the fifty-first.' From which I extrapolated that someone else *could've* written the other seven manuscripts. And it was true! Neither the plot nor the characters were that remarkable. Nick Hornby (to choose at random) could've done a better job. Only when I wrote something truly unique did I warrant a publisher's attention."

Many editorial decisions can be changed later on. But if you haven't started writing the book that only you can write, then you need to go back and get clearer on why this is your project. That's where your *why* comes in. Figure it out. Own it. Lean into your you-ness. Only then will someone else want to share your world, get inside it and live there, and share it with others.

Michael's debut, *Queen of Spades*, also passes this "only you" test. Together, we wrote this description of it:

> *Queen of Spades* revamps the classic Pushkin fable of the same name, transplanted to a mysterious Seattle-area casino populated by a pit boss with six months to live, a dealer obsessing over the mysterious methods of an elderly customer known as the Countess, and a recovering gambler who finds herself trapped in a cultish twelve-step program. With a breathtaking climax that rivals the best Hong Kong gambling movies, Michael Shou-Yung Shum's debut novel delivers the thrilling highs and lows that come when we cede control of our futures to the roll of the dice and the turn of a card.

Michael had worked as a poker dealer at a casino in Washington, and his lived experience informed every scene and chapter. Another writer could have never imagined the novel or, if handed the first fifty pages, been able to write the fifty-first. Michael explained:

> Like Jamie, prior to the manuscript that became *Queen of Spades*, I had embarked on many different writing projects, but for me, each would reach a point where the falseness, the contrived quality of the content, would overwhelm my sensibilities and I would write into a dead end, usually after several chapters. Only with *Queen of Spades* was this not true—in fact, the book "wrote itself"—which leads me to believe there is a certain naturalness that comes with material and story that only arise when it is truly your own. It was a joy to write *Queen of Spades*, and the hardest thing for me as a writer in its aftermath is writing when I don't have this feeling: that's when writing begins to feel like actual work, and the falseness creeps back in.

So now: You've considered your why. Maybe you've written a mission statement. You're reading like a child—for fun, just because—and also like a writer, learning techniques and scrutinizing authorial choices. And you're writing! (Woo-hoo!)

So here's another tool, a question: Could another writer imagine the fifty-first page?

If no, you're likely pushing yourself to write like you. That's amazing! Great job.

If yes, why do you think that? Is it because you're working within a genre and there are tight, conscripted rules for that genre? There's a sound and a certain pace to best-selling fiction and if you're going for that, maybe it's a good thing to say yes at this moment. Yes isn't necessarily the wrong answer.

But if you say yes, ask yourself: Are you hiding behind the lines, not yet confident enough in your storytelling to take risks and be authentically, weirdly *you* on the page? If we as readers delve into books to find connection, to *feel* things, and you are holding yourself back, that's something to know now, before writing the next three hundred pages.

I have battled forward with manuscripts that didn't hold up, plot-wise, because nobody told me to pause at the fifty-first page. To consider: Is this what I want? Is this what I mean? Is this what I want to put into the world?

Is this who I am?

I kept going without knowing those things. Without knowing to ask myself those things.

It's great to finish a manuscript because it teaches you so much and can give you a blaze of confidence. Jamie might not have written *Froelich's Ladder* if he hadn't written all those earlier novels. But if you pause here, before you spend the next few years following what you've started, and ask yourself these questions, you might adjust your story plan or get clearer on how your *why* is informing your work.

You might even find yourself, like Nastashia did, getting braver on the page. Leaning into what makes your work special instead of pulling away from your you-ness.

FIRST READER

I STARTED FOREST AVENUE PRESS in 2012 to publish the kinds of novels I love to read. Just to give authors a chance, I read hundreds of pages of submissions that didn't appeal to me. After all, I had been sitting on the other side of the editorial desk for years, dreaming of acceptance. How could I say no to a novel without reading fifty pages and seeing if the fifty-first was where the story really started?

Eventually I learned to trust my instincts. If a novel doesn't interest me from the query letter and the opening pages, I probably don't want to spend the next eighteen months working on it. If it's offensive to me in concept or execution, I don't want to put my shoulder against it and move it forward into the world. Trusting myself made me a more efficient and honest reviewer of manuscripts.

This insight trickled into my writing life and helped me make a terrifying decision. After several years of writing, I cut my protagonist out of my novel.

 **PROTAGONIST**: The lead character in a book. There can be multiple points of view, but usually one

character's experience is the center around which the rest of the story revolves. There are exceptions, though. Some novels have ensemble casts, like Sequoia Nagamatsu's brilliant *How High We Go in the Dark,* with no clear-cut protagonist. There's also a trend in contemporary romance to have dual, equal POVs, instead of one character dominating the narrative.

 **ANTAGONIST**: The lead villain. There can be multiple antagonists, but usually there's one extra-bad baddie. The antagonist is usually human but doesn't have to be; it could be a terminal disease or climate change.

Jean-Jacques Blanchard, my original story star in *Singing Lessons for the Stylish Canary,* had a mean streak and an overload of self-confidence. Everything came easily to him, the oldest son of a master craftsman in a small village in France. Everyone liked him (well, except for me). His little brother Henri preferred the company of girls and wished to learn the feminine art of lacemaking. Henri was always sick or getting in trouble with the schoolmaster for not paying attention. A savvy developmental editor suggested that Henri ought to be the protagonist. The awkward one should inherit the family business because he doesn't want to. That would raise the stakes immediately.

Slice, went my cursor, cutting deep into the story. Exorcising a bully of a brother.

Poor Jean-Jacques.

Although in truth he already had everything he wanted, so I didn't feel so bad for leaving him out in favor of bequeathing the story to the underdog. *Singing Lessons,* with Henri as the protagonist, came out from Lanternfish Press in 2022.

When I made the decision to eliminate Jean-Jacques, I had

a total reframing to do. At first it felt overwhelming, but I had so much more fun imagining the new version. If this were a true nineteenth-century novel, of course a boy like Jean-Jacques would be the hero. The central focus of the plot. He had a confident swagger and good hair. But in my modern, magical version of nineteenth-century France, I could make the shy, curious boy the hero. It took an outside editor to adjust my trajectory, to help me get clearer on what I wanted to say. To teach me that I could write the kind of story I wanted to read.

Forest Avenue Press has a catalog of nearly thirty books, and many of them are sad or have hard moments. (Because plot! And life! Plus, joy falls flat without contrast.)

CATALOG: The list of books a press has published. Publishers used to always make print catalogs but now most rely on Edelweiss, a platform that aggregates metadata about each title. Catalogs include a *frontlist*, books that haven't been published yet or are within their first three months since publication, and a *backlist*, books that are already out.

At some point (around 2016) I grew into choosing projects that delight and inspire me. Books with characters I want to spend a year or two ushering toward publication, written by authors who have conjured a positive view of the world despite all the horrible things happening. I don't publish for *me* so much as for community, but I can do that while picking manuscripts that don't trigger existential dread every time I open the file.

These days, our press editorial guidelines state that we are looking for "literary fiction on a joyride and the occasional memoir." When we're open to unsolicited manuscripts, my committee of readers and I make explicit lists to give writers the inside scoop. Things we like. Things we really *don't* like. That helps writers find us—or to bypass our open call if they aren't a good fit.

What does this have to do with *your* project? You're committing to spend time with your story. We stack the deck against ourselves when we try to write something because we feel we *ought* to, not because we *want* to. You might lose interest too fast if you don't truly love what you're writing. Reading a trendsetting book and deciding to write your own witch story or postapocalyptic tale or whatever's hottest now can backfire because publishing is glacially slow. If you try to jump on a topic train, by the time you finish the manuscript, your project may feel outdated—likely by several seasons—to the agents and editors you query.

Dana Haynes, the thriller author, said it this way: "The First Reader for your story is you. You'd better enjoy it. Later (the gods willing), you'll write for a literary agent, and for an editor at a publishing house, and for a publicist, and for a bookstore buyer, and for a book lover. But first you gotta write for you. Find a protagonist and a story that appeals to you. You're going to be living with this story and these characters."

That's another way of saying *write for yourself*. Not for an agent who doesn't know you exist (yet). Not for a publisher whose taste you can only guess from a distance. Not for your writing group because they're writing a certain genre or style.

And if you get feedback from a friend or editor suggesting you make a sweeping change, ask yourself: *Is that the story I've been meaning to tell all along? Is that how I want to spend my time?* If not, let the advice go. Because you are your own first reader, like Dana says. When other voices come into your process, you have to center your vision while trying to imagine the story from the outside.

If this reader feels this way, is my writing doing the work I expected?

Why or why not?

What needs to change?

What needs to stay?

VOICE

*V*OICE REFERS TO THE WORDS you put on the page, how the story sounds. Your characters also have their own distinct voices; readers should know who's speaking without an attribution. But here we're talking about the big-picture voice. The manuscript's music. Voice is a pastiche of choices, made over months and years of a project, reverberating on every page. It comes from within you—your subjects and obsessions and mission statement and the way you see the world—and how your *you-ness* rubs up against the story you're telling. It's why nobody else could write the fifty-first page if you're leaning into your *you-ness*. Nobody else has your voice.

A nonfiction reporter book might have a narrative voice that's restrained, pulled back in an effort to tell the *truth,* not opinions. Or it might be jaunty and curious—a much more personal sound—depending on who the writer is and what the topic is. A fantasy novel might have languid, long sentences full of made-up nouns, or it might sound like a modern-day memoir, just with talking axolotls or something.

Voice creates a cohesive sound for your manuscript.

Different characters *sound* different, as do different genres, but you the writer are the guiding hand, moving the puppet strings not only of your plot and characters but of the language itself. Voice includes the words you reach for, the sentence structures you favor, and punctuation tics.

"I know I'm not the copyeditor, but there are waaaaay too many em dashes!" my developmental editor Liz Prato wrote in her first-pass edits for *Imagine a Door*. "And I swear, that's something I never thought I'd say. I love the em dash, trust me. Just dial it back."

Oops. I'm so glad Liz caught that before we went to press.

That tic is one of my voice things—usually when I want to fit a thought inside a thought, or when I take a sentence beyond its natural ending—that helps me refocus and create structure. The em dash. My neurodivergence leads me there, every time; my brain pops and pirouettes. I think in big brushstrokes, and then I want to add extra details within those strokes. Parenthesis work well too. (I'm also pro-semicolons and colons and the occasional exclamation point!)

Liz, in reviewing my pages from outside my brain, did me a huge favor in pointing out this tic. Without someone to intercede, I might not see how those choices get loud on the page and overwhelm the content itself. "I love voice," Liz said, "but if it's distracting, then it's done the opposite of what it should do."

Imagine looking through a telescope. Where you choose to focus, and how close you get to the action, is stance. What you want to share with readers when you look through that portal, and how you describe it, is voice.

Authors with multiple books—especially those in different genres—may sound different in each one, but the connective thread between them is also part of voice. The reader knows, *Ah, this is by* her *after all.*

YOU, THE WRITER, PUT PEOPLE on the page in a way that honors their identities, your voice as an author, and your *why*'s intersection with those variables. That should include clues on how your characters see the world, how they choose to interact, and the editorializing about their choices that you, as creator and artist, decide to make.

Your characters must have their own voices to live and breathe in readers' imaginations; they need to sound like themselves, even if you're working in a made-up land. *Especially* with world-building fiction, characters need to be fully realized so the emotional stakes feel like they matter.

Amy Stewart, author of the wildly popular Kopp Sisters series, said: "I wanted this series to read as if it was actually written in the 1910s, particularly [like] novels by Mary Roberts Rinehart, who wrote a great deal of what we would today call 'women's fiction,' as well as crime fiction. I kept a whole shelf of old novels like this by my desk and read from them all day long as I was writing. As I read, I made lists of unusual words and phrases that just aren't used as much anymore. I also made it very clear to the copyeditor that this was a voice."

Amy said her characters learned to speak in the late nineteenth century, so they needed to sound "a bit baroque." She added, "At first, my copyeditor tried to find more concise ways to structure sentences, and I had to remind her that this was not the goal! Sometimes I even sent her examples of unusual grammatical choices from hundred-year-old texts to show her that what I was doing was not 'wrong' for the period."

With nonfiction, you have the nuts and bolts of reported material, newspaper articles, interviews with your subjects, photographs, diary entries, and so forth to help create a cohesive, "true" sound. But you have to stitch the paragraphs together with your insights and voice, otherwise the reported parts won't feel organic to the story you're telling. I had that issue in the earliest drafts of this book, relying on others' voices instead of my own.

SO. THERE'S YOUR VOICE AS the author and also making sure your characters sound authentic. But how do you figure those pieces out if you're new to writing?

Any guesses?

Put yours here:

Now turn the page for the answer . . .

Practice!

That's right!

(Did you make a guess?)

(Did you peek? No shame if you did!)

When you're just starting out and you write something you love, think about what's on the page.

What makes this passage sound more like you?

What do you love most about this sentence?

Could anyone else have written it?

You're on your way to finding your voice every time you think, *Aha! I love this!* or, *This sounds exactly like the character I'm imagining!*

In 2023 I participated in a library panel about voice where all of us, three midlife writers with vastly different upbringings in different countries, talked about our childhood landscapes as primary influences. How those places and times molded and changed us. If you need a hint about where to start digging for your voice, the genuine you, try going back in time. What did your voice sound like before the world tried to change it? Imagine a door to your childhood and walk through it. Do you feel safe there? Scared? Bored? Sick? What did it smell like? What did it *feel* like? What did grown-ups misunderstand about you?

My grandmother saved all the papers and stories my parents sent her, dating each when they arrived and later organizing them into three-ring binders for posterity. As a result I have proof that I have long been pulled into imagining the past. When I was twelve I wrote a paper on Chopin that sounded like this:

> One cold and stormy night, the maid burst into Nicolas and Justyna's bedroom crying, "God Almighty! There are ghosts in the drawing room!" Fryderek's parents jumped out of bed and ran through the bitter cold rooms. When they peered into the drawing room, it wasn't ghosts

> they saw, but little six-year-old Frycek. He was sitting on the piano bench clad in his nightshirt. Frycek smiled to his parents as he continued to play the music he heard his mother play for her dancing guests. What was extraordinary was he was adding his own embellishments as he went along.

What twelve-year-old uses language like "clad in his nightshirt," do you think? Or knows both the formal name of a long-dead composer, Fryderek, as well as his family nickname, Frycek? Maybe someone who doesn't belong in the *now*. Someone who feels closer to the past, the slower tempo of *then*. Someone, perhaps, who might grow up to write a novel that sounds like this:

> Our story begins with the grandparents of our hero, who believed their village to be as normal as any other, despite its pervasive gloom. Mireville had a tailor, a jail, a church, a baker, a doctor who did the best he could, and a midwife who did better.

That's the opening of the first chapter of *Singing Lessons for the Stylish Canary*. It's so cool that I can look back at that Chopin essay—not to mention a weird, Vonnegut-inspired parable and a letter supposedly from 1772 that I wrote around the same age—and see the playful historical tone that foreshadows my published work.

These passages match because the voice matches—from my child self to my fortysomething self, there is change in how I express myself, but there also is a clear through line. And discovering that Chopin essay speaks so deeply to writing what is true to you and what interests you, hitching your plot to the particulars of your imagination and your lived experience instead of trying to write like (or for) someone else.

You can write about anything you like; authors of horror novels don't (hopefully) sever their neighbors' hands to get a feel for the gush of blood. But what will make your voice feel authentic is owning the messy blob of lived experience, research, and language patterns that have led you here, in this moment, to write this particular piece.

Regardless of genre, voice is the artifice you must create to make a bridge between the wild cries of your brain and the person willing to spend time with your words.

MY FIRST NOVEL GOT REJECTED by a press I admired. The rejection said it read like a product of a specific workshop. The way I chose to tell the story matched the style of my teachers in a way that felt recognizable to the editor.

I don't sound like anyone else, I insisted. *This is my story! This is me on the page!*

Years later I understood that criticism. At that time I had been studying with a consistent group for a few years. As an unpublished writer, any sentence of mine that earned laughs, handwritten stars, and verbal kudos meant *good*. These discoveries felt like little tricks. If I do *this*, my peers and/or teachers will love it, so where else can I do these things? I needed that love to help me feel like a real writer, just like I craved report-card praise in high school. And just like in school, I studied what got a positive reaction and repeated it in my manuscript. I started sounding more like the group and less like me. That's what the rejection referred to.

Besides, back then I was still scrounging around for my *why*.

I didn't have a mission statement. I had completely blocked out trauma that might have informed my voice or given some weight to the playfulness of my prose.

Once I had a bit of distance from the critique, I understood that writing within a closed community can create a kind of sound that attuned editors might identify. People talk, sometimes, about MFA writing in this way. I didn't go back for that degree in part because I got rejected from the one school I applied to in my twenties, but mostly because I found ways to write in my everyday life and then jumped onto a raft on the publishing river. And now here I am, writing a chapter on *voice*. Without an MFA.

How dare you? You didn't study this in graduate school. Who said you could write this? Who gave you permission?

I carry that type of questioning into my work, regardless of genre; that's part of my voice. The vulnerability. The times when I forget to be gentle with myself for my shortcomings. Those thoughts show up on the page whether I'm writing a historical novel or a personal essay. It's who I am as a writer. Maybe I didn't show enough of that vulnerability in the novel that got rejected for sounding like a particular workshop. I had figured out how to earn praise from my mentors. But I hadn't (yet) figured out how to write like me.

VOICE CHANGES AS YOU EVOLVE. It's not static. I guarantee if you write a few manuscripts and then look back at the first one, it won't sound the same as you sound to yourself in the present. You might even cringe at your sentence structure or a superfluous number of adjectives. Perhaps you loved adverbs and now shun them. Or there's a tic you used to rely on that isn't necessary to your storytelling anymore.

There's a reckoning that happens between finishing a manuscript and seeing it on the shelf, because publishing takes so long, and your life and voice continue after the story work ends. You have to learn to let what's there rest. As is. To let go.

My manuscripts that didn't find homes are resting in dusty boxes in the basement. And I'm okay with that. I have no interest in pulling those pages out because I've lived—and written—past those points in my life. I don't wonder about the same things I obsessed over back then. There's a lot in those files that still sounds like me now, though. I've changed but I can hear threads of my current voice and theme preferences in those early novels. Kernels of self-expression, moments of humor, or the unexpected reach of a metaphor.

I wrote my senior thesis at Vassar on F. Scott Fitzgerald and how the social climbing affectations he described in *This Side of Paradise*, the stilted and awkward ones, created the framework for *Gatsby*. I posited—ha, a thesis word—that he couldn't have written his masterpiece if he hadn't yearned for social status in particular linguistic ways in his first novel and his collected juvenilia.

When I read pages of *Singing Lessons for the Stylish Canary* now, after several years of touring and appearing at book clubs, the language sounds like me and not me. I recognize me, *then*, in the throes of parenting and figuring out health challenges and pushing against writing advice just to see if I could do it *wrong* and get away with it. My voice and identity changed a lot in the fifteen-year writing process of *Singing Lessons*. If you know to look, there is a palimpsest effect, with earlier iterations of *me* (as a mother, as a daughter, as a storyteller) hidden behind plot choices and text. Like I did with my Fitzgerald research, I can find through lines between my earlier projects and this one. Even though they're wildly different from each other and spaced out by many years.

It's a little different when you're working on a series featuring the same characters. I asked Amy Stewart about the seven books in the Kopp Sisters series. I wanted to understand her process for keeping the voice consistent over the years she spent writing them. "Of course, I read the previous books and listened to the audiobooks to get a handle on the voice from one book to the next," Amy said. "I have a terrific audiobook narrator, and she brought those voices to life in a way that I hadn't even heard inside my own head as I was writing. Sometimes I even sent her draft passages from the book for her to read and record, so I could listen to them and get a handle on whether it sounded authentic or not. We had an unusually close working relationship."

That's a great technique anyone can use when you're looking at voice—read your work out loud and record it, or have a friend read the pages to you. Amy said she read every book in the series out loud two or three times. "This really helped me find anything that sounded unnatural, especially with dialogue."

When we look at the same words over and over again, we don't really *see* them anymore. Changing the format to speaking offers a new way to investigate what you've put on the page. It gives a new perspective when you're too close to the story.

What sounds flat or off? Can you figure out where and why it's not working?

You can also change the typeface and spacing for a fresh look at voice and to see what sticks out. I usually draft in single-spaced documents because they look unfinished to me like that. When I work on a double-spaced manuscript, I'm more reluctant to cut whole swaths or move chunks around.

Double-spaced, to me, is too formal a format for drafting. There are lots of options for changing it up. You could try changing a serif font to sans serif or from double-spaced to triple. Anything that makes the work look fresh to your eyes.

I'M AGAINST APPROPRIATION

FIRESTORMS OF CREDIBILITY HAVE ERUPTED in recent years over identity, particularly when authors have chosen to write from cultural or racial perspectives that are not their own while authors with those exact identities are told by literary gatekeepers that their characters are "not relatable" or "too complicated" or their characters' names are too "difficult."

A few years into my publishing career, after I had tuned in to more conversations about race, gender, and accessibility, I made a choice to only publish novels that have some connection to the author's lived identity. Yes, of course, there can be characters who aren't like you in your stories, and yes, imagination is a grand thing, but I always seek genuine lived experience to anchor a manuscript.

I often say *we* when it comes to the press, but that's a boundary *I* choose to set. I am sharing this decision here because it might help you avoid spending five years on a book that an editor doesn't want to touch because you are speaking for—speaking *over*—other identities to privilege your own.

My learning happened because of DEI training in my volunteer work and because of women and nonbinary folx with marginalized identities who have helped read submissions over the years. Their perspectives and insights helped me realign and clarify my mission as a publisher; I can't thank them enough for their patience with me, for doing the extra emotional labor of sharing what made them cringe and why we shouldn't publish manuscripts that don't align with the author's identity in a fundamental way.

A novel about an adult returning to her hometown of Shiraz written by someone from Shiraz? You bet.

A novel by a woman who identifies as a cultural Muslim, writing characters who aren't traditional Muslims? Yes, of course.

A fantasy with a trans protagonist written by a trans man? Yes please. And sure, I'd love to see characters of color and other kinds of queer identity represented within that story.

Authors often bemoan this kind of thinking as restrictive or reductive; shouldn't *anyone* be able to imagine *anything*? And what about representation? A white person doesn't necessarily want to fill a book with white people. Great. Put lots of characters in your book with different lived experiences and hire sensitivity readers to critique those representations, but something of yours needs to be at the center.

Joyce Maynard set *The Bird Hotel* in Guatemala, where she has a home, and her protagonist is an expat who travels there because of grief, which is also part of her lived experience. It's tricky to write about other places and cultures, but this book worked for me. I loved it.

How about a novel by an able-bodied person who wants to investigate disability from a place of physical privilege? Why would I put money and time into that project when I could work with a disabled author? Especially when there's a scarcity of published disabled voices? Until more disabled people get book contracts, it doesn't make sense to accept a project about disability from an able-bodied perspective.

Recently I heard about a white person who penned an essay about an indigenous practice that changed her life. The idea is connected to her identity; it's an essay about what she learned. But it's also using indigenous culture to center the author's voice as a white person—and to try to make money from selling the piece. If you are using someone else's culture or identity to elevate yourself, that's probably going to be a hard sell to an editor. And if you somehow get it published, it might earn you vitriol from readers, especially those who belong to the culture you're writing about.

I'd rather focus my love on work of the heart, work that flows from and through identity. I realize that lots of talented intellectuals make layered arguments for writing anything they imagine. Freedom of expression and so forth. But as a publisher, I get to choose, and this is what I choose. I love imagined worlds and characters built from the ether. Fantasies are a favorite of mine as a reader. But too often this idea of imagination has been used to lift up white cisgender authors—to give them permission to take up space and attention instead of opening our eyes and ears to authors of color, queer authors, and authors who have lived experience propelling their storytelling. The counterargument about being able to imagine anything you want is most often used to quiet voices from the margins, those who have been historically underrepresented.

Not everyone feels that way, of course. There are many examples of New York houses putting crazy money behind books by people appropriating stories of other cultures. I have made a ton of mistakes in my writing life and as a publisher—in acquisitions, in editing with sensitivity and grace, in using checkboxes about identity in our submissions forms. Part of it is learning what feels okay and what doesn't. Part of it is tuning in to industry conversations. I can point to all the decisions in my past that make me cringe. And I'm sure some decisions I'm making now will feel like mistakes in the future. I keep correcting, trying to do better.

LEAPING FROM CONCEPT TO EXECUTION is part of why I believe this. It's where people working outside their knowledge get things wrong and where wrong is hurtful.

Disabled author and editor Annie Carl pitched an anthology of science fiction and fantasy stories by disabled authors to Forest Avenue Press, and I accepted her idea. She specifically wanted to push against the tropes that able-bodied writers tend to lean on when creating characters with physical and/or neurological differences. "People like me and other people with different disabilities are rarely represented in a positive way, especially when authors write about disabilities without a lived experience," Annie said. "So often, disabled people find themselves in the role of the villain, cured by medical science and technology, or outright killed. Very rarely are we allowed to have our story arc and experiences within books and storytelling." Annie's anthology, *Soul Jar*—featuring thirty-one stories, including some by first-time authors—came out in October 2023 and earned a starred review in *Booklist*.

I tend to avoid reading reader reviews, but occasionally I turn some up while looking for news hits. One that popped up for *Soul Jar* complained that the stories weren't each *about* a specific disability. In fact, some of the characters appeared—*gasp*—normal! Like, not *different* from anyone else. The audacity! Of disabled characters being . . . people! Ugh. This is the same tired logic that gets shoved in the face of marginalized groups by people who aren't members of that group. It's offensive to expect a certain kind of narrative from someone—for them to lean into their pain and trauma for the sake of entertainment. We specifically didn't ask authors submitting to *Soul Jar* to perform their disabilities in fiction—and we left it up to them whether they wanted to self-identify specifics in their bios. Every story is by a disabled author and reflects on disability, whether or not the character's conditions are named.

On a similar note, one review called Robert Hill's *The Remnants* not gay enough to be classified as a gay novel; that sentiment infuriated me. It felt absurdly judgmental and off-base. I wonder what was missing—a particular trope that all gay novels are supposed to have? If the author identifies as gay but doesn't include (say) a coming-out conversation, does that make the book *not* gay? Why isn't it *enough* for a person who identifies as gay to write a gorgeous novel?

When you get a negative review, you can never *ever* engage, so I had to wrestle those feelings to the ground on my own. I also never mentioned the criticism to Robert, who died unexpectedly in 2023. In 2019 Powell's named *The Remnants* one of twenty-five books by Pacific Northwest authors to read before you die. Looking back, I'm glad we celebrated the good stuff and let go of the rest.

It's slippery, this talk of inclusion, because I love books with lots of representation and characters with intersectional identities, but authors write from their particular identities, not *all the identities*. Even if they identify as an underrepresented group, they/we don't necessarily have an intersectional identity. You can't write *of* your identity and also be inclusive if your identity does not include historically underrepresented groups.

Can't we write whatever we want? you might opine. You aren't alone if you think that way. Running my own press, I need to touch base with myself on this topic every time we're open for submissions.

No! is my answer when, on the platform formerly known as Twitter, I see storms of outrage about a white author who has made boatloads of money imagining the experience of a person of color while authors of color with similar stories get rejected.

No! again, when I hear people with lived experience feeling frustrated that another author got it wrong and never bothered to check—and their editors never raised red flags or held up production to fix the manuscript.

No! when I hear yet another tale of a BIPOC writer trying to break into the industry and being turned away because her characters aren't "relatable."

This last example comes from Ramiza Shamoun Koya, author of *The Royal Abduls,* who received multiple rejections from agents over the years because of her culturally Muslim characters and the fact that her female protagonist was in STEM and didn't want kids.

By the time I accepted Ramiza's beautiful novel and we were preparing to go to press, her terminal cancer worsened. Her doctor gave her six months to live. I reeled and mourned and got angry all over again at the agents and editors who had said no years before because they didn't *relate*. The gatekeepers didn't share the characters' cultural heritage, or maybe they didn't relate to a woman in science, or maybe they had ideas for editing, and instead of stepping up to work with Ramiza, they brushed the book off by saying it was too *complicated,* too *unrelatable*.

I do think things are better now in publishing than they were when her manuscript was on submission. Maybe now an agent would see the genius and think, *I love this story AND we haven't seen this kind of representation enough in fiction, so THEREFORE, let's work on it together.*

Thanks to some dear friends of Ramiza's and Forest Avenue staff, we managed to get *The Royal Abduls* in print and on shelves in March 2020, right before the pandemic shut the world down. Ramiza passed in June 2020, knowing her words would continue reaching readers. She's not here to tell you why it hurt to have her work dismissed, so I'm going to quote from a letter she wrote for me that addresses what happened in her own words:

> While numerous agents said they "did not relate" to this character or the subject matter, Laura saw straight to the heart of the story. She has also been the most thoughtful and insightful editor that I have ever worked with. She read deeply, pulled no punches, and patiently helped me to craft the best possible version of my book. She respected what was unfamiliar to her and allowed my intentions to guide the process. At a time when I was unsure if there was room for a story about Muslims outside of those stereotypically focused on immigration or terrorism stories, she, as my publisher, has sold that same story as one about compassion and a family as American as any.

I especially want to point out the "respected what was unfamiliar to her" line, because as editors, we're supposed to question story. We're supposed to ask. And then we're supposed to listen and let the author guide the adjustments, if any. It was incredibly important to me that Ramiza felt heard and respected by my process.

YOU CAN SEE, MAYBE, WHY I take a pretty hard line on this lived experience question. New York told Ramiza there was only room for "stereotypically focused" Muslim stories about immigration or terrorism. They said no based on racist, outdated thinking about audience or who is allowed to identify as Muslim. If someone had said yes to her debut back when she started querying, she might have written and published more books. We wouldn't be left with just one.

I'm still angry about that. How the industry didn't make space for her when she first started querying. And I'm sad too. Ramiza had so much more to say. In her last days, when we were all sheltering in place, we had a long phone conversation about how living with a terminal illness had prepared her for the uncertainty of a pandemic. Her perspective shaped how I coped. How I changed.

CASE STUDY #2: Sensitivity Readers

If you want to write about a marginalized identity and that identity isn't directly related to *yours*, it can get sticky and awkward and, occasionally, awful. If you don't do the work to get it right. That's the key.

I'm able-bodied and want disabled representation in my book, you might think.

Or: *I'm white but I don't want to write a story full of white people. I want diversity! That's the right thing to do, isn't it?*

Sometimes these decisions, as well meaning as representation attempts often are, turn into firestorms of credibility, insults, and social media takedowns because the author got too wrapped up in their own head to see what's potentially fraught or downright offensive in their portrayals. That's where sensitivity readers can come in.

Neil Cochrane, author of *The Story of the Hundred Promises*, identifies as trans, queer, and white. He asked for two sensitivity readers during acquisition: one editor of color to focus on his characters of color and one aromantic/asexual editor to critique his portrayal of that identity. "Seeking sensitivity reads is an expression of respect for your readers, and it was important to me that my publisher shared that respect," Neil said. "Many readers that I've worked with are happy to consult *before* writing begins. In exploring an adaptation of the 'Rapunzel' fairy tale, I consulted with a blind reader to discuss my idea for incorporating the blinding of the prince by thorns. Based on our discussion, I decided not to and saved myself the effort of writing a whole book that would end up not reflecting what I hoped it would."

Neil and I incorporated his two requested sensitivity reads into the editorial timeline. "I'd done plenty of reading on stereotypes to avoid, but nothing is too small to double-check, in my opinion," he said. "For *Promises*, one of the only notes I received in the read for racial representation was for a particular description, which was not wrong per se, but was enough to bump the reader out of the narrative and make them feel othered. It was an easy fix, and reassuring to both me and my publisher."

The Story of the Hundred Promises made the *Washington Post*'s Best Books of 2022 list! I might have dragged around the fear that such a bright spotlight on this book might lead to backlash for something we didn't notice if we hadn't taken these extra steps.

Here's another important facet of this conversation: if you ask someone to check your work for inaccuracies around identity or explain things to you, you should pay them market rates. It's not the same as trading pages with a friend, edit to edit. You're asking for emotional labor and potentially triggering labor. Know that when you ask and also be prepared to change your work if the reader finds parts that are problematic. If you've done the work of *why* before you start, chances are you're on the right track with your manuscript. A sensitivity read can only shore up what you have and help you adjust and clarify where it's needed.

Interrogate Your Idea

PERHAPS YOU'VE RECENTLY STARTED YOUR novel and are staring down the fifty-first page. Or perhaps you're on your third draft. Wherever you find yourself in the process, it's better to ask hard questions about your concept and its relevance to your cultural identity and lived experience instead of finding out later that you accidentally squashed someone else's identity and get hit with a social media firestorm for something you didn't even notice. Here are a few questions to get you thinking:

- How is the subject matter or storyline connected to your lived experience?
- What kind of off-page content could a publicist generate based on your book's themes and how they relate to your life?
- If someone else has written a similar book, how is yours different—concept, tone, voice,

execution? Are they writing from inside the experience or outside—and if outside, does yours come from the inside and correct the record?

- Sometimes we know in our guts when we've taken a wrong direction. What worries you about your book? Do you think that scene, character, or chapter will stop an agent from saying yes, and if so, is including that piece crucial to your story? Be honest with yourself in considering these things. Even a side character's flatness could be enough for an agent to pass without feedback.
- Will you need a sensitivity reader—and if so, what kind(s)? What might a sensitivity reader object to? Pay extra attention to your anxiety when you do this exercise. Sometimes our bodies know more than our brains.

PROGRESS IS PERSONAL

Some books fly into being in a matter of months or a few years. Others—like my debut novel—take more than a decade. There's no correct timeline, regardless of what writing coaches and your author friends say; if you decide on a self-imposed deadline, and that helps you focus, great.

But manuscripts take the time they take. In the early drafting of this book I gave my neighbor Chrysia daily updates during our dog walks. More accurately, I offered stagnation reports. I couldn't seem to get past the first ten thousand words. I kept adding and subtracting, refining and rethinking, erasing and rewriting.

Ten thousand became kind of a joke between Chrysia and me.

Sometimes I had 10,071 words.

Sometimes 10,842.

After paddling around that word count mark, surging over then dipping under, I decided to slice my draft into separate Word documents. I couldn't count words at the press of a button anymore! A more organic narrative began to emerge once I stopped trying to measure my progress numerically.

This felt a bit like an early stage in writing *Singing Lessons for the Stylish Canary*. I wanted to explore how toxic masculinity can be broken down through generations by strong women in heteronormative relationships quietly resisting their husbands. To play with these themes, I chose an omniscient point of view. I wanted to give voice to my protagonist's family and the community that encircled him. I also felt moved to create a fairy-tale, historical sound that felt accessible to modern readers and included a sprinkling of French from my AP grammar class days. In other words, I knew how I wanted the story to sound, but I didn't know *how* to do it. So I slowed down and brought chapter two to my writing group for an entire year.

That sounds extreme.

It was. (*Probably*, haha.)

Over those months, chapter two kept growing in size and scope and dimension. Eventually it spanned more than a hundred pages, which then needed to be cut and shaped into multiple chapters. Much of that material now appears much later in the novel.

My neurodivergence probably defined my process here—allowing me to get stuck, wholly, exuberantly, in one stretch of story for longer than most people would tolerate. But it worked as a technique. I look back now at the earliest drafts of chapter two and feel the woodenness there. Trying to sound like a nineteenth-century author with a tip of my hat to modern readers failed. Avoiding contractions (to sound authentically old) gave the text an absurd academic tilt. I needed to put readers first, let them in on the cheeky tone, writing for *now* while playing with the era's insufferably languid, romantic prose.

What felt at first like being stuck, like annoying my writing group (*sorry, Henry Writers!)*, was just pushing my shoulder against an immovable problem. Slowly, over months, the problem budged. Progress within a boundary made me feel safe.

Focusing on one chapter helped me slow down enough to play with the language and get constructive feedback that didn't overwhelm me. By narrowing the scope, I could become more inventive within the frame.

THIS CONCEPT CONNECTS TO A lecture given in 2018 by Gal Zauberman, a Yale School of Management marketing professor, about thinking *inside* the box. I went to New Haven for the Yale Publishing Course, a certificate program combining leadership skills and industry insights, on a scholarship from the Independent Book Publishers Association. During his talk, Gal urged us to consider how when we problem-solve within limits, we often access a deeper well of creativity. He used the example of the Dom Pérignon champagne brand.

"When do people drink champagne?" he asked our cohort.

My classmates raised their hands and shared their thoughts, speaking into the high-tech mics built into the desks.

"At night."

"When celebrating."

"In low-lit dining rooms."

Gal pointed out how the prestige of the brand is one of its selling points, but the label doesn't matter as much if you can't see it. So the champagne marketing team came up with glowing labels. Now customers could pay a lot for their bubbly, dim the lights, flip a switch on the bottom of the bottle, and their friends would be sure to *see* what kind of champagne was being served.

The constraints, Gal explained—an expensive bottle, dark rooms, hosts who want to impress their guests—caused the innovation. In other words, thinking *inside* the box can lead to more improvisation and creativity.

"Seize the limitations," he urged us.

In the context of revision, I used chapter two as my constraint. My champagne bottle, my dark room. Inside the box of that one stretch of story, I found myself free to push boundaries, experiment, and play.

KEITH ROSSON—AUTHOR OF THE Fever House duology (Penguin Random House), *Smoke City* (Meerkat), and three other Meerkat titles—revises each of his novels five to nine times, focusing on advancing the story in the earliest iterations. "Between the agent and the editor and copyedits, it's probably twenty times," he said. "Every time, I learn more about how people talk. More is revealed with every pass. But I've got to finish it first."

Keith can tell that a first draft is going well when he imagines the next two or three scenes. "It happens organically," he said. "If that stops, I have to backtrack. The biggest thing is letting first drafts just suck. I know so many writers who are insistent on making the first twenty-five pages perfect, but they never advance the story. By the time I finish the story in the first draft, I know so much more about the characters. That informs me about how they would behave in the beginning. I fill in those gaps, making the characters more real and adding tension, because I've finished the book and I know what the ending is."

I've definitely stranded myself in the early pages of a first draft. Keith sold four projects to Meerkat while I was still batting around sentences in chapter two of *Singing Lessons*. But I'm a different writer than Keith and my process is different—and that's just fine. The time I needed for *Singing Lessons* included coming to terms with deeply hidden pieces of my identity and understanding my *why*. Giving myself permission to be playful, whimsical, and entertaining on the page while writers in my community tackled what I imagined to be more "important" topics. I didn't know what I was writing about until I wrestled those things into the light. Now that I've done that questioning and digging, it's different. I have the courage to write this book about publishing. Even when my nerve falters, I pick it back up, feeling sure writers need the information I can offer.

And right before selling *Singing Lessons*, I wrote a complete draft of a new novel in four months. (A first draft, but still.) The idea had bubbled up in me five years before. When I finally carved out time to sit on the couch and work on it, my characters showed up. I managed not to get caught up in my usual perfectionist tendencies, being able to envision the next few scenes, to *see* what I wanted to write toward. When I got to the end, I knew what I wanted to fix and how to do so.

Singing Lessons has a storyline and a texture I couldn't have stumbled on with an efficient, short process. It circles around themes and personal growth and builds a secretly matriarchal society in a male-dominated village. These turns—instead of following a straight line of plot—mimic the barrel organs I set out to write about. The first draft didn't have any magic in it; middle drafts went into the history of hysteria diagnoses and a famous conductor with thirty-six first names (I still want to write about him someday); a late draft included a hundred and fifty pages set in the Five Points district in New York that needed to be axed. I researched and tinkered with so much that enough material for several other novels ended up in cuts folders, all while addressing and reconsidering my *why* and growing into my identity as a thirtysomething (and then fortysomething) mom and business owner. I spent much of that decade and a half letting experiences wash over me, coming to terms with my health, writing essays, parenting two kids, learning publishing by starting a press from scratch, and figuring out how to be kinder to myself. Much of that time wasn't active writing time, but the living I did filtered into the final draft that sold to Lanternfish Press in early 2021, about a year into the pandemic, when humans everywhere were seeking joy and hope. I had a book about that. A feel-good book.

LIKE ME, SARAH CYPHER, AUTHOR of the debut novel *The Skin and Its Girl* (Ballantine), counts a fifteen-year span between starting her first published novel and its launch. She started working with the characters in 2005 and finished a draft in 2009 so she could shop it around during her first writing conference. "I received a few revise and resubmit responses from agents I met there, but when those hit a dead end, I moved on to a different project," Sarah said. "I returned to it off and on until I started from scratch in 2018, working from the narrative strategy outward, and finished a draft on March 8, 2020, just as the world was shutting down in response to the pandemic."

During those in-between years, Sarah continued to grow her freelance editing practice. She wrote a different novel, worked on short stories, and earned her MFA from Warren Wilson College. The second draft of *The Skin and Its Girl*, she said, built on all the years of story work she had already done. "I needed to find the courage and confidence in my own identity before I could approach the work of telling a queer, unconventional story with the creative courage and confidence it deserved," she said. "Ever since the notion of a Palestinian American baby born with cobalt-blue skin came to me in the middle of writing a scene about something else, I knew I needed to find a way to write about that kind of magic, but do it in a way that gave that character full agency."

WHILE I WAS SCRAMBLING AROUND in those fifteen years of writing my debut novel while parenting and learning how to be a publisher, I found courage and hope in Selden Edwards's overnight success. In 2008 his debut historical fantasy, *The Little Book,* came out from Dutton and became a *New York Times* bestseller.

Selden had been working on the manuscript on and off, mostly in the summers when he wasn't teaching, for thirty years. "The story that is meant to be told percolates in between writings," he told me when I interviewed him for my blog in 2012. Near the end of that three-decade span, after rewriting with the guidance of a freelance editor, he quickly landed an agent and a contract with Dutton. (That's the *overnight* part.)

In a 2016 interview I asked Selden how much changed from draft to draft over those years, and he said:

> Of course, I didn't intend to take thirty years. Each time I did a draft I sent it out, each time hoping that this one was it. The rejections always depressed me, and so I abandoned the project for a while. But I kept the story in my head (I couldn't get it out) and kept thinking up new character details and twists and turns. Each new draft was probably about twice as complex as its predecessor. Do the math: over thirty years, and five or six rewrites, that's a lot of twists and turns. It was a relief to have it finally published so I could stop running the story over and over in my head. For novel number two, *The Lost Prince,* I had to work a lot more efficiently, but it was sort of the same process. There was a fifty-page draft, a one hundred fifty, a three hundred, finally a six hundred. Like that.

Like that.

I have felt relief in thinking about the ending of *Singing Lessons for the Stylish Canary*. I played with several different endings over the years, tearing whole chunks away and rebraiding when an attempt didn't work.

Is the landing that stuck the best of the bunch? Maybe.

I miss a whole parlor full of characters I cut, their bantering and antics, and the new (final) ending has a clarity to it that makes it feel a little short compared to the rest of the book. But I'm not carrying the story around in my head anymore, wondering, *Should I push the story this way? Should I send it that way?*

It's a relief not to second-guess my decision anymore. It's done. Printed. The characters have the lives they have. The old ones have fallen away.

ANYONE WHO TRIES TO TELL you that your writing process is too slow or too fast is probably battling their own insecurities. Or maybe they've made it big, and they want to pass on what worked for them, which is admirable, but it might not work for *you*. There's no such thing as one size fits all when it comes to art making.

I spent a lot of time listening to successful writers share their wisdom at bookstore events. I read how-to books and writers' life memoirs, sucking up wisdom through a mental straw, wanting to follow their paths. It never occurred to me that the slowdown—the hang-up in my career—wasn't learning a secret method; it was centering what worked for *me*.

And finding that courage took the most time.

I work this way, I tell writers now when I give presentations. *What works for you?*

KEEP TRACK

MANY MOONS FROM NOW, YOU might find yourself scrambling to remember specifics about your writing process, your research, conversations or news articles that shifted your book's focus, and editorial notes that have long been folded into the work like egg whites to waffle batter.

If you have writing friends, you know how sometimes a margin comment or an aside in an email can spark a whole new direction. You'll want to keep a record of those mind-blowing moments. When it's time to publish your work, you'll need to access that material. This goes for fiction *and* nonfiction manuscripts. Especially if you're borrowing books from the library or a friend, keep a list, labeled clearly, on your computer, in your desk drawer, or both places.

You should cite all sources in the finished book and have them available for proofreading and fact-checking purposes, so you may as well start that process as soon as you read this paragraph.

SOURCES I HAVE USED SO FAR:

You should also write down the names of people who help you along the way. This informal document can be turned into a source list or blended into your acknowledgments.

When my novel's back matter was due, I thanked my past self for jotting down names and book titles in several Word docs. Were they complete or organized? *No way.* But they helped me cobble together the information my acquisitions editor needed to finish preparing the manuscript for layout.

BACK MATTER: Anything that comes after the last page of the book. Also sometimes known as *end matter*. This usually includes the author bio, acknowledgments, source list, afterword, book club questions, index (for nonfiction), and may include extras like a playlist, a recommended reading list, recipes, or an essay related to the making of the book.

FRONT MATTER: Yep—you guessed it! This is any material that appears in the front of the book. The copyright page and title page(s) are front matter, as well as the dedication, a foreword, and table of contents. Previously published excerpts of your book may be listed on the copyright page or on their own page. Usually the front matter has its own page number convention (i.e., roman numerals), and the actual book's page numbering begins when the story starts.

Thanks to my notes, after a few panicked weeks of searching I was able to locate the name of a French museum curator. I had disabled and deleted the email account where we corresponded, so I lost some valuable information, but I did have his name written down. Serinettes are high-pitched, piccolo-sounding barrel organs made with the purpose of teaching songbirds to repeat man-made melodies. This curator sent me a CD of serinette music recorded at his museum as well as information about how it felt to turn the crank. *Singing Lessons for the Stylish Canary* is about a family of serinette makers; I *definitely* needed to name that curator as a source. I also had kept a list of historical resources and the start of an acknowledgments page with the names of friends and writing group members who saw the earliest drafts. I would have omitted or forgotten many of them if I hadn't thought to write them down more than a decade ago, back when I thought I'd get published quickly.

It's also useful to take process notes for future tie-in essay ideas. Having extra material filed away will help you make an organic connection to the book you're trying to promote.

While researching her debut book, *Under the Henfluence: Inside the World of Backyard Chickens and the People Who Love Them*, journalist Tove Danovich kept notes about possible companion pieces. She landed an article about adopting battery hens in the *Guardian* in April 2023, a few weeks after her book's pub date, with the title "Want Free Eggs? Don't Buy Chicks—Rescue Hens." Tove told me:

> I knew early on that it would be one of the pieces I wanted to pitch closer to publication, though it took a while to find it a home. I think it would have had a hard time getting accepted if it weren't for attaching the news hook of avian flu making the price of eggs high and baby chick sales increasing as people looked to start flocks

> of their own. It's also a subject I was very familiar with. I did all new interviews for the article—including many organizations I'd never spoken with before—but the writing process was easy, a lifesaver when you're juggling postpublication anxiety with trying to also do new work.

In addition to that tie-in essay, the *Atlantic* requested a piece on feral chickens in Hawaii after the acquiring editor heard her interviewed on a podcast. "The story of chickens in Hawaii was similar to what I had written in a chapter on feral chickens but not *so* similar that it felt like I'd be rehashing the details," she said. "I went back to two sources I spoke to for the book about this question specifically and then was able to broaden my research with new reporting. It was an easy piece because I basically knew what the narrative would be from the book research."

Not only are these prestigious bylines but the subjects matched Tove's book perfectly; it's an easy and satisfying hop from reading one of these essays to buying *Under the Henfluence* for more chicken-related content.

CASE STUDY #3: Thank Your Sources

WHILE ADDIE TSAI DIDN'T TAKE notes when she wrote *Unwieldy Creatures* (Jaded Ibis), a queer Asian *Frankenstein* retelling, they are shifting their process for the sequel. (Addie uses all pronouns; I've chosen to alternate them here.)

"I didn't keep track of much of the research that I

did and moved through the book organically, in terms of *Frankenstein* (although I did work through each chapter with my favorite copy in my hands, guiding the way), the science that I used for the creation (found through a Google search after I came up with an idea and discovered that it indeed already existed), and also Javanese wedding ceremonies that informed my Frankenstein's parents' wedding scene (also from Google)," she said. "I would grow to regret not keeping more careful track of those sources, having to scour my internet histories when readers wanted to know where I first discovered these sources, or when I prepared other companion essays to promote its release."

While working on the sequel, which involves research into the sociopolitical histories of Singapore and England and LGBTQIA+ people in Indonesia, Addie has devised a system to keep sources and ideas organized. "I'm currently using a formal and informal system," they said. "I'm using Scrivener to keep track of more formally found sources and I'm using my Notes app in my iPhone when I've been told something more informally that will relate or when I hear or witness something out in the world (or am reading a book that I don't want to stop reading) that I need to jot down quickly. This includes books and films that provide insight for constructing this novel, as well as conversations with writers and artists."

I love that idea of having a formal source list and an informal jotting-down place and am already wishing I had done that for this book! (Next time. That's the great thing about deciding to write books *plural.*)

During our conversation over email, Addie also made

a great point about ethics and the importance of sharing meaningful appreciation for sources.

"As information becomes more readily available, almost too available in some cases," she said, "I find citational practices that much more important. I was recently reading Jerome Ellis's *Aster of Ceremonies* and I was moved by how he thanks artists in his community in the footnotes that have helped in some way, such as 'I am so grateful to you, Iya Milta Vega Cardona, for teaching me about time.' Or 'Thank you, Luisa, for the reminder!' I think we could all think more deeply and intentionally about how we cite all the forms we come to consider as 'research.'"

WITH *SINGING LESSONS*, I KNEW I wanted to pitch the Research Notes column at *Necessary Fiction*. My scrambled files of notes and acknowledgments, compiled over the fifteen years I worked on the novel, became the bones for that piece. My author friend Sarah Cypher visited the Musical Wonder House in Wiscasset, Maine, because I asked. The museum had a serinette, and I kept Sarah's written report of the visit in my novel notes. I got to quote her in my essay, making it less static (and less about me-me-me). Moreover, quoting Sarah was a way to honor her impact on my work. "Given the lack of other entertainment available to women at that time," Sarah told me, "their canaries were their pride; and many homes had a large, soaring aviary to let their birds fly 'free.' As with any status symbol, some canaries were boasted to be better or smarter or prettier than others, so women would enter their canary or collections of canaries into contests, and would seek to buy the best canaries for their contests and for showing off to their friends."

I had never heard about canary contests before! Sarah's report changed the direction of my novel and helped me invent Mrs. Delia Dumphries Stanton, a specific songbird collector, who became a key element of the plot.

Have I convinced you yet? Or have Tove and Addie? I hope so, because there's another reason to take notes as you write:

IMPOSTER SYNDROME

(Cue nefarious organ music.)

We writers, especially those of us laboring over full-length projects because we love them, sometimes lose sight of our work. When struggling in the messy middle, or beginning the fifth rewrite, or holding notes from a beta reader, our hope and curiosity can turn to shame.

Why did I ever think I could write a book?

Nobody's going to want to read this because I don't know what I'm doing.

I'm obviously no good at writing.

I've tricked everyone who thinks I'm good.

Really I'm a fraud.

Imposter syndrome is where self-doubt gets stuck on repeat, where you stop seeing all the great things you've done and replace them with the skewed belief that they don't actually count. Moreover, publishing your work doesn't disrupt the cycle.

Get a poem accepted? *It's just one little piece. It doesn't really count.*

Get an essay published? *I pitched the right idea at the right time to the right editor.*

Publish a book? *Yeah, but it didn't sell that well.*

Publish two books? *But neither got a Kirkus star.*

The shame loop is a hard one to extricate yourself from

once it gets going. My fifteen-year novel took that long because I stopped believing in myself for years at a time. I let the story hang out in my computer while parenting and running my business. At some point I decided I made a better book publisher than an author.

Who do you think you are, trying to write historical fiction?

On a really bad day, I might add, *Stupid!*

On a really, really bad day, I might add, *You are not a real writer anyway.*

So many of us battle negative self-talk, but when we are open about it with other writers it helps with the sting. To realize doubting ourselves, as artists, is often part of the process. Sometimes negativity can push us to work harder, invent new ways of solving problems, or even—eventually—build up our confidence. But just as likely, it can shut us down.

In those early years when I was wallowing in my not being a published novelist *yet,* my writing community might have reassured me if I had been brave enough to ask for help. But I might have brushed off their belief in me. I've always written strong, strange sentences using a kind of firecracker style that pops and crackles and lights up the page, so it's easy for me to wave positive comments away.

They're just saying nice things because I've tricked them with my voice.

Imposter syndrome is fiendish like that. It sneaks in all the cracks and fills them with "logic" that feels true when you don't say it out loud to someone else.

True, genuine community, as you'll see in the next chapter, is a wonderful tool for dismantling harmful thinking, which can feed on silence and separation. But keeping notes about your work is another powerful way to wield your hard work like a flaming sword of justice.

In other words:

You can't argue with the hours you've put into your book!

They are incontrovertible proof that you are writing. Even if you're stuck or you can't stand to look at your draft, even if you can't bear to call yourself a writer, or an author, or a novelist, or an essayist, or whatever word you *meant* to use but find yourself ignoring, you can look at the pages and files and calendar notes to prove yourself to yourself.

It doesn't have to be fancy, either, to get this point across.

If you are super organized, you might track your writing sessions and set goals or celebrations once you accrue a certain number of hours. Even us chaotic-brain types can keep a notebook with updates or insights into the process or what we want to say. When I flip through my previous years' calendars, I can spot all the times I met with friends at a coffee shop, carved out a meeting-free day to write, or went on a retreat.

Imposter syndrome can rage in your head, but when you look at all the research notes you've compiled, all the interviewing you've done, all the hours committed to your project, that's proof.

You are a writer because you are doing the work of writing.

You have a book in progress.

Here are the words, and six or eight or twenty-seven files of quotes and notes and cut material that you might add back.

Here is your *potential,* not an abstract quality or a possibility you see in yourself but actual evidence.

You are putting in time, energy, and imagination.

Your manuscript may not be finished, but it exists, and you deserve to call yourself a writer or an author or a poet or an essayist or whatever term you've chosen.

NOW . . .

You've started a book. Great work! Why don't you celebrate with a cupcake or a plate of nachos or a juicy apple. Or how about a dance party? A tea date with a friend? Or take a walk on a new trail in the woods.

You can be as formal or informal as you like with your celebration. Finding times to pause and appreciate the work you're doing is important because later, when rejections come into play, you'll be better fortified if you've honored your journey along the way. Having memories of enjoying the process and hitting milestones will help you remember a rejection is just a small piece of what it means to be a writer.

Publication is a journey, but as soon as you start on that path, you have to rely on others—readers, for sure, but probably also publishing experts, agents, editors, writers who are willing to blurb you, graphic designers, publicists, and all the people you ask for publicity support (bloggers, podcasters, Bookstagram influencers, BookTok personalities, and so forth). It gets harder to keep your sacred creative flame going when all that talking is going on. All that back-and-forth, all that *please look at me*.

You have to believe in yourself now, honor how far you've

come, find pleasure or catharsis or satisfaction in the process of word after word. You have to marvel over your own flame. Even if you want to throw your hands up in despair because you can't get a chapter to flow right.

So many times over my writing life, I've hit a certain milestone—the first fifty pages, say, or the third rewrite—and I didn't pause to acknowledge that moment. I just got back to work. That creates a false sense of impermanence about the work. A manuscript is always changing until it's out in the world, interacting on its own merits without you, the author, explaining your reasoning. But the work itself, the cyclical nature of grinding through a scene one more time, lifting out a character who has become redundant, dropping a new plot point in—all of this is a constant. The work is the work.

If celebrating a scant handful of pages or a rough draft that's more *rough* than *draft* feels too preliminary, why not host a celebration of your self-doubt? Raise a glass to your worries. Write your top fears on pieces of paper, then cut them into strips with scissors. Tell a friend, *I don't think I can fix this character*, and let that person hold on to your worry for you. Tell yourself, *If I want this book to work, I need to figure this out*.

Now keep writing.

Take notes on your process and research.

And keep reading—any book that inspires, grounds, or delights you.

We're all choosing to spend our time writing (facing ourselves at close range!) over, say, another hour of scrolling on social media or watching a show. And if we want an audience to read our work someday, if we are writing because we love reading, then we need to keep carving out time to discover new books. I think of my reading time as feeding the sourdough starter. If I don't add input—flour and water, *food* to nourish what's fermenting—that bubbly creativity will sour and soon it'll be easier to walk away from my project than to keep going.

Some writers swear by not reading midcreation, and if that works for you, great; you get to choose. I need books to cherish, to talk about, to lull me to sleep. They're the fabric of my days as much as dog walks, publishing work, and driving to and from my kids' schools. I don't go a day without reading, let alone the years it takes me to write and revise a whole novel.

If you find material close in concept to yours is distracting to your process and are thinking about quitting reading for a while, try picking something in a different genre. Writing a space opera? Borrow a cozy mystery from the library. Use your reading as a way to play, to surprise yourself, to break out of what you think you know. Use it, too, like another celebration. A gift to your brain and heart.

You've been working hard learning the craft; you still can indulge *in* the craft as a reader. Writing is about filling your heart and coddling your spirit, and what better way to do that than to pull a book off the shelf and dive into someone else's story for a while?

Beginning, for you, might be starting to write for the first time. Or it might mean opening an old draft and revising because you love the process, because now you have some tools to keep you focused on the work, not what might come after. Or you might be working on your fifth book, after getting four of them published, trying to chase that elusive want-to-write spark that got doused during the pandemic. It all counts as a beginning, and once you get going, you have to figure out where you're headed.

COMMUNITY

BELONGING

WRITERS USUALLY WORK ALONE. WHEN we feel brave enough to seek connection, it's the word wrangling that draws us together.

The word *community* has been overused and stretched out of shape, but it feels more inclusive than other names for congregating writers. *Community* can refer to a huge group of people or just you and one critique partner. And it has horizontal appeal—nobody's in charge in community. We all belong as equals.

I don't like *literary citizen* because it insists that there are people who can be cast out, or disallowed *in*, by whoever gets to decide these things. *Citizen* itself, as a concept, reeks of politics. *Team* carries a sense of rank and implies there's a way to win, plus it sounds like workplace software. And I don't use *tribe*, because it has been stolen from Indigenous people and it's not mine to use as a white person.

Writers can be *readers* for each other, exchanging pages, but that term definitely insists on a hierarchy: the person presenting the work is the writer. Everyone else is a reader, expected to share feedback. *Coreaders* seems cozy but without context, it's nonsensical, almost Seussical.

So what if we started using *imaginarium* to describe our gatherings and connectivities, all those brains buzzing? Maybe that sounds too much like a science museum. A *murder* of crime writers? A *fugue* of music journalists? A *cloud* of poets? A *camaraderie* of novelists? *Deskmates*? A *picnic* of prosemakers? *Cloud* feels right to me today, because it matches the weather and my sense of the outside world muffling while I revise. I can picture all of us floating around in wispy tugboats of imagination, of grief, of yearning, put-putting toward the next scene or verse, occasionally bumping edges and asking, *Do you need me to tow you for a while?*

Or, *Do you have a breeze to spare?*

IN CRAWLING OUT OF OUR brain caves, bleary-eyed and sick of a chapter we've revised a million times, it's exciting to connect with others who have been struggling with plot points or how to render dialogue from the 1870s. Sharing your insights, frustrations, and fears helps a solitary pursuit feel less lonely.

When you're on submission with a finished piece, fretting and venting with others who have been there helps a lot. So does hearing praise for your work—getting that reminder that taste is arbitrary.

Sitting at a coffee shop, laptops open, with another writer or two, can be great for focus and a sense of belonging. Working together is one of my favorite things. I usually start such sessions with some general catchup chatter and then we get down to business, followed by a postwriting wrap-up conversation. These meetings make me think of parallel play—a toddler development stage—where kids are engaged in separate activities while in the same space. It helps with focus, but it also banishes those self-doubt demons. (If you're working on a novel with someone else nearby, then you must be a novelist, right?)

Community can gather in a specific physical space like a rec center, a bookstore, or a library; or it can be entirely digital. Social media platforms have clusters of writers who find each other, where people can exchange information and cheer for each other.

I lean toward in-person relationships but also use social media, email, and Zoom to interact with writers and publishers. Many writers, especially those who work night shifts or those with disabilities, prefer online communities because they're accessible. I belonged to a group of 2022 debut authors that had a website featuring everyone's work, themed social media weeks, and a discussion board.

I don't think there's a wrong way to connect with others, unless it's with intent of making yourself more popular or successful at the expense of others. Sometimes groups create or insist on an us-versus-them mentality—a wall keeping some people inside and the rest at arm's length. The precious belonging inside the moat might feel good to the insiders, but they're missing so much by not looking beyond each other's shoulders. Other times our own insecurities keep us from connecting with people we admire.

When I first moved to Portland, all I could see was the wall. The moat. The *them* of the writers who had made it. The *us* of everyone who hadn't. It never occurred to me that

I could walk up to an amazing published author and say hi, so I didn't. I waited. I wanted someone else to spot my work ethic, to call it *talent* and usher me inside the literary circle of fancy people.

I paced, inside my head, waiting for my name to be called. For someone inside the circle to notice me on the outside.

Hello?

I had the same outsider feeling with the agents and editors at New York publishing houses.

Hello?

Don't you see me?

While I waited to be discovered by the big-name authors working in the city, I wrote novels and attended bookstore readings. I sent fan letters to authors, interviewed some of them, shared photos of books I loved, and penned painstakingly upbeat reviews.

Then my friend Liz Prato asked a question. Sometimes a moment is so powerful, you remember what it felt like to be asked, even if you can't remember how you responded. One summer evening Liz and I and a few other friends were walking on the graveled edge of a street without sidewalks, heading back to her house from Annie Bloom's Books, where we had just attended an event.

"Why are we waiting to be invited to the table?" Liz asked.

That felt revolutionary to me. *To become part of the community? Without someone inviting us?*

Of course by then we had developed our own community, joining together to attend a reading or to edit each other's pages. Liz probably meant it as a rhetorical question, but it felt to me like a blazing torch. I had been waiting for permission to participate in the literary ecosystem instead of observing. She gave it to me.

 **LITERARY ECOSYSTEM:** A group of writers, readers, and booksellers who support each other. It's a phrase borrowed from the natural world that incorporates the idea of symbiotic relationships. Each group benefits the others.

Liz began teaching and speaking and earning a reputation as a consultant, freelance editor, and submissions expert. I didn't know how I wanted to interact, but as she became a force in the local literary world, finding her way and teaching others, I started imagining the possibilities. I could do something just because I wanted to. Just like Liz.

She reminded me that we all have agency. That we can act. That the work created outside the powerful center is art—often more surprising or startling or delightful than what's found in the center. It's certainly as valuable, especially in the context of publishing's long history of centering white, cisgender, able-bodied, straight people as leaders and thinkers. The people who were in the center of the circle for decades never looked or acted like me.

Why had I wanted so badly to be among them?

It took a while to crawl out from under that hidden toxic thinking, but I did.

Now I imagine a line on a graph connecting Liz's question to my decision to start a publishing house for authors who weren't getting the attention they deserved in New York.

Permission came first. Then the idea of running a press surfaced. Then I did it.

You can too—start a writing group, curate a reading series, host a book club, whatever you think would be fun. If you need an invitation to make what you want to make, to show up in literary circles without being handed a ticket, consider this section your permission, handed from Liz Prato

—published author, editor at large at Forest Avenue Press, longtime literary community member—

to me

—published author, publisher of Forest Avenue Press, grateful friend of Liz—

to you.

THE COMPARISON TRAP

I'VE SPENT MUCH OF MY career watching other writers and learning from them. The ones who seem like they have it all, who have done it *right,* have helped me set goals and work toward them. They're shining examples.

It can be inspirational to feel admiration, but sometimes this kind of thinking can get in the way. For a long time, whenever I earned an accolade, I found a way to minimize it because someone else had done something even more impressive.

Featured reader at an annual event! Oh yay, an exciting opportunity, but one of my writing group members was featured at *three* events.

Five published essays! Great, but *real* essayists like [insert friends' names here] have more than ten credits *or* they've broken into markets that are more prestigious than what I've managed so far.

Published debut novel! Well, yes, huzzah for accomplishing my lifelong dream, but that was last year, and it seems like everyone else is publishing their second or third or fourth projects.

Longlisted for a major award! Fantastic, sure, but my friends' novels were short-listed for multiple awards.

We move our slide rule of success based on what we have achieved—minimizing our accomplishments, always wanting more, always judging ourselves based on the people around us, even if we work in different genres and our creative trajectories cannot be compared.

This pattern of undervaluing ourselves based on examples of success is perhaps connected to being sensitive artist types. Or perfectionists. Or maybe it's just human to feel jealous or bitter instead of acknowledging how far you've come compared to when you started writing seriously. This is one of the facets of the creative life that I love to discuss with other artists.

Especially because sometimes, when we take ourselves down we start taking others down. Instead of judging ourselves to be smaller or lesser, we find fault in our peers' work to make ourselves better. This feels awful, especially when you truly want to support other authors in your life.

But remember, publishing is where personal art making and capitalism meet. Publishers pour bestseller money into some titles, with high advances and prerelease media tours, while relegating other books to minimal support from one overworked publicist. Booksellers recommend certain titles over others. Readers choose what to buy. These decisions are all market-driven, not because one book is objectively better than the other. It's no wonder that the system of publishing makes most of us feel bad about ourselves at some point or another.

IN 2018 I HEARD FONDA Lee, author of the wildly popular Green Bone Saga, deliver the keynote speech at the Terroir Creative Writing Festival here in Oregon. Fonda told us:

> There is no career path in writing. Everyone's path is different. There's no one way to compare your path to that of anyone else. I have seen writers that failed to sell their first five books get a six-figure deal on the next manuscript and debut on the *New York Times* bestseller list. I've seen writers with established careers have their series canceled and be unable to sell their next book. Selling a project is no guarantee that you will sell the next one. Likewise, rejection and failure today are not indicators of the future. Trying to compare your progress to anyone else: that way lies madness. So much of what we do is done in solitude; you have no way of knowing what it took each author to get to where they are now. There's room for a lot of stories in this world; keep your eyes on your own paper.

In putting our work into the world, we are asking readers to engage with our deepest beliefs. Writing is our way of sharing how we see the world. To do it well, though, without hurting ourselves, we have to quit battling jealousy and nerves, measuring our work against what we think it *should* earn for us.

All the wants and should-haves and side-eyes we cast at other better-known books and authors distract us from the work in front of us. *Our* work. The stories that nobody else could possibly put down on the page, because they haven't lived in our bodies.

We're not competing against other writers, not even in our local communities or in our specific genres.

We're fighting for attention with movies and shows, social media, sports, news, after-school activities, workouts, all the ways people spend their time that *isn't* reading.

With that in mind, what if we could shift away from measuring ourselves against each other and instead focus on our own projects? Our own sentences and pages. The ones right in front of us. And what if we could train our brains to count every good thing in our careers? Instead of minimizing our wins and accolades, we could hold space for even the smallest of them and make sure they count.

Think of an abacus. You push some beads from left to right, each representing a writing accomplishment, and now what? It's time to push some more beads across—to tally more good things. But the first set of beads, the ones already on the right, still *exist*. You still get to count them.

Trying to weigh the value of our work against other writers only leads to feelings of embarrassment, jealousy, and frustration. It's a lot more productive to ponder your character's next move than to fixate on why so-and-so got a six-figure advance while you're still plodding through your third draft.

WHEN WE JUDGE BOOKS, WE'RE evaluating brains and artistic sensibilities and access to writing teachers (or not) and a million narrative choices. Not every decision will resonate with every reader. When we try to pin a value on a book, we usually skip right to talking about sales. Capitalism has taught us that value ought to be measured. But it's different—or should be—with art. A piece of beautiful writing can be given freely and make a difference in someone's life. Isn't that value too? Your work doesn't have to *sell* to matter to you and the people who are fortunate enough to encounter it.

Objectively, some books cost more than others at the bookstore; does that mean they're *worth* more? Does the answer depend on how many copies are sold, how many people are buying and reading it? An author's work can be valued in dollars counted up on royalty statements, but its *worth* is not as clear-cut.

You don't have to be inside the circle of popular people—or best-selling authors, or even published authors—for your art to matter. What you make matters because it's yours. As soon as you invest time and spirit in the work, it exists, and no gatekeeper can devalue it. No rejection can make it wink out of existence. Only you—in losing hope, in giving up, in listening to the critics, in trying to take down other people's art as a way to elevate yours—can make your work worth *less*.

And even then, even in letting go of a manuscript you once believed in, there's worth in having done the work.

I lost a lot of writing years to anxiety and uncertainty. Questioning my storytelling, my way with words. Trying to understand the market so I could create for it and find the worth I had trouble ascribing to myself. Waiting for someone to call my name.

It took more years to understand the inherent power in creating work outside the mainstream. On my own terms. In my own way. That's the power of story. Of voice. *Your* voice.

IF YOU FIND YOURSELF MARINATING in jealousy, reread Fonda's words. Log off social media for a while. Make more time for your writing—all the delights, frustrations, and surprises that happen when you sit quietly with yourself. Or step away from your work and take a nap or a walk or cook a delicious treat or pull out your old watercolors or think about an accomplishment you achieved recently at work.

And you can—you *should,* if you know them personally—congratulate the person with genuine appreciation for whatever you *do* admire about their work. You are secure enough, stable and grounded enough, to deliver this act of kindness. It can be a quick text message; it doesn't have to be a major public declaration for it to count. (Just like I didn't *need* to take five hundred photos of every single book event I attended over ten years and crash my desktop computer and riddle my hands with pain.) You can congratulate and be kind without trying to ingratiate or compensate for how small you feel. Your art matters too. You can afford to honor someone else's art and say you're glad for them.

And someday, if you win a prize or secure representation with a fancy agent and people congratulate *you,* you'll remember how you handled this blip of disappointment. How someone else's good thing *almost* made you feel like a failure. Almost made you scream or quit. And how instead, you transformed it into more energy: golden hope energy. Writing energy. And you carried on. And now here you are, coveted prize in hand.

List Some Achievements

Sometimes when *community* turns into a jealousy mosh pit, or there's back and forth scrabbling on social media, it's time to reestablish boundaries and sense of self. Think about all the things you've written over the years—for pleasure or school or work.

What compliments have you received?

What challenges have you overcome?

Write your answers here, in a notebook you keep for this purpose, or a set of index cards that you can shuffle, add to, or recycle as your thoughts change.

You can count something as small as an hour spent at the local coffee shop, researching for a project, writing a letter to a grieving friend, preparing a statement for your local school board, or revising a piece after it has been rejected.

You can count an invitation to speak at an online event, getting feedback from a critique partner, or digging in to that feedback and beginning to see a new draft emerge.

Count whatever has made you feel good about your writing. Try, especially, to find some memories you might not have counted before.

Once you have some notes, start celebrating these moments. Sonja Thomas, author of *Olive Blackwood Takes Action!*, puts it this way: "It's important to celebrate all the successes, big and small, especially those outside of our control. You can't control an agent, editor, or reader loving your book, but you can control showing up to the page and working on your craft. So celebrate writing for an hour or taking a writing workshop or sending out query letters. It's all about loving the [writing] journey, always celebrating and finding those pockets of joy."

You can honor each step solo or loop in your friend or your partner. One idea is to decorate a glass jar. Write each good thing on a slip of paper, fold it, then deposit it inside the jar. Imagine yourself feeling fuller, more seen, as an artist. Weeks or months later, when you need to boost your confidence to start submitting or when you're heartsick over a rejection, you can pull out the evidence that your work matters to others, not just to you.

Or why not hold a party for several writer friends who have achievements of their own?

If you wait until something bigger comes along to celebrate, you'll skip acknowledging so much good stuff and downplay (or forget) a lot of special moments.

A poem accepted? Worthy of celebrating.

A full manuscript request? Worthy.

Receive your friend's feedback? Celebrate the work left to do and the fact that you have a pal willing to inhabit this revision space with you.

THE FAVOR ECONOMY

So many writing resources conflate *community* with *audience*. Yes, we can be both. Of course we can! When you're on submission, being able to list potential blurbers or conversation partners helps you prove that you have a *platform*. But as writers, we open the door to each other for support, interaction, and getting through the hard times—not because we want to be on the receiving end of your sales pitches.

Besides, writers almost *always* aren't your target market. (Books like this, about writing and publishing, are the exception.) Your audience might be someone living with severe illness, or kids who are obsessed with outer space, or a person on the other side of a divorce, or a nonbinary aromantic person, or someone who loves cozy mysteries or otherworldly quests or contemporary poetry or fermenting vegetables.

When a writer follows me on social media and I follow back, and then they message me a form letter about why I should buy their book on Amazon, I unfollow. I am actively anti-Amazon, for one thing. Plus this kind of messaging tells me the author sees me as a potential sale. A target, not a human being or a creative peer.

There are examples of this kind of behavior all over the internet, with writers shilling their products without engaging in conversations, sharing other people's links and news, or interacting in *any other way* than asking for attention. Those are the people I tune out. It may be well intentioned, but it feels like spamming.

When there's no attempt to shine light on other authors before or after the sales pitches, these attempts read as *me, me, me*. Not community building. Not interacting. These posts read more like commercials. Annoying and better off muted.

WE DON'T BUILD COMMUNITY JUST to *sell* to community.

READING EACH OTHER'S WORK, BLURBING a manuscript before it sells (to get an agent's attention) or after it sells (to get the public's attention), attending an event, and posting reviews are all ways a community can support its members in quantifiable ways, but there are so many other ways to show support. I have a few friends I call when something's really bothering me and I can't get past it. I have friends who are willing to sit and listen to me run numbers about the press's financial health and offer suggestions. I have friends who will join me outside, wearing blankets and hats, for a work session when my immune system is low and I need the tether of company to get some words down.

A lot of coaches, how-to-publish experts, and the like encourage giving back to writers so they will blurb you or show up to your events. That's trading favors and there's nothing wrong with it. But if you go into building community expecting a payload of material value for the time you put in, you should join your local chamber of commerce, not a camaraderie of novelists or a fugue of music journalists.

Nikole Potulsky, a fabulous business strategist, helped me understand how to talk about my outsider approach as a publisher: it decentralizes the power structure. We can shake up the status quo by creating an alternate structure based on our position as outsiders instead of trying to force our way into the inner circles.

And if you do get invited to the center circle, do what you can to use your voice to elevate and support those who aren't in the room. Then, like in the hero's journey, bring the information back to the clouds who are waiting for it.

Or the fugues.

Or the whole dang imaginarium.

It turns out this is my mission as much as publishing books. To introduce writers to each other, and writers to readers, and to break down the walls by sharing information I've gathered as a publisher. To help writers who are spinning because of something they read online to gain context and put their creative selves back into the center—not the noise.

We don't need famous authors to hold the door open for us. We don't even need gatekeepers in New York to offer us a two-book deal for a six-figure advance. That would be nice . . . but we are valid as writers, as makers, as long as we are committed to the work.

In 2016, when I started putting notes together for *Imagine a Door*, I wanted to collect what I knew about publishing in an accessible format. Print and ebook and audio would increase access; writers wouldn't have to pay money for a class or a conference to hear me share these things. They wouldn't have to be able-bodied and immune-strong to brave a public appearance. Or show up at a certain time online. They could borrow a book from the library, from a friend, or buy a copy and then pass it on to their friends.

It took years to move that idea into the world. From scrappy, assorted files to a cohesive enough first draft to hire an editor.

Those in-between years were spent publishing, writing, getting my first novel out, and becoming clearer about having something to say. About my identity as someone who has been on both sides of the desk: published and publisher.

Before Covid I had gotten to the point of waltzing into a bookstore, feeling excited to see two people I adored in the same space, starting to introduce them to each other, and then feeling sheepish because they were already friends. (Sometimes because *I* had introduced them a few years back. Oops!) But the more these moments happened, the more I felt like I had done what I set out to do. Now others were building off that work and growing roots, and I didn't have to be *quite* so zealous. Community had become more vibrant, lush, and exciting over the years since I first jumped in, thanks to collective effort.

Community makes me happy. And braver. I used to focus on building community as a way to keep myself in the shadows, but over the years I became okay with showing up, even standing in the spotlight sometimes. And the more of us who do this work, the more we keep reading centered in the cultural conversation, even if it's a group of friends saying, *Have you picked up XYZ title? What did you think?* while other friends are discussing the latest Hulu hit series.

You don't have to wait for someone in the literary ecosystem to ask you a question. You can do the asking. You're here, writing, aren't you? By existing as a writer, you are part of the whole, even if nobody notices you in the corner at the coffee shop, doing your work. You don't have to get invited in. You can invite. Or sneak in yourself, then hold the door open for everyone else.

If you participate in a group of people who love the same thing you do, you will get all kinds of benefits. Most of these will be intangible. They might not buy the week's groceries, but you can bank them in your heart.

Cheesy, right?

But in the hardest times, when rejections sting so much you want to turn away from your project, to disown the work you've loved the most, you won't be alone. You'll have all those people. All those moments where you've boosted each other. These are your buoys. Your buffers. I imagine an inflatable raft coming to rescue you from your island of shame, just as soon as you call for help.

I think of this as the best part of the favor economy; if you help others, they will be there when you need help. But that's less about finances and selling books than it is about human decency, kindness, and connection.

WRITING GROUPS

WRITING GROUPS ARE OFTEN MORE about skill building than socially focused literary gatherings. Both are great for your development.

Feedback-focused groups help you get regular responses to your drafts if you are midproject and need reassurance or redirection. Your peers will help you figure out where you've gone off track, what's working, and what could get cut. And it's usually free to participate, which is great because conferences and workshops, where you can get similar experiences, are paid opportunities.

When it's not your turn to share, there's plenty to absorb. As each member gets their pages critiqued, you can roll those lessons into your own work.

A good one—where you feel heard and safe to share unpolished work—is gold. But part of having a successful writing group experience, I've noticed, is figuring out when it's time to leave. Sometimes groups can become stagnant or divisive; neither status is ideal for creative output.

I've only briefly participated in online groups, after two of my communities moved to that format during the pandemic.

I ended up exiting both pretty quickly. My best school friend from fifth grade died from COVID-19 in April 2020, and that summer I found myself sobbing when I peered at the faces of my peers in little digital boxes. Being together in an online space reminded me too much of the terror of contagion. The following spring I ended up writing a new novel without any group support, just getting it done in a few months because we adopted my sister-in-law's dog and he wanted to sleep in my lap.

Since leaving my groups, I've participated in parallel play sessions and occasional multiday retreats, where we work alone and then come together for progress reports. Other times I chat or text with a friend on the phone about how our projects are going, where we're stuck, what the research is like, and that's enough to keep me going.

When I need feedback, I hire a professional developmental editor to respond to the whole project. I used to thrive on paragraph-by-paragraph responses in writing group because that feedback made me feel good, but at this stage in my career, I need a clearheaded editor to respond to my whole manuscript not in short chunks but as a whole. The way a reader will experience it.

WORD OF MOUTH IS A great way to hear about which writing groups are open to new members in your genre or local area. It's hard to find a group that works for you, so if you don't immediately luck out, try again. Don't stay out of obligation or stubbornness. If going makes you feel awkward, stick with it, but if it makes you feel *bad*, maybe it's not the group for you.

Sometimes groups have an acceptance procedure to vet new members, hoping to avoid the awkwardness of the not-a-fit conversation a few months later. I recently visited a children's book group with an invitation from a longtime member, knowing it would need to be a fit for them and for me to continue. Ultimately I joined, but we all went into it with open communication.

Groups may pass out pages in advance, which means homework. You have to read work (and often jot down comments) before you meet, in addition to readying your own pages when it's your turn. Other groups pass out pages during their meeting and/or read those pages aloud. I've mostly been in read-aloud groups, which has helped me develop as a writer. Immediate feedback in terms of gasps, laughs, or total silence taught me what my fellow authors liked about my work. I can also experience how they react to other people's words in real time. Sometimes, though, experiencing the material in the moment is hard, especially if it's traumatic or your brain is focused on something in your real life.

Usually, regardless of how the pages are shared, there's a page-count recommendation or a maximum number so everyone has a turn. For a year or two I belonged to a novel group where we shared our full manuscript, had six or eight weeks to do the reading, and then we came together to discuss that one project for a few hours. We devised it as an antidote to the workshop method where we maxed out at ten pages. I could write a great ten-page section, but I didn't know how to fit ten pages next to another ten pages and manipulate the story in a way that would keep readers hooked. The novel group helped me see those patterns and fix them.

If you're working with short pieces of text, frequency of meeting matters—not that there's one best way, but it's helpful to find a schedule that matches your time, availability, and writing process. My output was always greater than what I could share in my monthly group. I kept my shares to under five pages, not wanting to take up too much time, but as a novelist, I was often grappling with twenty-page chapters. Getting feedback on three of those pages helped, but I often needed to explain what came before and after. Weekly meetings might have fit my creative output better, but I didn't have the time in my caregiving schedule to miss a few hours of home life every week if I wanted to keep writing too.

If it feels like a scary thing to ask to join an existing group, you can try starting your own. I did that with flyers, but my favorite way of low-key finding like-minded creatives is taking classes and looking around at who's there with you. (You get to try out the other humans! Without committing to them long-term!)

Within the structure of the class, if you appreciate someone's work or the way they talk about writing, you can ask if they'd be interested in trading pages or starting a group with you. The benefit there is you can talk to people whose work fuels something in you. Find those areas of overlap first, then see if that person wants to write with you. Who knows, they might have a group and invite you to check it out.

CASE STUDY #4: Finding Your People

SO HOW DO YOU FIND your people? I had no idea in 2002, after I had moved to Portland, Oregon. I only knew one other writer: my roommate's childhood friend.

So she and I started a writing group. Sharing the responsibility felt safer than starting one on my own. We put flyers up around the neighborhood to advertise.

Much to my surprise, people showed up for our first meeting at Annie Bloom's Books. We congregated in the cozy upstairs room.

Our group setup cost time and the printing of a few flyers; the bookstore didn't charge for their space. We didn't have a social media presence or an email list or even a name. We just showed up when we could, sitting with each other's stories on couches. I used *A Writer's Book of Days* by Judy Reeves to supply freewriting prompts. After that warm-up, we shared work and talked about it. We didn't have a rigorous critique protocol. We just sat with each other and listened.

It didn't feel like creating community so much as committing to myself as a writer. Marking those dates on the calendar. Bringing a page or two to read aloud.

A writer named Steve Arndt showed up at our first meeting and told us about studying fiction with Tom Spanbauer, founder of Dangerous Writing. Tom had worked with Gordon Lish at Columbia and written many books, *The Man Who Fell in Love with the Moon* (Harper Perennial) among them.

Thanks to Steve's love of connecting writers to each other, I wrangled an invitation to visit Tom's basement workshop. Steve also invited me to attend a session run by Stevan Allred and Joanna Rose.

He opened those doors to me—doors I didn't even know existed until he showed me. I decided to join Stevan and Joanna's workshop, which became known as the Pinewood Table. I was a newspaper editor at the time, putting in late nights on deadline and for board meetings, so I could afford to leave work early on Wednesday afternoons.

Paying for a class and carving out that time made me feel like a real writer. I brought in pages of my first *good* novel—the first one I actually finished. I learned so much about the craft of writing while getting and giving feedback. But most of all, I met my first best Portland writing friends there. Being a writer in that room gave me a sense of belonging. A belief that there was a place for me in Portland, my new city.

"Writing can be numbingly lonely," Steve said. "But! We share similar sensibilities and desires and so, friendship is a garden waiting for you inherently tilled with support, kindness, fun, and safety."

Years later Steve invited me to a just-formed group with people who had met in Dangerous Writing. We got together monthly and worked in all genres. One day, novelist Dian Greenwood mentioned her friend Judy Reeves, and I said, "Wait! Judy Reeves who wrote *A Writer's Book of Days?*"

And Dian confirmed: indeed, *that* Judy Reeves, founder of the San Diego Writer's Circle. I explained how I used Judy's prompts back when I ran my own writing group, and how Steve Arndt showed up one day.

Circles overlapping with other circles.

It only takes one person saying, *You should meet someone . . .* to change your life. And if that happens to you, you might find yourself wanting to make your own introductions. To be like Steve Arndt. To grow community because it benefits everyone.

Steve, besides introducing lots of writers to each other over the years, is the founder of the annual Portland Writers' Picnic. As you might guess, everyone's invited. Everyone's welcome.

PAID WORKSHOPS THAT RUN MULTIPLE sessions can be excellent alternatives to writing groups. There's a natural structure and a leader to enforce the rules like page count or to encourage specific (positive) critique methods. If you can afford to put money into your writing at this time, there's the security of having a leader making sure the conversation stays on track and that kindness and respect are centered in every critique.

We have multiple nonprofits and for-profit businesses in Portland that hold classes for writers. There are options that fit different budgets, schedules, and genre needs. Literary Arts, Corporeal Writing, the Attic Institute, Write Around Portland, and others all run classes in my community.

But here's a tip: you should never invest in writing instruction expecting to earn the money back someday with your writing career. It could happen, but there's no guarantee. Classes and conferences and retreats and developmental edits all add up. So do all the hours you spend writing. If and when you sell your debut someday, it may not sell enough copies to earn back those investment costs, but maybe your second or third book will. But probably not.

Instruction can teach you craft and help you get words on the page and hopefully lead to deep friendships. You're investing in your career, putting in time and money to level up as an artist. But that doesn't mean you're going to sell your book, someday, for more money than if you hadn't taken classes.

So join a workshop to learn. To make friends. To get better at the craft. To have an expert leading the conversation with skill.

These are all great reasons to invest in yourself if you can afford it.

If you can't afford it, look for free workshops, scholarship offerings, and local bookstore events, which are almost always free to attend.

What to Consider

HERE ARE SOME QUESTIONS TO think about when you're trying to find a writing group.

- Where does the group meet? If it's in person, can you access the location easily?
- Does the time and date of meeting change, or is it a set schedule?
- What's the meeting frequency?
- Is there reading homework to do in advance each meeting, or do the writers read aloud during sessions, or some combination?
- Do writers take turns sharing pages? Is there a page limit?
- Can you commit to the hours necessary to attend a group and also work on your own writing?
- If it's a paid workshop, can you visit the class and/or talk to a current student before committing? Can you afford the fee for multiple classes or sessions?

Here are some things to keep in mind.

- Sometimes people who share writing regularly start sounding like each other. You'll want to be aware of this and avoid it if possible.
- There are often members who talk more than others. You'll want to find the right balance of speaking up, sharing your thoughts, and listening to what others have to say. It's more like a "to taste" recipe when it comes to how

much is too much, but you don't want to monopolize or veer the other direction and stay totally quiet in the corner. (I did the latter for about a year in one of my groups.)

- If there's a page limit in your group, watch yourself for writing *to* that page number.

VISIT THE LIBRARY

If you aren't writing group inclined and don't have the cash to sign up for a class, there are plenty of other ways to find your people. Libraries are incredible community hubs. Even better: they're open to the public and free! Usually the county or city infrastructure provides public transportation stops near them, allowing for more accessibility than some bookstores provide.

Check your local branch for writing-related programming and become one of the regulars. By showing up to author talks, you'll be part of the community, even if you sit and listen in the back row. Slowly, as you feel more comfortable, you can start asking questions and meeting other people in the room.

These sacred spaces in your community provide a safe and welcoming place for readers and writers to gather. If you can't afford to buy your friend's book, you can request the library carry it by filling out an online form or talking to a librarian. Often this results in a multiple-format buy—the audiobook and ebook in addition to the physical printed work.

Sometimes readers feel apologetic about borrowing an author's book instead of spending money on buying their own copy. From the author and publisher side, libraries are the very best customers because they don't return books.

Returns happen when a bookstore or gift shop agrees to carry a book and it doesn't sell. The shop has the opportunity to ship the book back and get a full refund. Each of these transactions cost publishers a fee in addition to the full refund. There are exceptions—consigned books, for instance, are on loan with no money changing hands up front. If they sell, the author gets money. If they don't, the author gets the books back. If they get damaged, that's the author's problem since ownership hasn't transferred. Some publishers refuse to allow returns, but usually the booksellers refuse to carry those titles because it's financially risky—or they only take them on consignment.

RETURNS: Books that are sent back to the publisher, or the publisher's distributor, when they don't sell to customers. The customers (bookstores and other stores that carry books as merchandise) get full refunds. Sometimes books are damaged while in stores and get returned and credited back to the store anyway, making the loss the publisher's problem.

When libraries buy books, they don't return them. Patrons can come, check out a book, and return it, but those books are library property. End stop. They aren't in danger of being sent back for a refund.

I think of bookstores' shelves of books as temporary sales. If a customer comes in and decides to take a title home, then it's a point-of-sale sale, also called POS, an *actual* sale that counts toward royalties. Until that point, though, the book is just hanging out on the store shelves, temporarily in the bookstore's custody but not representing a *true* sale because it can be returned. Or it can be damaged, which doesn't count as a sale either. It's important to know about returns because often publishers tell their authors how many books have sold into stores, giving a falsely high number of "sales" (and hope!), when really the numbers don't count until the books go home with customers. Even though many returns happen at the three-month period of a book's life cycle, many can be returned months or years later. The expected return rate for books used to be 20 percent. In June 2024, the Association of American Publishers released data for April 2024, citing an 18.8 percent return rate among companies that contributed data; the July return announcement, for May sales, was 13 percent (down from 21 percent in 2023). All this to say, it fluctuates. Whenever a major chain or corporation restructures its buying program (think Barnes & Noble or Amazon), returns can skyrocket way beyond these numbers.

Libraries also provide access to books, DVDs, and audio editions to readers who otherwise wouldn't discover the material. Thanks to online portals like Libby and OverDrive, people can check out ebooks and audiobooks instantly without leaving their houses.

Your local librarians are also excellent writing resources. When you're looking for something to read, if you're trying to figure out who in your community is writing and publishing, or when you're working on research for your book, librarians can help. "Writers are of course generally readers themselves," said Heather Waisanen, adult services programmer at the Garden Home Community Library in Oregon. "I've known quite a few that have used the library for research for their books. Whether I know who they are or not, they get the same level of service as a patron who is placing a hold or asking a reference question."

In addition to all these (free!) wonders, libraries with community rooms have long been hosts to writing groups and book study groups. They're also excellent for writers seeking a free, quiet space in which to work. Unlike going to a restaurant or coffee shop, you aren't expected to buy anything. "Libraries are often referred to as the third place," said Tamara McIntyre, director of the Waccamaw Neck Branch Library in Pawleys Island, South Carolina. "We offer space, space to write (work), quiet and collaborative; space to create and share—author readings, local author collections—fostering a love of books and reading, creating lifelong readers (and book buyers); and space to learn, libraries offer resources and knowledge to help authors research for books—making for a more authentic reading experience."

SUPPORT YOUR LOCAL BOOKSTORE

I LOVE BOOKSTORES. THEY'RE MY favorite. (Along with libraries. I have lots of favorites.) Bookstores are also a major component of many authors' dreams of publication.

Seeing your book on the shelf!

Doing a reading!

Signing copies!

Speaking at the same venues where your hero writers have spoken!

If this is what you want, start establishing relationships with area stores now as part of your community-building project. Being present in the store as a familiar face will go a long way toward establishing a relationship.

Here are some other great ways to build a bookstore-centric community:

Attend author events

These are almost always free—the exceptions are ticketed

ones where the book is part of the price. If you become a regular, the booksellers will start recognizing you, especially if you ask questions or remember to say thanks. Then you can post a few photos on social media, tag the store, and your handle will be seen by the people you just met.

It's great to attend bookstore events for out-of-town authors with big fan bases, but if you start showing up at some of the events featuring local authors and publishing houses, you'll tap into those networks. You'll begin to recognize who likes the same kind of work as you, who knows everyone in the room, and who you might sit next to and say hi. Some regular attendees always sit in the same place. And many of us bookstore regulars love to meet new people and introduce them around.

I always encourage writers to have business cards on them for such meetings. (They're also great to remind you that you are a writer. *See? It says so on my business card!*) I went through a thousand a year for a few years. Not everyone is paper centered like me, though; if you prefer dropping names, numbers, or emails into your phone, that works too. Or exchange social media handles.

Preorder a book

When you place a preorder, the publisher sees sales numbers and the bookstore gets income and notices that there's demand for the title. A preorder puts the book on the store's radar; that might mean the store decides to carry a few copies. It's a great way to support your favorite authors and small presses that might not otherwise get the attention of the store.

Plus: whoever is taking down your information, and whoever helps you with pickup once the title arrives, will see your name.

Someday, the book being ordered will be yours! And the staff will be excited for you.

Walk in, say hello, and be kind

Ask for suggestions or help locating a title you want. Don't push in front of another customer. Don't ask a bookseller to throw your trash away. Don't ask for a long explanation or favor if there's a line (or if it's December, when stores are slammed with shoppers). Get a frequent reader card if they offer one. Admire the special sections or pick up a face-out book. Be appreciative.

Pay attention to shelf talkers

Shelf talkers are those paper signs with booksellers' recommendations on them. They might be tucked under a book or slipped into the cover like a bookmark. As you visit your local store(s), see what's being recommended and which staff members like the kind of books you do. If you buy a recommended title and love it, next time you see that staff member, you can thank them for a great read.

Visit indies when you travel

If you have the health and budget to go to other cities, plan to visit their local independent stores. You can, years later, reach out to let them know you visited when you were in town, you loved their store, and now your debut is coming out and you hope they'll consider stocking it. It's so much easier to make an ask if you've been to the bookstore.

Tag the bookstore on social media if you share content related to the store

Comment on store posts when you want to read a book they

feature or if you like an image of the bookstore cat. Sharing pictures or adding a comment on the store's feed are great ways to interact and boost book culture for free.

Buy books when you can afford to!

After all, writers need to support other writers and the culture of literature, and one way to do that is to spend money locally. Just remember: spending money doesn't mean you'll earn it back with your own book sales someday. That's not an equation that works.

Here are three additional easy—and dare I say *essential*—ways to show your appreciation for your local bookstore in your online life:

- **Opt out of sharing Amazon links.**
- **Opt out of buying books on Amazon.**
- **Definitely don't tell people to buy *your* book or your friend's book on Amazon.**

I've mentioned my feelings about Amazon before, but it's an important enough topic to take a deeper look. Amazon doesn't need your dollars or your friends' dollars. People who shop there all the time will find your book without you having to give them the link. By sharing Amazon links, or encouraging people to review your book there, you are acknowledging their power and promoting them over local stores.

I understand that especially in rural communities with few brick-and-mortar stores, Amazon can be a way to get products shipped to your home at a major discount. But spending your money through Bookshop.org or Libro.fm (for audiobooks)—two sites that return a percentage of sales to independent stores—shows your commitment to their survival. Independent bookstores keep so much more of each dollar in the community. They're being run by people who are invested in the place you call home. They're being staffed by your neighbors.

Even though years ago, Barnes & Noble was considered a threat to independents, it's now one of the proverbial good guys. Publishers are united in wanting the chain to survive because if it fails, it'll mean a large part of the bookselling market has dried up. Remember those returns? It'd be catastrophic to publishers to have a chain's worth of books come back. For decades, Barnes & Noble and Borders were competition for local independent stores. But then Amazon came along and let books be a loss leader—discounting them far below what brick-and-mortar stores could do. Borders went bankrupt in 2011 and closed all its stores.

Throughout the 2010s, Barnes & Noble struggled to survive as Amazon continued to grow its literary market share. Return rates skyrocketed. As an example, our first book to make a national splash sold in bulk to Barnes & Noble. More than six hundred copies came back as returns, the bulk of them in 2016. That volume could have tanked my tiny press—and lots of presses did go under in that decade because of overzealous sell-ins. It took a long time for my balance sheet to right itself, and that was just the impact of one chain on one particularly successful title that didn't perform as expected in chain stores.

Barnes & Noble's trajectory has been upward since selling in 2019 to a hedge fund and letting local stores decide what to stock. These days, it's kind of everyone versus Amazon. If you want to learn more, read Danny Caine's *How to Resist Amazon and Why: The Fight for Local Economics, Data Privacy, Fair Labor, Independent Bookstores, and a People-Powered Future* (Microcosm).

While Forest Avenue Press sells books on Amazon, per our distribution agreement, we don't promote the site and we encourage our authors to share links to independents and Bookshop.org. Not just *along with* but *instead of*. Amazon doesn't need us; playing the numbers game, trying to get a bestseller in a niche category just so we can share a screenshot on our socials, isn't worth turning our backs on the independent stores.

Forest Avenue Press shares our love of independent stores in every call for manuscript submissions. It's astonishing how many times we get a letter from an author saying they love their local stores—hurray!—but a quick check of their social media shows Amazon link after Amazon link. I don't think the authors are misleading us so much as they're buying into the common "wisdom" that you *have* to share Amazon links. That Amazon sales are important.

So I'm saying it here: you can opt out.

I BEGAN MY PRESS WITH a mission to bring readers and writers together inside indie bookstores. That creates conversations around reading, keeps dollars in the local economy, and shows the booksellers that you care about their store. So as we sign our authors, we urge them to share independent store links, not Amazon ones.

Because I have national distribution, though, our titles populate to Amazon automatically. I don't push sales there, because people who use Amazon know how to search their database without me having to help them, but I also haven't asked my team if I could stop the data flow. I just ignore it.

Publisher Michael Heald, who runs Perfect Day Books and distributes his titles to independent stores across the country, has made the choice to completely opt out. I'm so impressed by his ability to create these individual connections with store buyers, one store at a time. I asked Michael for more information about why he works so hard to have this hands-on indie model and he said: "We've never sold our books on Amazon and never will. Frankly, I find their business practices Machiavellian and anti-community, and I'm only sacrificing a small percentage of sales by boycotting them. I believe that every neighborhood in America should have a brick-and-mortar bookstore, and in this one small way I'm attempting to contribute to that goal."

Bookstore Etiquette

First-time authors have to get brave and ask bookstores for favors. Those favors could be stocking the book, taking it on consignment, hosting an event, or some combination.

In asking, and *before* asking, you'll want to avoid behaviors that mark you as troublesome or entitled—especially if you plan to be a multipublished author! If the staff rolls their eyes when they see you approach the cash wrap, you're not going to be welcomed back with as much delight as authors who are kind and courteous.

Don't ask to be put on the staff pick list. This puts booksellers in a very uncomfortable position. Maybe they haven't read your book. Maybe they read it and *didn't like it*. So. Just don't.

Don't ask to be displayed face out on the local author shelf. You can walk in and mention you're local—hopefully they already know you—and ask to sign stock. This works best if you first look around the store and see if they have your book.

Lots of writers tell each other to flip your book face out if you see it at an independent bookstore, but unless they work at a bookstore, they're trying on an entitled behavior from the outside of the business.

I say *don't*.

Booksellers get to choose who to promote. That's their job!

Especially if you negate one of their face-out picks—flip it so only the spine shows—to make space to feature yourself, booksellers will *notice* and *remember* when you come to ask for an event. They will suspect it was you or maybe a friend who acted entitled on your behalf—and either way, that's not a good look, is it?

Don't share Amazon links on social media—or your Amazon bestseller status in some obscure category. Instead, share independent bookstore links and photos. Sales of your book really matter to them. And chances are, if you have an Amazon bestseller status, you got there because a handful of books sold (unless you are an Amazon-focused author and have chosen that practice over your local stores, in which case you are probably arguing loudly with me in your head). Besides, gaming the numbers used to work better for indie authors before everyone started talking about how to hit those lists.

Which would you rather have: a screenshot of an Amazon list or your book face out in the window of the local store or on the staff pick table?

I choose, every time, the local store.

If you feel pressured by your publisher to link to Amazon on your author website, I encourage you to list other independent bookstore links first and put Amazon last. That sends a message to stores: the indies matter *more*.

Don't try to negotiate about the consignment policy; chances are whoever is working the counter didn't make the rules but must enforce them. If you can't afford the discount the bookstore requires for shelving your book (usually 40 percent of the cover price), you can say yes anyway, if you want your book in that store. And if it's not financially doable—if you'll lose money per sale and can't accept that as a business expense—go back to your publisher and see if you can negotiate your terms with them. In almost every case, bookstore policies won't change because you want them to. The best way to handle this issue is to understand your book contract language and how your press works with bookstores *before* you sign. I'll share a lot more specifics about distribution in the PUBLISHING section.

Don't ask friends and family to call (pester) the store until they stock your book. If you're local and you aren't getting in, it's probably a distribution issue. Especially don't encourage this if all the people calling already have your book and won't be buying it from the store anyway.

Don't complain about how little stock is brought in for your event. If your book sells out, great! You had a successful event! It's worse for the publisher and bookseller if they bring in way too many books and have to return a lot. Returns cost money and time. You can always carry a case of your books in the car just in case they run out and are willing to accept some extra copies on consignment. Also, most bookstores will special-order copies if they run out, and that'll mean they—and you—still get the sale the night of the event, even if the product isn't there. You can always leave signed book plate stickers or swing back (if you're local) to sign when the new stock comes in.

There are some other things you can do, specifically if you have a book coming out that you want a store to carry.

Do bring in an advance reading copy or galley to share with bookseller staff. If they already know you, great, but if not, identify yourself as a local.

Do encourage your friends to order (or preorder) your book from their local indie if it's not in stock. That shows actual demand and interest; pre-orders will get you on the buyers' radar.

Do get used to asking the staff for advice on what to read or even comp titles for your work in progress. Obviously, coming in mid–holiday rush expecting concierge treatment isn't okay. But showing up on a quiet Tuesday evening with thoughtful questions about what sells and what books might match yours, could be fun for the staff and you. Unless you're a regular customer, asking for that kind of favor means that it would be awfully nice if you could spend a little money. A discounted trade paperback or a bar of chocolate or a greeting card could show your appreciation and goodwill, but if you can buy one of the books the staff recommends, that'd be even better.

Do see if your local bookstore ships to other places, and if so, see if they would be willing to be a hub for autographs and personalized inscriptions. Broadway Books in Portland does this for Cheryl Strayed and many other local authors. Likewise, Annie Bloom's, my local store, sets up autograph pages for local authors. When I get an email saying a signature order is in, I pop by at my convenience.

Do share links to local bookstores, Bookshop.org, Libro.fm, and maybe a few other bookstores that offer shipping. This can be a great option if you live in a rural community without a local bookstore. You can choose to spend your money at a specific store you visited or in a city you used to live in.

Do visit independent bookstores when you travel. Especially if you don't have a local one, browsing a store when you're visiting another town or city will help you get a feel for the consumer side of the industry in a personal, nonalgorithmic kind of way. And if you want to leave a postcard or a bookmark or an advance reader copy of your new book, that kind of gesture is appreciated as long as you are polite and not belligerent about them accepting your material.

ADVANCE READER COPY: An advance reader copy—also called an ARC, an uncorrected proof, or a galley—is a pre-release version of your book. ARCs can be sent out to reviewers and booksellers in digital form (PDF or ebook) or in paperback form. They are not for sale and they usually carry a statement about checking any quotes against the finished product; content may change during later editing stages. At Forest Avenue, we call coverless ARCs "galleys" to differentiate them from the more-polished ones.

If you are feeling bashful when you visit a bookstore, or if you don't have material to drop off yet, visit the store anyway. You can jot down a few notes about what you like and plan another visit for later. You can then use those notes—especially specific and positive words about how you enjoyed their staff picks or the cozy vibe of the store—when you give them an ARC or ask for an event.

The best way to reach booksellers before your book comes out is to attend your local independent bookstore trade show. The Pacific Northwest Booksellers Association, the Mountains & Plains Independent Booksellers Association, the California Independent Booksellers Alliance, the Southern Independent Booksellers Alliance, and the New England Independent Booksellers Alliance offer regional gatherings that feature authors talking about their forthcoming titles, usually every fall. Some of the associations host smaller spring events as well.

THE DIY APPROACH

MUCH OF WHAT'S EXCITING ABOUT community comes together because of one person's vision. You can totally join that vision and attend a new reading series or buy a copy of a brand-new lit journal.

You can also add your own project to the mix. Building something new can take a lot of energy, effort, and time you might spend on your work, but it's a great way to positively impact writers around you.

Skyler Reed, a Klamath Tribes poet and artist, is one of the local community builders I admire most. They were the Northwest Folklife poetry slam champion early in their career, which led them to found Moved by Words in 2013 as a community project to document poetry gatherings in the Willamette Valley in Oregon. In other words, they started asking writers to show up and speak, and they started asking readers to come listen.

Skyler gave Moved by Words a three-pronged mission: making space for writers to debut new and experimental work, connecting writers under the Moved by Words umbrella, and documenting writers' achievements and readings. The events they create are intentionally inclusive, especially in terms of inviting new voices to take the stage.

Skyler said:

> Without the high bar of commercialism to clear, and a willingness to push the edge of acceptability or challenge art norms in person, there has been feedback from writers over the years that Moved by Words is by far their most favorite space to be in or event to be a part of. At the festival events, everyone rises or falls together.
>
> With the documentation and promotion project, groups and writers come and go but there never has been a year where the acceptance of new or experimental work on a stage in front of a willing crowd hasn't produced some of the most breathtaking and exciting moments. Because the work is so fresh, the writers are so new to it, there does not seem to be an audience or writer in recent memory who did not deeply feel the presence of a moment greater than ourselves.

"A moment greater than ourselves," Skyler calls these events they produce. That's a clarion call to community right there. We can write by ourselves, hold ourselves against the hot burn of our stories until the words melt into place, but only in community can we take in the words of others and share our own.

And don't we write to be with others in the liminal space of the mind? To touch others' lives? And maybe, hopefully, feel the zip and pull of another's mind working in response to our own?

CASE STUDY #5: Small Press Champion

WENDY FOX HELPS SMALL PRESS writers by promoting their books on national platforms. It's a niche she knows and appreciates as an author; her most recent titles, both from Santa Fe Writers Project, are *What If We Were Somewhere Else*, a story collection, and *If the Ice Had Held*, a novel. As someone who has held day jobs in marketing and public relations, Wendy started pitching articles about small presses and their authors. "I figured, instead of writing one-off reviews for tiny lit mags (open letter to lit mags: *please* make your reviews process easier), I could do roundups of all the crazy good books I was reading anyway and pitch to national magazines. I totally know that the review work I do is not true literary criticism, it's marketing; that's fine, too!"

She landed a small press column at *Buzzfeed*, which then moved to *Electric Literature* in 2023. "Ultimately," Wendy said, "what has happened is the more I put energy into shining a light on other writers, the more and more I find the entire enterprise of writing more satisfying. I think we need to bust the myth that this is a solitary practice."

It means so much—I'm tempted to say *everything*—when you're a small press author and your book gets covered in a mainstream publication. Wendy knows this. So often, the trade journals ignore small press titles or only occasionally review one. That's something we can't control—and something we as outsiders can't begin to emulate in terms of scale. But Wendy, in committing to this small press–championing space, has made a huge difference to many authors and their presses. Getting on a list on *Buzzfeed* or *Electric Lit* is often the biggest boost of a publicity campaign.

For a small press author, and for independent publishing houses, every recommendation matters. Every photo shows *this book is in the world*, and that's a gift. Wendy said:

> Of course most people want to be thought of as skilled in their genre; that's fine. There are a lot of fabulously talented writers that I guarantee most people have never heard of. I asked myself: *What makes you happy on the business side?* Anyone who writes is a writer. I was a writer before I had a single book. Yet, publishing is a decision to interact with the commercial side of art, and it can be hard to find joy in the monetization of one's heart and soul. I began to understand I wanted to be someone who is active about creating connections between writers and readers. I wanted to be someone who, instead of lamenting that small press books don't get deserved attention, tried to do something about it.

Anyone can help lesser-known titles get a few more readers by telling other people about books they like. Share a photo of your current read. Stop by the library and check out something from the local author shelf; those circulation numbers matter. Write a review when you're done. Add a line to your author newsletter where you list your latest read or the titles in your to-be-read stack. Loan your books out to neighbors and then talk about them while you're walking dogs together. Take photos in bookstores of small press titles, then tag the author and press. Invite a friend to coffee and ask if they've read a certain book. Or better yet, host an informal book exchange!

What you choose doesn't have to be an extravagant gift of your time; any energy diverted from consuming mainstream media into *admiring* or *promoting* the work of someone in your community, matters. Whatever time or energy you can expend. Give back just a little when you are able. Not because you expect the same from your peers—or because you desperately need to accrue favors so you can cash them in when you get your book out. But because you acknowledge that the central powers of publishing keep some people out while letting others in, and that you as a reader, as a *consumer* of books, can choose to read outside the lines others have tried to draw for you.

More Ways to Find Friends

- Is there a writing conference held in your area? If you can afford it and access the location, consider attending. Learning from publishing professionals and maybe even pitching some agents or editors will teach you a lot. Aside from the programming, you'll meet new friends during the meals, before each workshop starts, and so forth. If you can't comfortably pay to participate, reach out to the organizers and find out if you can volunteer in exchange for a pass. (Volunteers = instant belonging!)

- Ask someone you admire to have coffee or lunch. I (eventually) had to start saying no because I didn't have the energy or the immune system to keep it up, but for many years, this was my primary way of giving back to the publishing pros who taught me: teaching the next group. Modeling how we can exchange information and lift each other up instead of competing. I've shifted more into a consulting model these days because book sales aren't always reliable income, and I push most of my volunteer work onto online meetups, which carry less health risk than in-person ones.
- Read literary journals published locally. Who is doing the publishing? Who is writing? Send a compliment to one of the editors or authors and you might make a friend. Subscribe to the newsletter so you'll be notified the next time submissions open.
- When I feel insecure or disconnected, I like to volunteer. You make a difference—yay!—but you also hold space for yourself by showing up as an expert. Schools love having writers come talk to their students. Community nonprofits bring formalized writing instruction into classrooms and prisons. See if a reading series near you needs help with promoting their events or scouting for readers. Or volunteer to sort books at the local book bank.
- Reading a friend's essay and giving feedback,

or exchanging one of theirs for one of yours, is a great way to spend your time. It builds your writer brain to do that kind of critique, and it's invaluable to your friend. Some writers luck out in finding partners to trade pages with on the regular.

BECOMING A PUBLISHER

WHEN PEOPLE ASK ME WHY I started a press, I often quip, *Nobody told me how hard it is.*

I definitely took the get-involved idea further than a neurotypical person might have; in 2012 I realized I couldn't change New York publishing or influence acquiring editors with my personal taste, but I *could* publish Oregon writers. I set up a small press to do just that; the thought came from an outsider place combined with the privilege of a pot of funding I had intended to use for an MFA (back when MFAs cost less).

I couldn't afford to lose the money or to *spend* it all, but I could invest it in authors I believed in. I also had a spouse with a steady income and healthcare, so the fate of my family wasn't riding on whether or not I could sell enough books. Publishing seemed like a fun thing to try. If I worked hard and figured out how to make and sell novels, that would be good for my community, not just the individual authors I published. And this plan would earn me access. I could learn about the industry from the other side of the desk, and I could share all that information with the rest of us, the *community*. At the time I knew too many talented novelists banging on East Coast publishing doors and getting ignored. We wanted to grow up and be writers, and here we were, full-blown adults, grown-up as heck, *still* committed to writing but unsuccessful in getting agents and editors to care about us.

Why are we waiting for New York to pay attention? I wondered. *We want to read each other's work. Isn't that enough?*

I didn't know about the financial realities of the business, how to make a profit and loss statement to calculate which risks are worth taking, or how many hours I'd need to spend. The questions propelled me; that was enough.

Most people can't take a risk on starting a business that creates and tries to sell objects because there's so much money that goes into developing the products before they're even available for purchase. I realize what a privilege that opportunity is. I also realize how laughably small my efforts were compared to Elizabeth Koch's; as a billionaire's daughter, she invested in Catapult in 2015, which began its existence with lots of staff and the money to pay everyone, advertise their books, and sponsor housing for booksellers at Winter Institute. I spent the next few years watching Catapult's business decisions, how they chose to spend their money, and figuring out how I could react to the market at the micro level.

Portland in 2012 had many thriving independent publishers, including Hawthorne Books, Future Tense, Perfect Day, Tin House, Timber Press, Microcosm, Eraserhead, and Ooligan, a student-run press that's part of Portland State University. With a background in community journalism, public relations, and freelance manuscript editing, I had transferable skills—layout, managing freelancers, localizing pitches, writing press releases, and editing full-length creative works. And I had a very fussy three-month-old child. I needed to harness my heart and brain so I could fixate on something besides that rigid, arching body, so obviously in discomfort no matter what I did.

Sleep deprivation might have been *how* I decided to start a press, but the why had everything to do with Powell's Books getting an Espresso Book Machine. Like a glorified, state-of-the-art copy machine, it could print and bind real books inside the bookstore. I loved the idea of getting local authors' work into a major US store not because we had a track record or connections but because the mechanism of printing was already inside. Our first project, *Brave on the Page: Oregon Writers on Craft and the Creative Life,* was an anthology with cover art by graphic artist Gigi Little, who has designed the cover of every Forest Avenue book.

I named Forest Avenue after my elementary school in New Jersey; in fourth grade the librarian invited me to print and bind a long story I had written about a red recess ball. My first published work! Naming my press after that school seemed like a fitting tribute to a woman who saw me as a real writer.

A FEW YEARS AFTER I started Forest Avenue I found evidence that this decision to start a publishing house without any experience wasn't as random as it seemed. The proof: handwritten correspondence from the nineties saved in shoeboxes. At age sixteen I had sent letters to poetry editors seeking advice on starting my own poetry publication. We didn't have online databases or QueryTracker yet, so my requests for help were enclosed with original poems I sent for publication consideration. I also included the requisite SASE—a self-addressed, stamped envelope, folded in thirds—which is how editors responded yes or no back then.

I knew I wanted to be a writer in elementary school, but as a teen everything I knew about publishing I knew from reading print books and magazines and taking high school classes. I figured: How better to learn about publishing, as someone committed to the author life, than to start my own journal? It didn't seem impossible to me then, a junior at a new-to-me high school. I needed to anchor myself. I wanted to learn about publishing. I still thought of myself as a poet. (This was before other people's voices got into my head and convinced me I wasn't, *couldn't possibly be*, a poet.)

Entrepreneurship runs in the family. Both my parents ran their own businesses. In 1982 my dad founded a magazine, *Horn & Whistle*, for air-horn hobbyists, collecting train-related paraphernalia. I remember watching him do paste up by hand in his home office after work, moving segments of text and black-and-white photographs around.

If he could do it at his desk after work, then surely I could do something similar after school and between homework assignments.

Much to my surprise and delight, my SASEs returned with notes stuffed in them. Busy poetry editors and publishers took the time to write back. Some of them accepted my poems; others rejected them. But with the yes or no answers came information and encouragement about my project of creating a home for other people's poems.

Ira Rosenstein, founder of Starlight Press, sent me this handwritten note in 1992:

> Do whatever you do with energy.
> Put out an excellent, really professional-looking publication. Don't stint on quality of paper, typesetting, cover strength, etc.
> In choosing poems, choose for yourself, not unknowable others.
> Try as hard as possible to find a distributor.
> Don't expect to make a dime.

The industry has changed significantly in the past decades—especially due to technological innovations such as ebooks, audiobooks, and print-on-demand services—but energy, quality, taste, distribution, and tight profit margins continue to be primary factors in publishing.

"Don't expect to make any money—you will be lucky to break even!" wrote Michael Northen, editor of *Chimera Poetry Magazine*, in 1992. "It has to be something that you do because you love doing it."

Sparrow, a renowned poet, activist, and musician, took the time to add lines to the poems I had submitted—an act that mystified me at the time, someone trying to twist and tamp my work into a different mold. He heard me, though, and took the time to offer advice in his own peculiar way, advising me to make my cerebral teen poems more grounded, something I wasn't ready to hear.

"As for putting out a poetry mag, here is my theory of that," Sparrow wrote. "Put it out so cheaply that it doesn't matter if no one buys it. Walk around with extra copies of it, and give it out to anyone who seems interested. Do it for maximum fun."

Those letters I received meant *a lot* to me as a young writer and potential publisher. And they taught me about access. The people with power, who get to decide, can build community even if they don't accept your work. I wrote to these poets with a dream; they wrote me back to make sure I knew how hard it was. How much time it took. One even said she'd give up her journal soon because the work wasn't worth it. She had more poems to write.

Exactly twenty years after receiving those honest replies, I launched Forest Avenue Press to publish the kind of literary fiction I love to read. Too many talented, hardworking writers in my personal community had been turned away from the shiny New York gates because their novels were too *this*, or not enough *that*.

Besides, publishing sounded like *maximum fun*.

IN 2014, WITH THE HELP of advisors and the dawning knowledge that I needed to change my business model if I wanted independent bookstores to continue being our primary sales channel, I signed on for national distribution with Legato Publishers Group, owned by the Perseus Book Group. But then Perseus sold its distribution holdings to Ingram and Legato folded into Publishers Group West, a well-established, prestigious distributor based in Berkeley, California.

I would have never gotten PGW attention, I don't think, if I hadn't tiptoed through the back door in the Perseus days; as a result I'm among their smallest (tiniest) clients, with a title or two per season. But being represented, having a sales team in place to sell our books into stores, made the stakes higher—financially and emotionally. Once I got distribution, my little project didn't feel like such an outsider place anymore. Forest Avenue didn't feel so *small*.

Our books started getting major trade reviews, face-out placements in bookstores I hadn't visited personally, and an influx of submissions from established authors. Then we started showing up on lists of best independent presses from *Reedsy*, the *Nonconformist*, *Bookfox*, *Independent Book Review*, *The Milk House*, Powell's Books, Jane Friedman's blog, and others.

For a while I thought optimistically, moving the bar higher every time we earned a starred review or an award. *If I just sell X copies. If I just get a book on NPR. If only __________ happens, then I'll be successful as a publisher.* But the reality is that one achievement is exactly that: one. While I have grown my brand awareness and increased sales generally, I haven't yet procured a magic ticket that will change the course of my business. Maybe a movie deal with a major production company would do it?

WITH COMMUNITY POWER COMES RESPONSIBILITY—to create good things—and also the potential for being judged, misunderstood, or lambasted based on a half-truth. I didn't really step up to the proverbial microphone myself until after I did some deep self-work unpacking old trauma. At some point during that journey, I offered a free copy of a Forest Avenue title to a reader who said on Facebook that she wanted to review it. I chimed in with appreciation, asking for her address so I could send a note and the book.

Much to my surprise, the woman started a whiplash-quick feud against me on social media, claiming I had unfriended her years ago as a way to keep her out of the literary community. I honestly don't remember her. I definitely don't remember unfriending her. Maybe I hit the wrong button during my brain injury months? Or because she had attacked a friend and I quietly unfollowed her, rather than tacitly accepting her negativity about someone I considered part of my community?

I worried that responding or defending myself would make her angrier, so I said nothing and let her heap abuse on me. Her friends piled on, yelling at me from their cozy digital perches. Never having met me. Believing the narrative this one frustrated, angry person had decided on because she felt left out. Kept out. Like I used to before I started my own thing. Perhaps it's easier to blame an individual—to pour your frustration into a campaign against one human being—than to change a broken system.

One by one, my friends spoke up online. They shared stories of how we met, what I had helped them with, and why they like me. These notes were contextless—not even acknowledging her attacks. The outpouring of support was so great that when the agent I wanted offered me representation, the first thing she said was how powerful it was to see so much support on my social media. She didn't know what had happened, only that I had been buoyed by love, and that I had real, genuine *community*.

Up until that social media firestorm, I had been very careful to stay out of the public's way—to not take stands, to hide behind the work (or the newsroom wall in my journalism days).

And yet the worst happened—what I was always afraid of—and it made me stronger.

Later that week I shared a chapter from my novel in progress at a local wine bar reading series. We had a packed house. One friend showed up wearing a TEAM LAURA T-shirt she had made. And during the Q and A, when the moderator asked what had surprised us as publishers, I said it was realizing I'm a public figure now. I didn't want that power, I didn't embrace it, because I was afraid of being challenged. After all, I had started my own press. Nobody gave me that power. Nobody said I could. I just did it.

I had no idea that anyone could even look at me and accuse me of trying to keep them out when I had built something so far outside the center.

Takedowns don't build relationships; they break them. I didn't want the woman to lose respect or followers. I certainly didn't have the kind of power she attributed to me in her rage. I didn't speak up, defend myself, or yell back, so people made their own choices.

That was a huge moment in my understanding of community. I've always felt like my press—my publishing life—is entirely on the outside. This person perceived me to be *inside* the circle, so she made up a story about me that wasn't true. We do this all the time as writers, imagining being one of our superpowers.

Being the target of social media rage has definitely tempered my reactions to vitriolic posts that stir up drama and ask people in the literary community to take sides. I've become more aware of the stories I make up about other people. How, as an outsider to whatever is going on, I can only access what's made public. When I read an opinion online and then make value judgments about a person's character or about a book I haven't read, those thoughts are based on hearsay. *Perhaps* valid, valuable hearsay, but how can we tell? How do we know?

SUCCESS AS AN IMAGE

THE LITERARY WORLD IS FULL of "success" stories that hide the whole picture. It's rare that an author is as powerful, sales-wise and influence-wise, as their social media accounts make them appear. That's the trick of social media—cropping images, crafting entertaining reels, adding filters. We know this, those of us who engage in these platforms. Most of the time just the pretty parts show: photos of books on shelves, a smiling author signing autographs, a list of upcoming appearances.

Sure, there are authors who make it huge. Stephanie Land and Cheryl Strayed are two memoirists that come to mind for their graciousness and openness about their journeys.

A lot of the rest of us are investing time in *looking* like successes because that's what we're told to do by editors, agents, and published authors.

Build your platform!

Get your name out there!

GO, GO, GO!

But when we only share the flash and shine, the special moments without the struggles, we give a false picture to everyone trying to follow our lead.

If she can do it, I can do it, I used to think about authors I admired.

After I became a publisher I realized how much is a hustle. And I started noticing how many people were *pretending* success and feeling rather desperate and unable to share their worries or failed hopes.

I started counting how much of the literary reputation is *looking good.*

How much is having the health, money, and privilege to curate such an image.

None of that has anything to do with your talent or work ethic.

All of that feels daunting and exclusive to writers who haven't figured out it's all in how you present yourself. So this is my chance to tell you. Most of the time the writing life—the being-published life—isn't nearly as glamorous as it looks. There are some awesome moments, some incredible experiences, but most of the time, we're all just paddling through, doing the best we can.

LIDIA YUKNAVITCH IS A BEST-SELLING, award-winning author whose online presence soothes and inspires.

She doesn't deflect the success of her books, which include *Reading the Waves, Thrust, The Book of Joan,* and *The Chronology of Water,* but she also engages publicly in being human—sharing the good stuff and the hard stuff. Her connections with her friends and fans feel like everyone is writing, and *being,* together. Instead of reinforcing toxic power structures and using her success to put herself ahead, Lidia is constantly pulling everyone along with her openness. I see this with her writing school, Corporeal Writing, what she posts on social media, and how she responds to other writers in person and online.

I asked her to tell me her thoughts on success as someone who has attained that status and uses it in a community-building way. "The 'Image of Success' is a snapshot in a life," Lidia said, "with huge highs and lows constantly in motion like an ocean—it's a well curated and coifed moment in time where someone caught a glimpse of something shiny! Ha . . . completely fleeting and unreal. Our real lives are hard and sad and filled with ups and downs, struggles and wonders, beauty and brutality."

When we create an online persona, we're highlighting some of our characteristics and hiding others, the same as if we walk into a room full of strangers. Our clothing, our mannerisms, and how we choose to speak show only a small part of the real *us*. Those of us who are neurodivergent and those of us who have experienced trauma are often taught to *mask*, or hide our real emotions and reactions. I know so many middle-aged women, newly diagnosed with autism or ADHD or both, who are suddenly understanding how hard they've worked their whole lives just to perform simple social situations. And then we have to do it all over again, or a version of it, online via our Facebook author page, a TikTok account, the perfect Instagram reel, or a newsletter.

But instead of building what we think the platform experts want us to build, why don't we center ourselves?

"Ask yourself what you want," Lidia suggests. "What kind of life do you want to live? Who do you want to be in community with or collaborate with? When are you your best self? How can you keep conjuring and growing that storyspace?"

She continued, "Do you want to arrive at the end of your life having lived someone else's story, in someone else's clothes, with someone else's hair and uplighting? Who gives a shit about the image of success? Whose success counts and for what? Whose successes are made invisible by the rise of a single star? I'm for the whole constellation."

We should all be for the whole constellation.

I WANTED TO GROW UP to be a writer in a cabin in the woods, working away outside the everyday world of grocery stores and neighbor hellos and walking the dog. In my fantasy it was just me and my notebook. In the woods I'd have enough empty brain space, away from the clutter of other people's emotions, to do Serious Work.

I thought a lot about Serious Work.

(I was a very Serious Child.)

Many writers are introverts. We have chosen to use words on the page because it's a way to connect to others from a safe distance. Writing as a way of communicating means connecting with people without having to listen to them chew loudly over lunch. Without the messiness of relationship, of bodies in a room. But the first thing we hear when we start investigating publishing is that we need to establish an audience.

And audience brings us right back to large groups of people—the ones we needed to step back from to do the work of writing. The ones we're purposefully avoiding to carve out the emotional and mental space to write.

It can be great to gather with writers because we can all be awkward and anxious together, and we can lament having to interact. But the pressure's on when it comes to proving there are readers for your book. Audience means social media followers but also connections with people who might blurb your book, social media influencers who might do a shout-out for your project, readers who are excited to tag you in a post about your book, and booksellers and librarians who might recommend your book to their customers and patrons.

This is where the idea of *community* intersects with words like *platform*. It's a legitimate, even important, connection, but they are not the same. *Platform* is something to be used, to be leveraged, a concept that puts you at the top of the heap, relying on everyone else to do their parts to keep you way up high.

Community is about relationship. How you fit within a larger group of writers. Do you flit around the side of an established group? Start your own outside circle? Walk boldly into the midst of the existing power circle and say hi? When we hear success stories about platforms and audience and customer/reader engagement, those of us who aren't trying to become famous can often feel left behind, dejected, or even hopeless.

Even when the person isn't bragging but is giving information to help other writers, their success can feel abrasive or like you'll never catch up. Capitalism works that way—fueling those thoughts of *value*. It's easy to forget we are talking about a deeply personal art: writing.

The best antidote for this kind of thinking is chatting with your writing friends. Sharing your hurt feelings or your jealousy or asking them how they handle all the feelings that go along with trying to get published.

Not only is it helpful to commiserate, but often what you *think* is going on isn't entirely true. Processing with your community can sometimes help you move past it and get back to work. With community comes anecdotes—an excellent antidote to feeling small or lesser. Writers can share stories of the real happenings behind the social media posts. What it's *really* like when you win an award or what the first month postpublication really feels like. In sharing and being receptive to others' journeys, we can see behind the flash and mirrors and gilt edges.

IMAGINE A SELFIE ON A conference hotel balcony. It seems glamorous with that glittering hotel pool in the background, and it is! But likely the author paid their own way to the conference and will end up selling three (or maybe, if they're lucky, *ten*) paperbacks, which won't even recoup the cost of the first morning's breakfast. And they had to pony up for the plane tickets, the hotel booking, and all the other meals as well.

Many of us are volunteering or paying to get access to the room. It costs to be at a conference or workshop. I have privileged my way into some of these rooms by running a press, elbowing my way there among agents who do six-figure deals all the time and authors whose books pop up on bestseller lists.

Having the title *publisher* earns me access and invitations, but I've also paid for airfare and hotel or accepted a teaching gig for free in exchange for getting to be part of something that will look as good on my CV as it does on Instagram.

And when I'm in those spaces, my priority is to glean information to share with writers who don't have access, especially authors and publishers of color. If I choose to pay to get there, I want to bring back information that will help people who couldn't afford access. In other words, with access comes responsibility to open the door even wider—not just to carry information back to those outside the room but to invite more people into the room, then step away yourself. Giving up your spot to let someone else in.

THE SYSTEM FEEDS ITSELF, AND you don't have to be part of it. But if you choose to participate, you can also be transparent. You don't have to create a veil of secrecy around how you achieved these things that other authors haven't.

You don't have to call your book best-selling because one time, on one website, it moved into the top hundred in a very, very narrow category.

You don't have to only share the good stuff. You can be human too. Share the hard stuff or information on how you got to that fancy hotel room in the first place.

As Lidia reminds us, "Flubbing is the human default. Ha. Falling on my face and getting up to try again is WHY I'm still a writer, because I had to figure out how to get up and give it another try endlessly. That is such a different ethos and effort than aiming for the still shot of celebrity, which is a false fiction in the first place."

Online Etiquette

It feels important to address some community-related behaviors that can come across as petty, unnecessary, and just plain mean. Remember, you have a choice about how you want to be seen by others. Here are some things to consider:

- If you want to post something negative just so you look smart, step away from your phone or laptop and think about your intent before proceeding with care.
- Don't tag an author in a bad review. It feels awful to see a notification pop up, a reader wanting your attention, only to find a scathing takedown. It's like waving a flag, trying to get someone's attention, only to laugh at

them. Authors who search the interwebs for mentions of their books will find your review, but they'll be emotionally prepared (ish). They decided to look; they decided to take the risk.

- You don't have to review a book you don't love. Everyone's taste is different. You can post a picture of the cover of a friend's book on social media or share a link to an upcoming event. That's supporting your friend too! I personally stopped reviewing because I kept reaching for the same adjectives. If I had to rate another writer's language as *luminous* or their storytelling as *deft*, I would have screamed.
- If someone misspells your name or mixes up the title of your book, don't criticize or ask for a correction unless it's a major newspaper. Nobody likes to be told they're wrong. Instead, say thank you. If you really can't stand the error, reach out privately so as not to embarrass the error-maker, who has done you a huge favor in mentioning your book in the first place.
- If you take an unflattering photo of an author, don't share it. These things live on (and on) and the subject will either have to politely ask you to take it down or just let it float around out there. That being said, many times I've taken what I thought was a lovely portrait only to be asked to take it down. When I was deep into author photography, I learned who was self-conscious of what body part

or imagined flaw, and I worked around each request. I spent so much time trying to caretake everyone's perspectives of themselves.

- If you find yourself in an unflattering photo, thank the photographer. I know, I know, you hate it! But the well-meaning person who took the picture will feel a little stab of embarrassment or regret and likely they shared it to please you, not to hurt you. Probably you're the only person who thinks your chin looks too big.
- Don't post pictures of people's kids without asking first, even if the kids are in the front row at a book event. Not everyone puts their families online.
- Consider sharing some real-life, noncurated photos of your life. That could be a blanket pile in the middle of a snowstorm or a disorganized bookshelf. If you're real online, your followers will connect more intuitively to your content than a polished version of you.
- If your book makes it onto a list, or into a bestseller category, you might write about that experience, how it happened, on your social feeds. Let people into the *how* instead of concealing things to make yourself look bigger or more famous than you are. Or share one of the many struggles you went through to get to where you are now. Let other writers and your fanbase see the process, not just your progress.

WHERE ART AND COMMERCE EXIST, there are expectations, hard feelings, jealousies, and people who get ahead by playing the game. People who leapfrog over others because they are better at leveraging relationships or happen to query the right project at the right time. People who tell stories about successful writers, imagining their lives instead of keeping their eyes on their own pages.

But you—*we*—don't have to be against each other. We can be *for* writers, all the time. The ones signing two-book deals for big bucks and those still in the query trenches. Because we're seeking companionship. Because we like to learn from our peers. Because it's lonely to sit at the desk for hours without anyone to commiserate with when you are overwhelmed. It feels great to have friends you can exclaim to when a frustrating knot in your story finally comes undone, friends who get what you are going through. Real friends who care about the craft, the process of writing and the results of the process, as much as you do.

Yes, if you pay into the community by reading other people's books and showing up for their events, hopefully someday people will support you in the same way. But it's not like a bank where you keep depositing your good deeds. They don't accrue and become more valuable over time. They don't automatically earn you extra sales or starred reviews when your debut book hits the shelves.

I used to have this kind of magical thinking every time I attended an event and bought a book I wouldn't have ordinarily chosen. I was banking one more good deed. Taking care to uplift and appreciate one more person's hard work.

Maybe it should work like that. But that's not how the economy works. An author who has put twenty years of love into their local writing community may sell a thousand copies of their debut novel, while another debut novelist whose work sells at auction to a major New York house might sell ten thousand copies without showing up for her peer authors even once.

The trick is to feel good about those thousand copies if you're in the first situation, to understand and appreciate that every one of those readers has spent time and money on your words. That you, the author, have worked hard to get every one of those copies to every one of those readers. It's a balm, if you think of it that way, instead of doing the math of how many thousands of dollars and hours you've spent writing, taking classes, attending conferences, paying for developmental edits, and so forth, to sell a thousand copies.

And if you find yourself suddenly in the spotlight, feel good about that! You're living the dream so many others want!

You can also think about how you can use your newfound fame—your platform—to shine light on other creatives who don't have big platforms like you. The ones making art in quiet spaces, in the margins. Use your power to say, *This book matters too.*

Keith Rosson, while he was on deadline writing the sequel to *Fever House*, squeezed in the time to blurb our *Soul Jar* anthology. I've followed Keith's career since his first book came out from Meerkat Press because I admire him, not because I expected someday he'd be in a position to do me a favor. But then he got a big deal from Penguin Random House, and when *Fever House* came out it landed in airports, on media lists, and on front tables in bookstores across the country. More people started talking about his work, so having his endorsement on the front cover of our collection of stories by disabled writers meant even more than it would have a few years before.

THE CURIOUS CASE OF THE PAID REVIEW

One service that can be useful to authors is the paid review. But it's often not something publishers and authors are transparent about, and that can hurt community. We all do it—call a review a review, whether or not it's paid—and only some of us, some of the time, explain how we got that review.

Reviews are important to share because they are, ostensibly, from outside sources writing objectively about a piece of art. When small presses, self-publishing authors, and hybrid authors tout a fabulous new review in a major trade journal, everyone celebrates in the comments with emojis. That's great, because we should be celebrating everything.

Hurray, author so-and-so!

Great job!

But there are so many authors with all sizes and styles of presses that want reviews and a shrinking number of outlets that publish reviews. For many decades, having a review in a trade journal was a marker of real success for a book. It proved that the book mattered, and a good one also increased sales.

But there's this whole service economy that's sprung up too. Don't get enough trade reviews? You can pay and get one that looks almost identical to the organically chosen books' reviews!

As a publisher that doesn't always get our books reviewed, seeing other people's reviews makes me second-guess myself.

Did I not pitch well enough?

Did I pitch too early?

Did I pitch too late?

Should I have sent a hard copy instead of a digital one, or vice versa?

Do they just not like Forest Avenue Press as much as __________ Press?

And then I take a deep breath and actually go look at the review. And frequently I find that the author, publisher, or publicist has paid for this coverage. It's called the pay-to-play model. I can tell because instead of a review saying *Publishers Weekly* or *Kirkus Reviews*, the website version says *BookLife* or *Kirkus Indie*. The press and author sharing the text generally use the more official, more prestigious name of the publication, so it looks like they have been chosen. In fact, *Kirkus* currently encourages all paid review recipients to list *Kirkus Reviews* as the source, not *Indie*.

In an industry where reviews really matter, paying to get coverage is an increasingly useful option. It's marketing (paid), but it looks like organic publicity. (Your book is great! We choose you!)

PUBLICITY: Placing information about the book, including interviews, features, and reviews, for free. The cost to the publisher (or the author, if you're bootstrapping it) is printing, mailing, and the time to research where to submit.

MARKETING: These are the paid opportunities. Contest entry fees are marketing. Paid review services? Marketing. Advertorial, where advertising is created to look like news, is also marketing.

Paying for a review is an absolutely valid and useful option, but it's not always obvious when that's the case. Recently, I spotted a several-year-old book with its first sentence highlighted in a trade journal. There was nothing new or *newsworthy* about the book. I couldn't figure out why it had earned this placement. *How?* I wondered. *And* why? I followed a rabbit trail of evidence to the source: a paid placement. A service. The author paid for the space in the journal, then promoted that her first sentence had been published, then accepted all the congrats and compliments from her friends instead of saying, *Thanks, but actually I paid for it.*

I totally understand why this kind of paid promotion can help writers reach audiences. It can also work for readers; thanks to the author being able to afford this service, readers who might not otherwise know about the book have a chance to discover it. Where I struggle is seeing all the other authors who didn't make it into that section. They don't know it was paid. They're thinking their work has been judged inferior.

So often these services and marketing opportunities are hidden behind several clicks, or explained in fine print, so the average reader or writer doesn't know the difference between the earned kind and the purchased kind. And then, as I've talked about a bit already, we make up stories. *The industry is unfair! That author keeps getting everything!* Or, *My book must not be any good.*

I'm sure the paid services at trade journals help offset the cost of publishing; I don't have a problem with them if they're labeled as paid. Paid reviews can help level the playing field at a time when there are lots of books and many of them aren't chosen. Presses that don't have distribution are often ignored, for instance, no matter how great their titles are. When I first started my press and distributed books out of my house, I asked *Publishers Weekly* how to get reviewed and they said, *Get a distributor*. (I'll share more about what that means and why it matters in the next section.)

Paying for reviews is, of course, a system built on privilege. If you have the money or enough room on your credit card, you can drop a few hundred dollars on a review. Then you can share that review like it was earned, like you (or your press) had its book chosen for its merits. It used to be that these were all disclosed, albeit discreetly, but I have seen that less and less in recent years. People outside the industry respond with joy when they see their friends' books reviewed—as they should—but people whose books got ignored often feel sour, sore, or lost. Sometimes they doubt their publicist's ability to pitch. *Did they pitch? Or did they just tell me they did?* Or they wonder if they signed with the right publisher. Or, if they self-published, they start second-guessing their cover design or the book description they reworked a million times.

They feel bad about their own work. And it's all because they're *imagining* that this other person's book got chosen as more worthy than theirs. When really the other author had enough money to pay to play.

When at all possible in casual conversations, I like to point out that reviews have been paid for, especially to authors who didn't get traditionally reviewed by the same journal. I always submit Forest Avenue titles to the trades and have only twice paid for a review. Our first, *A Girl Called Rumi* by Ari Honarvar, earned a starred review from *Kirkus* and was named a best *Kirkus*

Indies book of the year. Our second, *The Queen of Steeplechase Park* by David Ciminello, earned a star and a *Kirkus* Best Book of 2024 designation.

STARRED REVIEW: An honor given only to the best books. Reviewers at trade journals determine which ones receive stars.

Why didn't *Kirkus* choose Ari's book for traditional review if it was that good? Or David's? I haven't the slightest idea. *Kirkus*'s policy for authors using their paid review service is to label them as *Kirkus Reviews* so they are indistinguishable from the organically chosen free reviews. You have to click on the *Kirkus* site, look up the content, and then see if the page says *Kirkus Indie* or not.

I'm glad I did pay-to-play for *A Girl Called Rumi* because the review was excellent, but I also feel like it's important to share that it was paid coverage. We didn't buy the star, or the exact words about the book, but we bought the attention. Same with *Steeplechase*.

If you pay for a review and don't like it, you can cancel it. Make it disappear. Ensure it doesn't go online and haunt your future book deals with its negativity. That's another kind of privilege.

I GET WHY A PRESS wouldn't want to own up to paying for review. I don't always up front, when I first reveal the review, because that feels unfair to the author. It contributes to the problem, but the alternative is to say, *So-and-so's book didn't get chosen for review, so I put some cash down and look! It got reviewed!*

Which kind of negates the importance of the content, especially if it's a great review. Paid reviews are about buying access, not content; the actual review is written by a legit professional reviewer, just like the free reviews.

It makes the financial investment worth less if you say, *Hey, I paid for that!* when sharing a great review. But eventually I share publicly what was paid so writers who are sad they aren't getting reviewed see when and how I chose to play the game.

Even if you don't say so on social media when you reveal the review, or use a piece of a quote to promote your book, you can share the pay-to-play details with your writing group or your critique partner. You can write a blog post or a Facebook update a few months later explaining how that particular accolade came to be. Or you can comment on someone else's lament about not getting reviewed and share your experience.

Be part of the transparency if you can.

PAYING FOR AWARDS

BOOK AWARDS USUALLY HAVE FEES—not all of them, but many do. Some of the bigger award programs allow tiny presses to waive the cost if they send in an affidavit about the press's income. I love that option because it helps with accessibility and confirms the organization is focused on books, not the submission fees.

A whole lot of these contests are legitimate. And they can be a great way to boost awareness and sales. For small press authors, having an award to add to the cover is a sign that means their books matter. That their books have done *well* in a sea of new books. A gold or silver or bronze sticker might make up for slow sales or a disappointing lack of reviews.

But there are some less ethical businesses that rake in submission fees and dole out awards in a million categories without any real meaning behind them.

If you see a friend's book winning more than one or two awards, they've probably entered a bunch of these pay-to-play contests. There are award mills that churn out new contests under related brand names; I got caught once sending a book to a themed contest only to find out it wasn't legitimate. When the author earned a top spot, she did some investigating and broke the news to me. I hadn't done my due diligence. Together, we opted not to promote the "award" to avoid encouraging other writers and publishers to dump money into the same machine.

Awards that matter are ones where the judges actually read the books. There are so many of those that are worthwhile. I usually study contest winners to see how selective a program is—if they are selecting books by presses I've heard of, books with great premises, books with professional-looking covers.

These are all great places to start evaluating a contest. You can also ask your community—see who's submitted, if they won, whether the win meant a sales bump or not.

CONFERENCES AND COMMUNITY

CONFERENCES ARE ANOTHER MONEY-RELATED PRIVILEGE. If you can afford to go to one in your local area or to pay for transportation and lodgings in another city, you might meet agents, editors, and other professionals whose interest in you might change the trajectory of your career.

Or you might meet a bunch of cool people who now know to look for your book on shelves someday.

By attending, you're buying face time with experts. You're getting the privilege of being in the room when publishing professionals and best-selling authors share their insights. And you're there to rub elbows with other writers, people like you, who are doing the work and want to find their way in publishing.

I love the Willamette Writers Conference in Portland, Oregon. It's in my city, they bring in excellent speakers, and they also invite local authors and publishers to participate. There isn't an us-versus-them mentality; it's all *us*. Warm, friendly, welcoming. Some of my favorite experiences at that conference have been sitting around chatting with writers and readers I haven't met before. For similar reasons, the Terroir Creative Writing Festival has my heart. It's small, it's also in Oregon, and it's a one-day event. Whenever I go, I have a feeling that we're all there together for community and to learn. When I did the Terroir keynote speech in 2023, I also attended Melissa Hart's middle grade workshop, which inspired me to try that genre—and I discovered I love it!

Conference Checklist

Sometimes we sign up to attend expensive events hoping we'll be discovered or get some kind of life-changing connection. That *can* happen, but it's not guaranteed. Instead of daydreaming about a conference, ask yourself these questions. The more yeses, the more likely it's a good fit for you at this time.

There's a teacher I want to study with. **Y / N**

I have friends or family where the conference is taking place. **Y / N**

I'm a caregiver and I could really get away for a few days. **Y / N**

Being with other writers makes me happy. **Y / N**

Wow! That hotel! I'd love to spend some time there. **Y / N**

I can afford the travel cost, the conference fee, and lodging without worrying about paying bills. **Y / N**

I can afford it without making the cost back in the next three to five years. **Y / N**

I'm stuck on my book and being with other writers might help. **Y / N**

There's a session I really want to attend. **Y / N**

I can volunteer and go for free. **Y / N**

BY THE NUMBERS

PROCEED WITH CAUTION WHEN HEARING about sales numbers—yours or others'. There's no objectively *better* or *worse* art. Some is to your taste, some isn't, and a lot falls in between. Not every project that makes it to print—even with big houses—is ready for readers. Some long-anticipated novels (I just finished one) fall flat because the author got stuck on the project, had personal changes to work through, or had to meet an unreasonably fast deadline. Good books can have small sales. Commercially successful books may be considered *bad* by lots of readers, despite racking up so much attention.

Sales depend on distribution, the marketing budget, and other factors that are completely irrelevant to the words you put on the page. So when we look at sales data, we're trying to measure what a book's worth is by comparing it to other books, but the concept is flawed from the start. It doesn't help that there are limited tools. Only people in the industry can access BookScan, the industry's point-of-sale report system, because it's so expensive to get membership.

BookScan doesn't include library sales or sales at bookstores that don't pay to report their numbers. It doesn't include ebook sales or digital audio sales either. Authors who have Amazon profiles can now see *their* BookScan numbers, I've heard, but without access to the whole database, it's hard to know what those numbers mean.

For instance, one of my debut authors had single-digit sales a month after publication. That sounds bad—and yeah, I'm a little worried when I see numbers like that so close to publication. But then I consider the situation.

Has the book gotten reviewed? Yes, plenty of traditional and consumer reviews, with a few more still to come.

What about events? Lots of well-attended ones! With more on the calendar!

Are books being reordered? I can look at my distributor's portal and see the answer to this: yes. I see new orders—a lot from libraries, yay!—and reorders stacking up.

So how is the book doing? Well, it's going better than BookScan says.

I knew this, of course, looking at the initial number. If ten to fifteen books sold per event, then none of those events reported to BookScan, or we'd see double-digit sales for a few of those weeks. But it helps to look at the data, to consider what's going on beyond BookScan. My assessment is that I'm doing the right things: drumming up more publicity, following up on my author's queries, and making graphics for our latest reviews so we can promote them.

THERE ARE LOTS OF INACCURATE ways to interpret sales numbers. Publishers often give their authors false hope, wanting them to feel good, without sharing the whole picture. Authors who disclose their book sales often misunderstand the paperwork they get from their publisher, thus muddling the conversation despite wanting to be transparent. Others totally avoid the conversation—not telling when people ask—and I fall into this camp because so often the people asking don't know what the numbers mean.

The most common mistake is when publishers tell their authors how many print books are sold into stores; with how the returns process is set up, none of those actually count as a true sale until customers bring those books to the cash wrap, buy them, and walk out of the store. In other words, your publisher can sell a thousand copies of your book to bookstores, but none of those counts as a true sale until a reader finds the book, brings it to the register, and buys it.

This leads to false inflation of sales numbers and eventual disappointment when the author gets the next royalty statement. Moreover, when authors excited about their sell-in share their numbers, authors who only can see their BookScan numbers or who have received a lackluster royalty report, feel terrible.

I don't have any great answers. Sharing all the numbers might help people be more realistic and not, say, spend twenty thousand bucks on publicity when they can't afford to lose it. But not all numbers measure the same thing. I do great with sell-in; those are good numbers because I'm a distributed press. But selling back out, having those books walk back out of the store under a customer's arm? That's what counts toward royalties.

RETURNS, I NEED TO ADD here, are crucial to allowing brick-and-mortar stores to take chances on new books. They are hard to stomach as a publisher and they feel harsh when you see them on a royalty report. A robust return rate for multiple titles in a row can sink a small press. Those things are true. But returns also allow a no-risk option to bring an untested author's book into a store.

"For our first fifteen years, we didn't accept returns at all," said Joe Biel, publisher of Microcosm. "When we signed with a distributor, we hit 25 percent returns and it was a massive sticker shock. But this is only a small part of the picture. Returns are a *good thing*. While this meant that our distributor was overselling to major accounts and tying up inventory at Barnes, Ingram, and Baker, when we resumed self-distributing in 2018, we used returns correctly. Done right, returns allow a bookstore to take a chance on a debut author. They don't need to commit forever."

In 2024, with their own distribution and sales team in place, Microcosm had a 1.5 percent return rate—way lower than the industry average. Joe is very happy with this percentage. "It means stores are taking chances on our authors. If we were at zero percent, it would mean that we weren't taking enough chances and stores weren't taking chances on our authors."

Microcosm's rate is extraordinary. It reaffirms my respect for how the press makes books that will reach their target markets and achieve high sales goals. The average return rate in the US hovers between 20 and 25 percent, I've heard; I've seen 30 listed as standard as well. If you work for two years on a title, as a publisher, and a third of the copies come back as unsold, that's pretty devastating. But it happens.

SALES NUMBERS ARE OFTEN A disappointment. Not always but often. No matter how many sell, it could always be more, right? Capitalism gets us thinking like that.

Singing Lessons for the Stylish Canary got a ton of press

coverage and social media shares because I've been active in the community, volunteering countless hours to support writers by taking their photos and promoting their books. My novel performed beautifully from the outside looking in—tons of trade reviews, excellent blurbs, packed events.

But my BookScan number is . . . disappointingly small. Less than a thousand. Even though I know I sold more than a thousand, I still eye that number with something akin to despair. I quickly earned out my advance thanks to an audiobook deal, so that's awesome, but I certainly haven't earned enough royalties to pay me back for the cost of all those writing workshops, conferences, professional edits, and DIY retreats I sprang for over the fifteen-year period I wrote the novel. There's no way! And I knew that was likely when I went the small press route. So I'm sharing that insight with you now, to prepare you in case your experience is similar to mine.

Standard print royalties are generally between $0.25 and $1.00 per book for paperbacks, because bookstores and distribution companies take deep cuts before the publisher sees compensation. Why don't authors get all the money? With distribution, publishers start investing in a book eighteen months or more before the pub date to meet all the required deadlines, and they get paid 180 days after the first books ship out. And still then, if books get returned, the publisher can start seeing negative statements—losses!—three months into the publishing cycle. Just think about printing and shipping heavy books—how much the logistics alone cost to get a book from the printer to a warehouse and then from that warehouse into a bookstore. Hardcovers have slightly different numbers—royalties are generally based on purchase price—but they cost more to make and ship because they're heavier. They're also, because of the per-book cost, less likely to be purchased on impulse unless they're by a best-selling author or a lucky debut who gets featured on the morning talk shows or picked up by a national book club.

Print publishing is a high-touch, high-cost business. And yet as a younger writer, when I signed up for classes and workshops and conferences, I told myself, *Someday, you'll earn money from your work, and you'll be glad you spent money on this.*

More specifically: *This is an investment! In your career! There wouldn't be classes and services targeted to authors if it's impossible to earn your money back and make a profit.*

Except that's not how it works. There are so many paid publishing services out there, not to mention classes, conferences, conventions, hybrid and self-publishing presses, and coaches. You could spend a fortune trying to amass information and still not make a dime from your writing. Some of these opportunities are great and can lead to finding an agent, fixing your novel's ending once and for all, or meeting a critique buddy. But before you spend money on membership or a specific service, make sure your goals align with what is promised and don't overtax your budget, because you may never earn those dollars back in book sales.

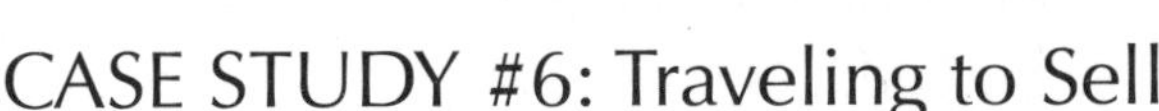

CASE STUDY #6: Traveling to Sell

In 2017 I spent big bucks (for me) traveling to Washington, DC, and shipping heavy books to sell at the Association of Writers & Writing Programs conference. It's a huge event and much anticipated by many small presses, MFA programs, and authors. I brought enough cases to cover my plane ticket, half booth cost, and hotel room—thinking surely I would sell them all. Otherwise going wouldn't make sense financially, right? Note, too, that I was purely looking at cover price, not subtracting the authors' royalties or factoring in the per-book print costs. Just cover prices.

It didn't work out. I ended up with a few hundred books stuck on the East Coast. I stashed them in my parents' garage, not willing to pay the exorbitant shipping fees to send them all back home. It was already a loss—the plane, the conference fees, the hotel, shipping inventory there. Maybe my press *looked* successful that year because we tabled at AWP and shared pretty pictures to prove it. We probably reached new readers and potential authors: intangible, possibly invaluable, benefits of being on the scene. Maybe our table inspired authors to submit who otherwise wouldn't have considered us a worthy home for their stories.

But I sure felt dumb. *How come I thought I'd sell all those books?* after some time had passed shifted to, *How come nobody warned me this isn't a selling show?*

Running the numbers after that conference confirmed my dejection: we took a significant loss. Other presses do great there; I've heard that! Maybe I didn't bring enough authors to sign in the booth, who would then have brought their friends to buy books from them. Or maybe our aesthetic didn't match what readers wanted at that particular AWP. Maybe—and I suspect this is true—most presses have that experience of going to be part of the scene, not expecting to earn back airfare, hotel, and food costs. But we don't talk about it, so more people show up and lose money to look successful, and the cycle continues.

I asked Leland Cheuk—author, reviewer, and publisher and founder of 7.13 Books—about his experience with event costs and other marketing spending.

He said:

> Book publishing is probably one of the only businesses out there where there are more ways to lose money than make it. You would think that if you sell a product for more than cost of production, you would be able to math out profitability pretty easily, but with publishing there are so many potholes in the road. Distributor fees and return charges are big culprits, but advertising, event, and travel costs can be significant as well, with very little direct return on your investments. It can be a vicious cycle: If you don't get "out there" in the literary community, fewer people will know about your books, but if you do get "out there," and it costs a lot, it can adversely affect your bottom line. I recommend a cautious approach to the many marketing opportunities out there, and to set expectations that the goal of most book marketing spend is brand awareness, which isn't easy to quantify in terms of increased book sales.

I love Leland's wisdom because it dovetails with the perils of the author journey. No matter how many quarters we put into the slot machine, spending money to make money, there's no guarantee of a payout of big sales. Those quarters have been used up. And hopefully you've earned a bump of visibility, depending on where you're focusing your marketing efforts, but money flowing back into the coffers? Maybe. Maybe not.

Now I'm at the point in my career where I don't feel obligated to pay for events; I want to be paid for my time and travel. I put the numbers first when I decide where to go and when to stay home. *A paid appearance?* Yes, if it works schedule-wise and fee-wise. And yes if I have friends or family in that city and can make that work as free accommodations. But I don't spend money just to be present out of obligation. Even if I can afford the booth fees and travel costs, I don't want to stress my body that hard if I'm not going to come out with a profit.

YEARS AGO, WORD GOT BACK to me that one of my authors was upset that her advance was way less than one of my new authors' advances. I couldn't understand how this gossip had spread, because I tend to offer small advances. Just tokens. There are so many expenses in publishing, I don't get underwritten by a college or university, and I'd rather spend the money on the author's book than overestimate earning potential up front.

So when I heard this, I couldn't understand where that misconception came from. A mutual friend explained that my author was upset because my new author's deal was listed in Publishers Marketplace. The website identifies "nice deals" as coming with advances of $1 up to $49,000. At the time I was offering $250 advances. My author saw the listing, looked up its definition, and imagined $49,000 going to the new person. Of course she felt terrible! Of course she started thinking about the distance between what I gave her and what this new person might have earned. Which caused her to rethink how much I appreciated her book. How much *I* appreciated *her*. Thankfully, I found out through a friend and was able to explain—a relief to us both.

Sometimes when we don't have information, or we get partial information, we make things up. Community can be a hedge against that, letting you bond with people you trust enough to ask, *What's really going on?* Your friends won't judge you for not knowing.

They might even say, *I wondered that too!*

HARD TRUTHS

THERE ARE DAYS I FEEL sick about publishing. I lose faith. I stop believing that a flawed industry is worth investing my time and energy in as a writer or publisher.

When authors of color are told their character names are too "complicated."

When white authors are paid significant sums for stories that aren't theirs to tell.

When autistic authors are told their protagonists are too *immature* and *naïve* to be believable.

When a review comes in that disparages someone's lived experience, written in memoir form, because it doesn't match their own experience.

When a literary conference promises accessibility but forgets to account for the raised speaking platforms that are easy for able-bodied participants to navigate but barriers to access for everyone else.

When able-bodied editors let disabled characters be objects of pity on the page instead of calling out the harmful trope or hiring a sensitivity reader from the disabled population.

When a hybrid publisher hides fees from their authors and calls their business model "traditional," then slams the authors with unforeseen costs.

When a publisher ghosts their authors. Or quits paying royalties. Or quietly closes up shop.

When a publisher keeps acquiring new books while breaking promises to existing authors, then a major trade journal slants their coverage to privilege the publisher's side of the story.

But then I take a deep breath and think about the people who are doing good work in their communities. And I remind myself that none of us is perfect; we all make mistakes, no matter how many years we have in the business (publishers) and how well intentioned we are (writers).

The industry may be broken and outdated, in desperate need of shifting certain practices, but it's also made up of individuals. And those individuals are part of communities, and those communities are part of the literary ecosystem.

Agents who work through multiple revisions with their clients because they see the work's potential.

The acquisitions teams actively seeking authors of color.

The freelance editors who actually know what acquisitions editors want and how to help you steer your manuscript to that place of readiness.

The book designers who conjure brilliant covers into being.

The sensitivity readers who help authors check their biases.

The independent publishers who are hustling for grant funding and Kickstarter campaigns just to get one more book out in the world because they believe in their authors.

The publicists who have connections and approach them with thoughtful, personalized pitches that turn into coverage.

The authors who show up for each other, over and over again. Not because they want to trade favors but because they believe in each other. And because they love to read.

OUR CULTURE UNDERVALUES ART OR, worse, ignores anything that doesn't make the bestseller list.

How we got here, putting price tags on ideas, feels like a whole other rant about capitalism. I don't want to defend the broken parts. Being in the industry means I'm part of the problem. But it also means I have the opportunity to actively push against the established norms, at least in my tiny, gentle corner of the industry.

WITH FOREST AVENUE PRESS, I'VE been trying to crack open the productivity model and replace it with an author-facing, mental health–focused model. Our goal isn't more-more-more books—even though that might make the bottom line a bit healthier, because more titles means more income. Our goal is happy authors—or at least well-informed, resilient authors who understand that returns happen and that putting creativity into the world shouldn't *only* be measured by sales numbers.

If I can help two or three authors per year have a good experience with publishing, maybe others will try to slow down and focus on one project at a time. But even if not, seeing the industry from the author's perspective while acknowledging the importance of publicity and marketing and metadata means I can report back to everyone else. In workshops, classes, keynotes, and now *Imagine a Door*. And, hopefully, sharing that perspective will make the publishing journey feel less perilous.

Mostly, when I see writers who feel awful about their work, it's not because of their relationship to their work in progress. It's because of something they read online about platform, or a particularly smarting rejection, or something else *external*. Something they—we—can't control.

So this is my attempt to rebalance the scales, pull the narrative of publishing away from the commercial underpinnings and refocus on our experiences as sensitive, funny, brave writers. To center community. To say, *We can do better if we band together.*

WHAT CAN WE CONTROL?

What we put on the page.

Who we ask to represent or publish our work.

How we take care of our delicate selves when rejections come in.

How we take care of others.

How we hold

space

for ourselves.

FINDING A GOOD BALANCE

SINCE 2020 THERE'S BEEN MORE conversation about the *cost* of in-person gathering. I love this. It has been part of the discussion all along for immunocompromised people, those with chronic pain and physical disabilities, and those with neurospiciness and sensitivities to crowds, lights, and sounds. I have always struggled with the cost of social experiences, but I just suffered through, not realizing I could opt out. Sometimes events set me back weeks because I got the flu from someone in the room, or I just couldn't catch back up on sleep or energy.

In the before-Covid times, I kept paying the price. Showing up even if I had rough days and elevated pain levels to show for it.

Nowadays, I still believe in local gatherings, the joy of being around your peers and other writers who are pushing the edges of genre or writing a best-selling multibook crime series. But I can't go out a few times a week anymore. I worry too much about getting sick, even while masked, not to mention emptying my small tank of energy. It can take weeks to recover. That sounds like it's an exaggeration, but it's not. I've had to unlearn a lot of my coping mechanisms to be able to say, *This happens to me.*

In having these conversations with myself, deciding which invites to accept and which to decline, I've gotten to a deeper truth. A kind of gutting one. About me. I used to show up with my camera at every book event I possibly could because I felt like I owed it to the people around me. I *wanted* to contribute to my community. To make local writers feel seen and heard.

That's a great impulse, but *why* did I feel so driven to do this, often when it cost me pain and hours of my time in sorting and fixing photos?

Here's what I figured out. I didn't believe I mattered, as a writer or a person, so I gifted favors of photos and social media posts in the hopes of being accepted. I didn't think my art was worth celebrating—after all, I hadn't gotten a book published yet. (I held that fact over my own head like a cartoon weight, ready to drop anytime I started feeling like a real writer.) The least I could do was clap and document others' big moments. To spend hours sorting and editing photos to share the best ones and tag everyone. To value everyone who turned out at an event, not just the writer at the mic.

To say *you matter* when I didn't believe *I* mattered. I couldn't imagine that people might like me for me. These acts of service grounded me and helped me cultivate longtime, love-filled relationships. I don't regret the hours or the wear that editing thousands of photos took on my now-arthritic hands. But I regret the deep sense of insufficiency, of cutting myself down, that prompted me to hyperengage.

I've been working on a balance ever since—offering support and also holding my energy close, investing in *me* and my work, not just other people. Not much has changed with how I run my publishing house because I'm still author-centric, and the steps of putting a book out are the same. But I'm definitely a much more low-profile figure in my community, especially when it comes to attending events. I just can't go everywhere. Being immunocompromised means I have to be careful; I can't expect to socialize and stay healthy for the following weeks. And I've mostly stopped bringing my Nikon when I *do* get out. Cell phone pictures are fine; other people can bring cameras if they want. I don't have to do it all.

Neither do you. But you can do something. You can show up—in a virtual space or a physical one. You can introduce two writers who might like each other. Anything you do to make community better will actually—*gasp*—make community better.

PUBLISHING PATHS

THE DREAM

WRITERS ARE OFTEN PORTRAYED IN films and TV shows as having glamorous lives that revolve around their craft. (Cue the string quintet and the sunrise at a lakeside chalet.)

That's just not true for most of us. Which means if you assess what you want from publishing through a clearer, more realistic lens, you'll be more likely to set achievable goals. Ones that relate to you as a person, not the *industry* or other writers. That's at the heart of this section.

You. And your mental health as a creative person.

We spend a lot of time imagining the opening door, the *welcome* waiting for us. Rejections can be terribly painful, but they're only one kind of response to your work. In truth, there will be reader responses at every step of the process.

First round: beta readers, freelance editors, and writing group members

Your friends and family might be part of this first tier, if you can count on them for honest feedback. Otherwise, try finding community members who are willing to volunteer their time or trade manuscripts with you, or hire a professional editor.

Developmental editing—the big-picture kind—is a great use of funds at this stage, if you can afford it. The goal with this tier is to build up your confidence, figure out what's working in your manuscript, and get actionable feedback on what's not working. Everything you learn from these readers will help you feel confident in your work when you send it out to the pros as a submission.

Second round: agents and acquiring editors

The stakes are higher with this tier, because you're asking for support from people in the business. Not only emotional support but also financial support and communication. You're more likely to succeed at this level if you have a professionally edited query letter, a dynamite manuscript that's been revised more than once, and a title that works. I'll share more specific tips about these elements in the QUERYING section.

Third round: readers of the published book

Acceptances and rejections matter a lot emotionally, but that middle tier is actually the gateway to the people we've always dreamed of reading our work. People we know! People we'll never meet! When we sit down to write and imagine an audience, this is who we're writing for. Readers and the people who preview books for them: the professional reviewers. It takes the first two tiers to prepare and revise so you're ready for this group to see your pages.

ONCE YOU GET A YES from the middle group, or open your own door by self-publishing, there are all kinds of judgments still awaiting your beloved words. Whether a favorite author will agree to endorse your book. Whether a trade journal will review it (favorably). Whether a book club will choose your title over all the others. Whether the sales are anywhere near what you had hoped. Or not.

Early feedback, if it's constructive and supportive, can help you prepare for publishing.

In a similar way, learning about how the industry works can help inoculate you against some of the big feelings that may come your way before you even have a contract in hand. Whenever I hear an author despairing about their career, it's usually because they've fallen into the crevasse between what they expected and how the book business actually works. It's important to know how it works up front so you don't take those unreached goals personally.

For instance, you probably won't earn enough money to quit your job and live happily ever after as an author. It's delicious to dream big, but if you prepare yourself for a twenty-dollar royalty check, you can use it to splurge on a fancy pen or take your best friend out for coffee. And that'll feel like a win! Even if you do end up one of the lucky few who ink a six- or seven-figure deal, you'll want to sell enough books to earn that out—not an easy feat.

EARNING OUT: Many publishers pay their author advances on royalties. Earning out means that you have earned back your advance and can now earn new money. A common misperception is that if an author doesn't earn out, the publisher has lost money. Your book can be a success commercially for your press even if you don't hit this milestone; publishers retain the bulk of the per-copy profit that comes back to them after booksellers and wholesalers take their cuts, so printing and labor costs can be recouped before you earn out your advance.

Who publishes your book also impacts what success metrics are.

If you sign with a small press, selling a thousand copies is an achievement worth celebrating. So is selling two hundred of a print run of three hundred. That's great!

If you sign with a big five press, though, and your print run is ten thousand, selling five thousand might be seen as a failure and hurt your chances of selling your next book.

How success is defined depends on who's doing the defining.

And even with the best possible experience, no matter how great your book is, there will be disappointments.

Like when you realize that trade reviews aren't rolling in . . . they're trickling.

Or another one-star "I don't get it" review shows up on Goodreads.

Or when the new bestseller lists come out and your book isn't on them.

Or when the lineup for your local book festival gets announced and you're not invited despite your years of supporting the festival.

Or when you get that first royalty statement.

Or when you get your first negative-balance royalty statement, reflecting returns.

That doesn't mean you can't dream.

I wish all the things for you! Sometimes a book makes buzzy waves at its announcement and that buzz turns into fantastic sales. It's great when everything goes right, because frankly, it's a relief to know real, hardworking people who have earned that kind of success. Their track record proves big things *can* happen for a writer. Even if they're not happening for you (us) right at this very moment.

Mostly, though, authors are disappointed in the experience

of publishing. Not because those manuscripts aren't well written or valuable to readers, but because of market factors and the sheer volume of projects moving through the many manuscript-to-book pipelines.

To combat the disappointment and bridge the gulf between expectations and reality, published writers often put a brave face on their journeys. This only sharing successes strategy may feel great for your ego, but it also encourages other writers to dream big, to think, *If so-and-so can ____________, I can too!* Only a lot of these "opportunities" are less about earning—and the quality of the story you're telling—and more about spending. Or, more specifically, who's putting money into promoting their books. Who has a stable job or family wealth or a successful spouse with a steady career. Who can sign a contract for $16,000 or $20,000 with a well-known hybrid press, book publicist, or both, and afford to lose the money.

WHEN I ASK WRITERS ABOUT their goals, they often respond with hopes that are dependent on other people saying yes. Usually these lists are focused on sales and pie-in-the-sky rewards.

A bestseller list!

A national book club!

Being interviewed on NPR!

The *Times*! The *Post*! The *Guardian*!

But there's a system in place that sorts, sifts, and rejects many wonderful books for all kinds of unpredictable reasons. Readers have their own specific tastes. Agents and editors are people too; they're readers too. A bad day, or a subject too close to a recent personal trauma, might get a no-response no that has *nothing* to do with your talent. Recently I reviewed a manuscript whose outrageous premise delighted me, but one of the lead characters relies on illicit drugs to get through his day. I don't relate to him at all. My spontaneous nope has nothing to do with the author's prowess and everything to do with my identity.

It can feel impossible, when you're waiting on the outside, to get anyone to pay attention to your work. And yet the goal lists writers share with me are all what *might* happen if they hit that jackpot position of being a much-buzzed-about debut author.

The traditional way into publishing—getting an agent who then sells your book to a press—is not the only path. There are so many others. Part of our journey needs to be identifying the options. Another part is being really clear with ourselves about our goals. What do we want and *why*? Are they realistic goals? What's the backup plan? How about a backup backup?

Then, with a bit of self-love and patience, we can identify goals that are up to *us* to achieve—ones that take work, not magic. Goals that are not bound up in earning a six-figure advance or a celebrity's attention.

Dependent on factors outside your control:

- Being interviewed on NPR.
- Being chosen for a celebrity's book club.
- Getting on the Indie Next list.
- Winning a major award.

There's nothing wrong with wanting those top-tier achievements, unless you bind your sense of self-worth and your belief in your work to achieving them. So many writers—with well-funded publicists! And celebrity editors! At the biggest publishing houses!—are all vying for the same few slots, the same exact recognition. The biggest presses have a competitive edge because they have connections, money to throw at earning recognition, and more staff members than smaller presses. These advantages are why, when submitting their manuscripts, an author might prioritize these houses. Sure, a small press or an affordable publicist can pitch you for NPR, send a galley to the buzziest book clubs, and create an Indie Next campaign, but they (we) are pitching at a disadvantage if we don't have preexisting relationships or a previous win in that category.

I've pitched NPR shows for years and only earned an actual interview for one of my authors in 2024, when *Chicano Frankenstein* received interest from two different shows. One of the two—*Code Switch*—ended up coming through. And neither of those opportunities responded to my dutifully sent press kits and sample copies. The requests came because NPR staffers had heard about Daniel A. Olivas's book; we had earned enough buzz to get attention.

I don't know where my initial queries landed—the recycling, probably. It's a great example, though, of putting in the effort to pitch and hearing nothing even though the book was coverage worthy. Someone *there* needed to want to read it. I couldn't insist on their attention from the outside.

So now let's look at the other side of this. What are some goals you can achieve because you work hard and because you've spent time lifting other writers up?

Dependent on you:

- Word-of-mouth buzz from people genuinely wanting you to succeed.
- Having a feature article run in your local newspaper or your alma mater's magazine.
- Placing an interview with a blog that's focused on a topic related to your book.
- Writing and publishing essays about related ideas or experiences.

Will those move as many copies as, say, a national book club? Doubtful. But it's all momentum. And getting a few press hits will help you, maybe, reach for some bigger ones, just like our early success with *Chicano Frankenstein* (and Daniel's catchy concept for his novel) earned NPR staff interest.

Moreover, anything you can pitch based on your existing connections is a way you can impact your book's sales potential in a real way. Reporters, reviewers, and bloggers are inundated with queries that are thrown out like so much spaghetti. If you've been active in your genre or interest groups that match your book's subject, you won't be brashly marching into a space asking for support from whoever might listen. You'll already be there; people there will know you or at least recognize your screen name or your interest in, say, heirloom candlesticks. I'm thinking of *space* here as digital but it could also be your local library or bookstore or knit night or aerobics class or a tech company's lunchroom. Anywhere you build connections and show kindness is a place where your book might find readers, because you have shown up there genuinely over time. You are a known quantity.

Before delving into the mechanics of how submissions work and where your project might find a home, it feels extra important to acknowledge all of this. If you work hard at your day job, you'll get a promotion or a raise. If you have a job that pays by the hour, an hour worked is an hour of earnings. But if you work hard at writing, even if you spend all your free time drafting and revising, there's no guaranteed payout. The brass ring of New York publishing may never get close enough for you to grasp it. Especially for those of us who break forms, who revel in our neurodivergence, who want to do something *different* than what's out there, who are too busy with other priorities to find time to research agents.

Some people earn the exact success they've always wanted—only to feel a huge sense of loss because the reality doesn't live up to expectations. A lot of this is because we, as human beings in a social media world, share only the good stuff.

We can write brilliant sentences. We can revise with courage.

We can identify our first-choice publishing path. But our brilliant, precious words aren't keys that automatically unlock the door to success. Maybe success is a variable, not a constant. Maybe our words aren't keys at all. Maybe they are seashells. Maybe they are ants. Maybe they are ghosts. Maybe, if we line up all our consonants and call them constants, we can appreciate their accrual. Their existence. We have put them where we want them to go. We have said what we wanted to say—or at least lunged toward that ideal we had in mind when we first decided to write this particular book.

Literary agent Susan Finesman, who opened Fine Literary in 2010 after her years as a film scout, said she wants writers to know how being a debut author can be "heart-bracingly hard." She told me, "In my experience, to a fault, almost all first-time authors are better writers than marketers. I wish they would spend some time thinking about the bookshelf, virtual or real, where their title would be at home. I wish they would take some time to study the competitive landscape. And finally, I wish they would embrace the fact of how important the query process is, and work crafting, recrafting, and crafting again. It is time well spent."

IN THIS SECTION WE'RE GOING to focus on the different publishing options and the importance of being clear with yourself about who you want to be as an author in the world.

If you want a place on a bestseller list, then you should go for it, and I'll tell you how. But you also need to understand why you want that, to imagine yourself living that life, the financial and physical costs to public appearances, and how to adjust your goal if external factors don't align. You might have the best dream but not get an agent. Or you might get an agent who fails to sell your book because there are so many manuscripts circulating, and for whatever reason, yours doesn't land on the top of the pile.

Publishing means relying on others—gatekeepers, if you like, although I chafe at that term's elitism. Most publishing professionals are earning small salaries and keep doing what they do because they love books, not because they expect fame and fortune.

Whether we're talking about agents, editors, or publishers, these in-the-know folx study how book sales work and learn what the latest metrics and best practices are. They know how to price an ebook in the current market. They know what type of comparison titles will help the sales team sell a book—and which won't. They understand how to talk about books that blend genres and books that adhere to a very specific formula but in a brilliantly inventive way. They know how to grapple with that terrifying word *audience* and nail down actual demographic data and make reasonable sales predictions.

What these industry professionals know takes up space between your book and its future readers. They're also human beings with their own lives and tastes. I recently sent a note to a querying author saying we can't look at manuscripts right now because we have lives and that's part of the small press world, at least at the micro level like Forest Avenue, where a lot of work gets done around school schedules and dentist appointments. One year, when I was teaching writers about submissions, I asked them to picture me in my parents' driveway, spreading a gigantic pile of wood chips around their yard one shovelful at a time. Anytime they felt themselves get moony about whether an agent or editor was considering their work at that exact moment, I told them to think of me confronting my big pile of chips. It's not just a good metaphor for being inundated with submissions; it's a reminder that we are real people who are focused on multiple projects, including personal ones. Your query matters, too, but we'll probably answer deadline questions for our existing authors, or turn around a revision draft, or shovel another wheelbarrow full of chips before we carve out time to read what you have to say.

Knowing the *why* behind your hopes will help keep your publishing journey centered on the story of *you* and the specifics of your creative work, instead of letting outside forces determine the way forward. (By *outside forces*, I mean the market, the people you query, how the economy is doing, and so forth.) Writing is often a painful process, but so is this unearthing, this awakening, this pushing of your inner self into the outer world. It's riddled with unpredictable criticism, being too exposed or feeling invisible (or both), false expectations of sales or sales goals that aren't being met. You open the door to your heart when you make a piece of writing public.

So much can go wrong, especially when you sign a contract and dream of pub day, only to find out the local bookstore can't carry your book. If your publisher's distribution method isn't indie friendly (and we'll look at what that means), the store says no. Not only to a reading but to carrying your book, something you never dreamed was possible, because your book is a perfectly good read, your publisher is legitimate, and you are a regular customer.

With enough information, authors can turn these pitfalls into manageable bumps, ones easily circumvented or borne with a sigh and a bit of jostling on the way to the next truly magical piece of the journey.

And yet there are moments where the right reader finds the right title and sends the author a fan letter about crying while eating lunch because they love—*love!*—your book so much. We have to hold on to those.

"The connection with readers was an intensely rewarding

part of the writing / publishing experience," said Jackie Shannon Hollis, author of *This Particular Happiness: A Childless Love Story* (Forest Avenue). "I mean . . . I think that's why so many people write, to connect with a part of themselves *and* with others. And for sure that is what reading is about."

That relationship—between the words you've written and the people who read or listen to those words—is what matters. Not sales targets and market penetration. One reader at a time, holding your words and feeling moved, entertained, or comforted by them.

To give an example, on the two-year anniversary of *Singing Lessons* I posted some launch photos and friends and acquaintances chimed in to say they had read my book two or three times. One had listened to the audio version *three* times. Why shouldn't *that* be my goal for all my books? To write work that urges one reader to start over from the beginning. Work that stands up to a second (or third) look. Work that feels different, that speaks in other ways, when the reader has new experiences to bring to the text.

I didn't know, on the brink of my first book launch, to wish for such things.

It's great to adjust expectations based on what we can achieve, to create softer markers of success instead of rigid lines we must cross *or else*. But on the other hand, when we gloss over the hard stuff and don't acknowledge it's hard, that's how myths perpetuate themselves.

So here's this for balance, cozied right up close to my warm and fuzzy words: publishing is, by many accounts, occurring within a broken system. If it worked like any other industry, we would earn livable wages for our work. Not just the celebrities or the mega-best-selling authors, but all of us. Intellectual property would be revered. Bookstores would never go out of business. Returns would be low, hovering around 5 percent, because everyone would be reading.

In the not-so-long-ago past, writers got sent on all-expenses-paid trips to do original reporting *plus* they got paid for the assignments. That's not happening much anymore. Reviews and book coverage continue to shrink with the decimation of print news, which disrupts a major way readers can find out about new books. Whole book coverage teams are still getting laid off—the *Los Angeles Times* among them. These days, newspapers mostly rely on wire services—content generated by other sources—to be their books coverage, if they have any. If you have the dollars, you can buy your way into what we call *advertorial* content—advertising meant to look like editorial—and reach that many more readers.

Success, as defined by making a living by writing, applies to an elite few that have written books the big presses identify as commercially viable or that the movie producers or streaming industries decide to turn into entertainment. And yet we all still wish for success, paying for conferences and consultations, setting ourselves up with costs that we may never earn back from our art. For example: Book tours should pay for themselves, right? They don't unless you're getting paid thousands of dollars in speaker fees. If you sell ten books at a bookstore in another city, and you earn fifty cents a book in royalties, that's five dollars. Maybe enough for regional bus fare, or to buy a snazzy sticker at the bookstore, but not enough for lodging and travel and meals. Or let's say your book is expensive enough that you get two dollars per sale from your publisher. That's still only twenty dollars. Your transportation, overnight housing, and food costs aren't covered. Ten books, that's great! But it probably won't feel great when you check out of your hotel and pay the bill.

Note how similar this is to my experience at AWP. The overhead to be there was higher—a tabling fee versus speaking for free at a bookstore—but I had multiple titles to sell, versus a new author touring with a single book.

Book tours can be amazing. They can make you feel great. Like a *real* author. They're great for seeing friends and family, celebrating your book being out, and getting press in local papers and interviews on local radio stations. But they aren't cheap. And they aren't the best choice for everyone.

IF WE CAN'T FIX WHAT'S broken because we're on the outside as the talent, what can we do?

Refocus on what's important: the work of writing.

Understand that sales numbers and multicity tours aren't the only ways to judge a book.

Keep reminding yourself that you don't have to compete with authors seeking the same dreams. You don't even have to set out to write something commercially viable; you can write something new and distinctly yours and you can relish the process.

You can measure success one grateful reader at a time. Every time a reader becomes a rereader.

I'd love to see writers and artists get paid for their ingenuity and resilience, for their leaps of imagination, for their use of color and their ability to conjure adjectives. And yet it's dreaming about money that hurts a lot of writers' self-image, because nobody told them how hard it is to make a living by selling your books in a world dominated by sound bites and YouTube

Shorts. Or how many writers make a living because of their speaking fees, the college courses they teach, and the writing workshops they spend hours creating and delivering.

WHAT IF YOU KNEW YOU'D make $1,000 from the book you're working on? Would you still try? Would you keep going? Why or why not?

Experiment with changing that number. Would $2,000 be enough? How about $500?

If you accept the idea of a thousand bucks coming back to you in royalties, would you still attend that writing conference? Would you still pay for a week's hotel stay as a retreat? How about that weekly class?

What do you get out of writing in the moment of doing the work and in community with other writers? Are those things, in and of themselves, *valuable* to you? Can you afford them if you know, for certain, you won't pay yourself back later? Will you invest in them if there's no six-figure paycheck dangling out there, tempting you to spend money to (maybe someday) make money?

I used to bank on my future earnings; I'd pay now for the experience and the privilege of being in the room with agents and editors, because surely it'd be worth it someday. Well, there have been a lot of somedays between those conferences and now, and I haven't. I'm still living *the dream*, reading and writing and editing, taking my kids to the local bookstore and pointing out titles I've worked on or seeing their faces light up when they recognize a Forest Avenue book on the shelves. What I've been able to control, creating a writing-centric life, has worked out. But, even adding my speaking fees to dollars earned from book sales and some consulting gigs, I haven't earned anywhere near enough to pay for my college degree, let alone all those not-for-credit community classes I've taken. So the experience has to be *enough;* go to a writing retreat because you want to be there instead of, say, the beach or your high school reunion.

I don't regret my time and energy spent in the literary world. I've met incredible writers and worked with amazing mentors and written work that makes me proud. I have more books to write. I have more authors to publish. My life is what I want it to be. I would love to land a six-figure deal or get a book (mine or one of my author's) on a major bestseller list, but the right factors have to align, and I'm not powerful enough to move the market or create my own luck. I can decide to wake up in the morning and write. I can pick another manuscript to publish by an author I've never heard of, and I can shower that author with appreciation and a small advance and the promise that I'll work hard for them.

I wish every artist got paid what they are worth.

I do what I can, and it never feels like it's enough.

It's not me that's mixed up or missing the mark, though. This is happening throughout the industry, even at the highest echelons.

Saying that out loud helps, I hope, even if the market factors are beyond our control. What we can do is acknowledge these truths, finish our work, and start new projects. Or as Reggie Watts put it when I interviewed him in 2024 at the Oregon Country Fair, "You've got so many things to make."

So don't talk yourself into stopping. You've got more writing to do. More thought trails to follow. Let yourself wonder and work.

REMEMBER, IT'S ART

WHEN WE TALK ABOUT GETTING published—whether we're looking for a home for a short story, a poem, or a full-length manuscript—we're really talking about making our art available within a capitalist economy. Commodifying our work. Our thoughts and insights, our use of language, the way we see the world. Earning money (hopefully) or at least visibility are often prime objectives when we talk about publishing. It's helpful, though, to remember we're weighing the *market* against what our hearts have made—our creative risk-taking, our brave storytelling, our research and hours of contemplation.

A manuscript sells or doesn't sell. If it doesn't sell, more pathways reveal themselves. Do you try another angle? Revise? Self-publish? Sometimes when we fixate on the plan, we are so close to the granular details about how to query that we forget our efforts are part of a larger conversation about culture and craft and who holds power and whether they look like us or not.

What art is considered valuable?

How is a creative work judged against other works?

Who is making these decisions?

How do these answers impact which books get big deals?

How can we, as expressive and intuitive beings, use this information?

Sometimes, in the rush of submission, in the throes of rejection, we forget all these questions. We obsess over the yes we crave, the no we dread. And then we begin to measure our flaws and failures. To imagine reasons we'll be rejected. Things we've done wrong. We lean into the system instead of acknowledging its failures. Our society's insistence on placing monetary value—or cultural value indicators like bestseller numbers or award seals—onto creative work needs to be separated from the process of writing or we, as artists, will lose hope.

As a publisher I didn't get into this business to make writers feel bad, but a lot of time, saying yes to one person means saying no to hundreds (and ultimately thousands) of others. It's hard. All of us in publishing know how passionately writers pursue their work. How they must conjure confidence to put words on the page. To stick with it. To prioritize time to *think* in a society that prizes speed and quantity of information over quality. Whatever the why behind your work (to entertain, to illuminate, to change the world), writing is a valuable way to spend your time because communicating with others leads to empathy and change.

Looking at it from another angle, selling our creative work—or gifting it to a publication that can't pay—is participating in the economy. Doing the work of writing—assuming nobody has bought your project on proposal—*isn't* related to capitalism. It's an investigation of self, a way of unearthing secrets and viewpoints and adjusting your identity accordingly. If you're not writing in the hopes of selling your work, it's even anti-capitalist. Cool! You shouldn't *have* to sell your work for it to matter. It matters because you put time into it. Because other people might be changed by it. We have to remember these things and hold them sacred, especially when we're ready to introduce our words to the public. To invite judgment. After all, if our work is our soul, and we talk about selling our souls as a negative thing, as *selling out*, then why do we lose hope and feel awful when a piece of work doesn't sell?

Why not just keep writing?

WELL, BECAUSE WE WANT ACTUAL people to connect with our words.

WE'VE GROWN ACCUSTOMED TO SEEING images of happy writers with their published books in hand and we want that too. To hold something we've made.

WE WANT PEOPLE TO FEEL less lonely or scared or sad because we've connected with them through this creative medium.

MAYBE WE WANT TO BE remembered.

MAYBE OUR PARENTS AND TEACHERS and other mentors are still alive, and we want to show them that their belief in us kept us going. That we have carried on with the potential they saw in us.

THESE WISHES ARE ALL BEAUTIFUL ones—and none of them have anything to do with buying or selling, bestseller lists or big advances. There's no mention of money in this list at all.

We don't need someone outside our experience to validate the time we spend writing.

Sometimes we forget that.

In a culture where everything is bought and sold and product advertisements abound, we tend to measure in dollars.

But we can measure in insights gained.

With the currency of a friend's hug.

By appreciating our words.

How nice and neat they look, lined up like that.

CASE STUDY #7: I'm Done

AFTER RELATING A PERSONAL MOMENT she experienced with one of her readers, Kate Gray, author of *Carry the Sky*, said her reaction was *I'm done*. Not in a frustrated way but in a fulfilled way, an *it couldn't be better* way. Like nothing could possibly top this surge of gratitude—no award or royalty report could come close.

My mouth dropped open when Kate said, "I'm done," because it's a phrase I've been saying too. It's a glass-all-the-way-full remark, an appreciation for what exists now, not what might come later. It also spins the furious, frustrated meaning of *being done* so it faces the opposite direction: toward positivity.

I mentioned this kind of *done-ness* to Neil Cochrane, author of *The Story of the Hundred Promises*, and he wrote back: "I feel exactly the same. And the concept of being done as an emotional pinnacle but in a *positive* way? Being done when the emotional journey of the book as an object resolves, not necessarily at the end of writing or the pub date? Love that."

If we can center our experiences with sharing our work on these intensely personal and beautiful gifts—from one reader's heart back to you, the creator—you can shift your publishing experience from anxiety and what you haven't gotten (yet) to what you have, right here. Right in front of you. So let's train ourselves to seek those moments. The ones given freely, with love. Let's remember and judge ourselves by *those.*

Not by a list of numbers or a spreadsheet of rejections.

Not by the no-response nos.

By the feeling of a fuzzy sentence coming into focus. By the gasp of a writer friend when you read the last line of a new story aloud.

By how great it felt, last weekend, to spend an hour writing with a friend, sipping tea, each of you lost in your own worlds.

AS MUCH AS WE TEND to focus on it, publishing isn't the only way to share our work. Performance is another. So is posting content online. Sending out a witty newsletter. Speaking to a class of creative writing students. Penning a beautiful letter to one person who will appreciate it.

Even a sweet text sent to a friend going through a hard time might arrive like a poem.

Every word is a gift of self, an offering of our time, our insights, and our intention.

A high school friend, Summer, sent a selfie she took with my novel. I realized that was my *New York Times* moment. What I should have been wishing for all along. As much as I'd swoon to get a mention in the paper of record, Summer reading my book was the *I did it!* aha that meant as much to me as anything. The *I'm done!* I needed, along with my other friends reading it and my parents flying out to Portland to see me at Powell's. To stand there at the microphone and watch the crowd listen to my words and clap.

Sometimes we forget to count all these other moments that really do count. Even if we aren't paying attention when it happens. Even when it takes a few days or months to realize what a special experience we had.

It all counts.

AS WE ABSORB ADVICE FROM the writers who have come before us, including the disappointed ones who found out that publishing didn't change their lives, even as we read other people's bad reviews, even as we tell ourselves we know—of course we know!—that six-figure deals are hard to come by, there's that inkling. A tiny, jittery inkling. Your book won't be like all the other books. It'll sell way more than the acknowledged small press rock star number: a thousand copies. Because surely, after all the time you've put into it, anything less would be impossible.

Your book will change the world.

Your book will earn you lots and lots of money, enough to ____.

It'll succeed!

It *has* to, because you've worked too hard to imagine otherwise.

Ann Rittenberg of the Ann Rittenberg Literary Agency says some incredibly sensible authors are happy with every step of the publishing process until publication day. "The book comes out and makes its modest way in the world, but they are terribly disappointed because—you don't realize this until afterward—their dream all along was that the world would stop and everybody in the US would read their book."

All of us on the other side of the desk—the agents, editors, and publishers—need you to know it almost never works like that. Because we don't want you to feel devastated on publication day. We want you to celebrate! Defining success in a realistic way means appreciating what you get instead of spending all that energy on mourning what didn't come through.

So many factors must align for your manuscript to make its way from desk to desk and eventually onto the shelf. There's so much to be proud of along the way, with every yes, with your box of galleys arriving, with your first review. Even if there are no awards, no end-of-year lists, no trumpets blaring and banners waving, your work still matters. Even if you don't get published the way you wanted, your work still matters.

Sometimes an exceptional event occurs, leading to major publicity or a bestseller campaign and you become the author everyone else looks up to, but almost always your book comes out and the world keeps moving.

Most people never find or read your work.

So many people aren't reading because they can stream visual entertainment that caters exactly to their taste in shows and music. Even the best publicity campaign can't guarantee who will find your book, and even if it gets found, there's no guarantee how those readers will feel about our words—or whether or not they take the time to review it.

These aren't my favorite insights. They remind me of advice that suggests if you can live without writing, just stop. I like the work, the sentence play, the imagining—all of it!—too much to quit. So I choose to keep going. And I choose to be honest with myself (and the writers who come to me seeking advice) about expectations.

With all that in mind, let's explore the avenues you can choose to take your manuscript down when you're ready.

AGENT OR PUBLISHER?

THERE'S A LOT OF INFORMATION online about publishing paths, much of it excellent, but the volume can make it hard to sort through. Everyone has opinions and wants to share them on their favorite platforms.

Big publishers don't care; self-publish!

Small publishers aren't going to get you any coverage; get an agent!

Self-publishing is so ten years ago; find an independent press.

It's not just experts giving advice; it seems like everyone has a newsletter, and the content beast needs constant feeding. Writers often share their experiences to help other writers, which is great, but the deluge of information can be hard to sort. And everyone's manuscript, and everyone's journey, is different. What works for one author might not be replicable for another, even one working in the same genre.

So who do you listen to? How do you filter all those opinions?

The next chapters are just one view on all of this—the perspective of a small press publisher and author who still daydreams about the big New York deal. But I'm also coming from the place of wanting you to choose for *you*, not because you read a disparaging industry article or an inflammatory headline or a Substack post claiming to share the truest truth about publishing. There are always new thought pieces going around, inciting controversy, causing authors to panic, or urging one specific way of being a writer in the world.

The best way you can be a writer in the world is the way that will make you happy.

That might not be publishing the way everyone says you *should*.

THE FIRST FORK IN THE publication path is a big one.

This way?

That way?

Both at the same time?

Frequently, writers hear that finding an agent is the *right* way to jump-start a career in writing. Or the *only* way. That's because there's a sense of clout and security in having an agent. Representation means someone in the industry believes in you and stands on your side of every contract negotiation. Even if your agent hasn't sold your book yet, they have connected their career to yours. They believe in your work that much. They want to put your work out there using their name to open doors for you. That's a huge confidence boost.

If you want a chance at a bestseller list or glossy magazine coverage or an invitation to a fancy network TV show, you should probably start with seeking an agent, because the more established, bigger-budget, well-staffed presses are only accessible via agent, and those are the ones most likely to have the kind of clout to make those dreams come true. You'll want the whole publicity machine of a major house or a top-tier independent press working for you—*if* you are reaching for big publishing dreams, and *if* you can find an agent who wants to represent you, and *if* that agent goes ahead and actually sells your book.

Another benefit to starting with an agent is that it's harder to get representation if you've already sent your book out on your own. If you have a fresh manuscript, not submitted anywhere, it's full of potential. It might be the next big thing! If you've already sent it out and it's racked up rejections, those venues can't be reapproached with the same project unless they've invited you to do exactly that, which is known as a *revise and resubmit* (or, informally, an *R&R*). This is probably why many people suggest you try agents first, then move to independent presses. There's a lower chance of big money at an independent press, for another thing. If you start with an agent, that person can knock on all the doors they want, in the order in which they choose, and they have the smallest presses in reserve if a bigger deal doesn't materialize.

But that's just one perspective.

Starting with independent presses because you don't want to jump through the hoops to find an agent or because you're feeling time pressure to get your work out there are legitimate choices. But what about negotiations? Agents help you get the best possible deal; that's one of their roles. If you don't have an agent, attorneys and publishing consultants can go over your contract and help you negotiate. The Authors Guild offers this service to its members—a great reason to join.

With independent presses you get hands-on attention, the benefit of working with a small but committed team, and a sense of belonging with your fellow authors. Of course, each press is deeply bound to the people running it, and not everyone is an excellent communicator. Giant imprints might offer some of the same benefits. But at a small press, you can be sure to have a direct interpersonal relationship with the person or people who chose your book and (likely) the founders of the press. Some of my proudest, silliest moments have been feeding my authors out of my backpack during conferences. The leader of a major imprint might not be your go-to for a protein bar, but as a small press publisher (and mom), I'm always equipped for emergency snacking!

As you think about your manuscript moving into the world, consider what you've written. There's a lot of room in the independent world for genre-breaking books, experimental prose, magical historical narratives, and offbeat, zany ideas. If you aren't sure if you fit into that category, think about it this way. The biggest presses are looking for books that will replicate the successes they've already had. Small presses often pride themselves on taking risks, pushing the status quo, and publishing debut authors. Knowing this may help you decide where to start.

What's best for you also depends on how your goals and your work intersect with the industry, your health, and your sense of urgency. If you want to get a project into the world so you can move on to other pursuits, your path might look different from someone who hopes to write a lot of books. Often online and workshop advice glosses over how personal this decision ought to be. We're talking about art! Creative expression! Our personalities on display! There is no right or wrong.

When we think linearly, like *this is the best way* and *this is the second-best way,* we impose a hierarchy that doesn't have to be there.

No one way is objectively better. They're different, just like your as-yet-unsold project and the just-sold manuscript your friend wrote. Use your energy to celebrate your friend's achievement and learn about how she got there, and then acknowledge that what you've written is on its own path because you, the author, are a different person.

AGENTS

IF YOU HOPE TO SIGN with a big publisher or need a life-changing financial deal, you should find an agent for your manuscript. Agents are essential to opening doors to the major publishing houses. The big five are Penguin Random House, Macmillan, Simon & Schuster, Hachette, and HarperCollins. Each of those has prestigious imprints with their own personalities and specialties. Lots of consolidations have cemented the grip the major houses have on the industry. They were the big seven not that long ago—and the big ten when I first started in publishing. All signs point toward the big four in the near future.

Many top-tier independent presses only take agented submissions. The biggest, most successful ones have a robust in-house staff and deep enough pockets to push a book onto the bestseller lists. Sourcebooks, Chronicle, Soho, Quirk, Gibbs Smith, Graywolf, Tin House, and Milkweed are among the many beloved independents publishing titles that regularly meet success metrics—sales, awards, and other accolades. Each of these presses has its own personality, as evidenced by their catalogs.

Some of the major independents are open to unsolicited, unagented manuscripts at certain times of year, but the most common approach is through an agent. You can find lists online; Duotrope, Manuscript Wish List, and Chill Subs are excellent tools, as is getting a one-month membership to Publishers Marketplace, which aggregates deal data by agent, type of book, and size of deal. Not all agents report all their deals, but Publishers Marketplace is the closest thing there is to an old-school phone directory, showing who has done what in their careers. If you're making a list of five or ten agents to query, you can find your top choices by seeing who has been active in your genre lately. You can get Publishers Lunch, one of their newsletters, sent to your inbox for free, but if you can afford the twenty-five-dollar fee, a one-month subscription can yield tons of information specifically related to your book. You can cancel once you have enough information about agents and the presses buying their books. Or you can commit for six months or a year and get a small discount.

SO WHAT, EXACTLY, DO AGENTS do?

Agents are hands-on guides and go-betweens for writers wanting to sell their books. They tend to be hands-on editors. They work with their authors on manuscripts and proposals before sending them out. After all, they want your material polished to a glossy shine before they pitch it. Every project is a reflection of an agent's identity and editorial prowess. Agents have to feel the books they're trying to sell are *ready* for top editors. They can't afford to waste their contacts' time by sending an early draft. This means that while we think of agents as taking phone calls and fancy lunches, they're often deep in developmental editing for their clients, preparing work to get sent out. This is, admittedly, time-consuming. And it's unpaid labor. No money changes hands until a project sells. Agents do this work with their authors hoping it will pay off down the road, just like we as writers put paragraphs together and hope someday someone will buy what we've written.

Erin Harris, senior vice president at Folio Literary Management, earned an MFA in creative writing. "It's had a major impact on my agenting career," she told me. "When I decide to offer representation to an author, it doesn't feel like much of a decision at all. If I have a gut-level response to someone's work—which is to say, if I fall in love with it, see a place for it in the market, know how to sell it, and have an editorial vision for it—then the decision just sort of happens very organically. I feel a bit like I can't live without the project, and it becomes the best kind of compulsion."

I wanted to know if an imperfect project would hinder this "can't live without" feeling, and Erin added, "This type of visceral response to an author's work can happen when the work itself is not yet in its ideal shape. Generally speaking, the voice and premise will be spot-on, but something about the plotting and pacing isn't quite 'singing' yet. That's what the author and I will work on together."

In addition to giving their authors editorial guidance, agents answer questions and demystify how the publishing process works. They buoy their writers through rounds of rejections. They broker deals and fight for better contracts and higher advances or generate auctions, where interested presses bid on a hot book. They push back on the wrong cover so the author doesn't have to.

In exchange for their work, agents earn a percentage of your sales, usually 15 percent for print and ebook sales and 20 percent for subsidiary rights. You don't have to pay them out of your own pocket.

SUBSIDIARY RIGHTS: These are all the rights that fall outside your primary-language print and ebook sales. They include foreign rights, translation rights, audiobook rights, and film/TV rights. Foreign and translation can be the same thing, but they might not be; if you're a Latinx author who writes in English, a US-based publisher might buy your book for Spanish-language translation, so that would be translation rights, not foreign rights. Likewise, if you are a US-based writer whose debut novel sells to an Australian or British publisher, there wouldn't be a translation needed, just spelling and style guide adjustments, so that would be classified as a foreign rights sale.

The more money you earn from book sales, the more money your agent earns. They have a stake in your career.

You succeed = your agent gets paid more.

Your book doesn't sell = your agent doesn't get paid.

Even if the major publishers took over-the-transom submissions direct from authors, it'd be hard to figure out who is looking for what type of book. This is another area where agents shine; they make it their business to know who is buying what types of projects.

There are so many editors and so many imprints; they all have their own personalities and project wish lists. Agents act as gatekeepers to these siloed editors. Not only can agents vouch for the quality of the work being offered for sale but they maintain relationships and accrue information about acquiring editors' tastes and preferences.

It used to be that New York agents held a home-turf advantage, but there are successful agents all over; especially since the COVID-19 pandemic, we've shifted increasingly to online meetings. You don't need a hotel room and a plane ticket to meet with someone face-to-face; you can both log on from home.

FINDING AN AGENT IS A coup for a writer who wants a shot at financial success. As we've already covered—it feels important enough to reiterate!—most writers earn money with full-time jobs, teaching, consulting, or freelancing; only the top-selling authors (or those with financial support from their partners or families) don't need to hustle with sideline projects and businesses. That being said, agents *can* get their authors big, juicy, life-changing advances. It's invaluable to work with someone who knows the New York landscape—and knows individual editors who buy books like yours.

Competition is fierce to sell a book at any level, though, and there are no guarantees that once you get an agent, your book will sell. You might lose months or years to revising with your agent's feedback, waiting those interminable weeks or months as your agent submits your manuscript, and still not land a book deal.

Keith Rosson, author of *Fever House* (Penguin Random House), wrote several starter novels before approaching agents. He earned representation after about a hundred rejections. "It's just one of those things where you tailor the work or the query to each agent and then take in what they have to say," he said. "Run it up against the flagpole of yourself and see if you can reconcile if what they say has value. If it did, I took their advice. If not, I kept submitting. I love submissions, flinging your stuff into the world and seeing what comes back."

Once Keith signed with an agent, the querying process began again, this time with the agent representing his work. He and his agent turned down one small press offer due to unfavorable contract terms and opted to sign with Meerkat Press. *The Mercy of the Tide* was Keith's debut, followed by *Smoke City*, *Road Seven*, and a story collection, *Folk Songs for Trauma Surgeons*, all with Meerkat.

After these successes and growing his fan base, Keith decided to change agents. He wanted a shot at a big deal, a New York publishing house, and he needed the financial stability that comes with that kind of win. Deciding to find new representation was scary, though. "Even if you don't feel like they're really getting you or your work, there's still that internal cushion of *I still have a literary agent, so something might happen.* Which can be so misguided."

Keith's new agent, Chad Luibl of Janklow & Nesbit Associates, sent *Fever House* out on submission, and it was quickly preempted by Penguin Random House in a two-book deal. Suddenly Keith had time to write—and a sequel with a pending deadline. *Fever House* came out to great reviews and buzz in summer 2023, followed by *The Devil by Name* in September 2024.

"To drum up an entire new story around this very specific world was challenging," he said. "But also: here is your shot at a career. Give them a sequel, you're now a pro author. Don't blow it. I muscled through it. It was still fun, just not as fun as writing a standalone where you get to go bonkers."

I love that Keith used the word *bonkers* about writing drafts without any expectations set on them. Being a pro writer, as he said, means more people expecting specific things from you. If you go the agent route, there's an expectation in place that you are going to write more books. That you are going to listen to your agent's advice and your editor's advice and treat this opportunity like a career. Because it is one when all the pieces align, and you get paid real money for your creative output.

SOMETIMES AGENTS LEAVE THEIR JOBS because they've decided to pursue a career in another field or a different aspect of publishing. Emme Lund's debut novel, *The Boy with a Bird in His Chest* (Atria), was a finalist for the Center for Fiction's 2022 First Novel Prize. After selling the book to the Simon & Schuster imprint, Emme's agent Cassie Cannes Murray left agenting to start Pine State Publicity.

I asked Emme about that experience and she said: "A week before my agent told me she was leaving the business, I was out to dinner with a writer friend who was explaining the difficulty of being assigned a new editor who didn't really understand his work. I expressed my sympathy. He waved it off and said, 'Editors and agents come and go. What remains is the work,' meaning that while our relationships with agents and editors are important, they're not what makes our careers. Our craft, our unique voice, our writing, that is what can't be replaced."

I love that idea. It comes back to the work. Not who's handling it but the work itself, and how it's a reflection of how the author sees the world. Editors leaving is a regular issue for authors who get deals at bigger houses. Suddenly the editor who loved the work—who *bought* it—isn't there, or isn't in the same role as before, and the author has to work with whoever inherits that job. Emme said:

> I was sad when I heard my agent was moving on, but my friend's words were a balm. Soon after she announced her departure, I set to work

finding new representation. I was pleased to find it so much simpler than my first time querying agents. Of course, things were different. I'd released a book. I had more connections. (My agent set me up with another agent she thought would be a good fit.) I had the confidence of having landed an agent once. I tend to not share work before I have a full draft completed, but I broke my rule and sent the first fifty pages of a novel manuscript I was finishing to a few agents who'd expressed interest. I wanted to know that my next agent was excited about my new project, and I wanted to get a taste of what their notes might be once a draft was completed. I held several meetings over the course of a few weeks. I asked a lot of questions. I chatted with existing clients. In the end, I signed with a new agent who is just as excited about my career as my last one.

BIG FIVE

OKAY, SO IF YOU GET an agent, what's next? They'll try to sell your book to a major New York publishing house, or a bigger independent that can offer competitive advances. Occasionally there's competition; hot properties sometimes lead to auctions, where each interested publishing house submits a bid. Other times one or two editors might make an offer, and your agent can help you decide.

If you get an acceptance, your agent will negotiate your contract and you'll sign, and then you'll be rolling through the process, including revising for your editor, filling out an author questionnaire for the publicity team, and getting your first peek at the cover art. Your advance will be paid in several chunks, the first on signing the contract, usually through your agent, who will deduct their share before sending your money to you. Your agent will help prepare you for the process and will speak up for you and fight for you, which will allow you to preserve your direct relationship with your editor.

This is the scenario that many writers dream of, so be sure to celebrate every step of the way.

I am *not* an author with a big five house, so I can't share specific how-it-is stories, but I do know this: big five presses will always get your book into bookstores. It's something we take for granted when we dream about publishing, wanting to see our finished work on shelves, at our local independent bookstores. And it's why getting an agent and a deal with the big five remains at the top of many authors' dream lists. Your book in bookstores! What you've always wanted!

A lot of online conversations around publishing, including preorders, publicity campaigns, and event booking are specifically about hurdles small press authors have to overcome to get into stores. We will get to those in depth in a few more chapters, because I'm passionate about cutting through the noise and misinformation around distribution. For now, it's important to confirm that a contract with a major imprint means your book will be available to the trade—in bookstores, libraries, and likely in big-box stores, grocery stores, museums, and/or gift shops, depending on the kind of book it is and how much money the imprint is putting behind it.

How books move from printer to warehouse to wholesaler is called *distribution*. The big New York houses have in-house distribution; occasionally a successful independent press can contract with the big five to distribute their titles. Central Avenue Publishing, a Canadian company, recently joined Simon & Schuster.

DISTRIBUTION: How a book gets to its customers, directly or indirectly. Presses that have full-service distribution have sales reps that go out and tell bookstores, libraries, and other book-carrying entities what the next season's titles will be. This sales pitch, delivered months before publication, impacts the availability of a press's books, which in turn impacts

> sales. Distributed presses either have their own warehouses and in-house sales teams under the auspices of the press, like the big five, or they might work with a company that provides distribution services, which is how Forest Avenue and other distributed small presses operate.

Bestsellers can be *chosen* and *made* by the big presses—and even independent presses with multiple titles a season pick lead titles, the ones that are going to get a bigger, more costly publicity push. Part of the reason why that's possible is because they have the mechanisms in place to get a book *everywhere.*

Let's consider Target for a moment. The big five can sell their titles into Target because they have a sales team that knows how to sell to those particular buyers. Independent presses with full-service distribution can also get their books to the Target team if it's a viable book for that market, because there's a sales rep tasked with knowing the buyers and how to sell to them.

If your small press author friend starts bragging about how their book is available at Target, it's likely they are confusing in-store placement (which impacts sales and is an incredibly competitive process) with noticing the book's metadata has fed out to the Target website.

METADATA: Digital information about a book, which can include the price, the ISBN number of each format, the cover image, the subtitle, the book description, blurbs, keywords, subject categories, and sales handles. Anything you see about a book on a consumer-facing website is metadata. The more robust the metadata, the more likely the book will turn up in searches.

I don't expect this book to be stocked at Target unless there's a stroke of sheer luck, but even before we send out galleys for reviews, I can look up the title on Target's website, and there it is! For preorder! That's because my metadata has fed out correctly to the Target website. This book is not *really* at Target, though. Not in the physical sense. It's just data population, just like it has populated to Bookshop, Barnes & Noble, Powell's, WalMart, and Amazon. When I make a change to my book's description, or I add a new review, those changes update and repopulate on the same sites.

From a small press standpoint, when we talk about being able to compete with the big five, that's up to a point. There's a lot we can do to create a professional product, enhance the opportunities for readers to discover that product, and support our authors. Having distribution means we can compete by having our books on shelves next to big five titles. There may just be one copy of one of our books alongside ten or twenty of a big-name title, but hey, we're there too. One of my goals with every book is to make it look *as appealing* as books by presses with huge footprints. Most readers don't shop for their next read by what logo is on the back of the jacket, after all. So if I can create a book that adheres to professional standards of design and concept, and if it's available in a lot of bookstores, and if I fill out all the metadata fields so it shows up in online searches, then it can compete with any other title.

We can also replicate the process, from early enough lead times to pitching articles about and profiles of our authors. Most presses with full-service distribution have in-house publicity efforts in place to drum up coverage of their books. As coverage comes in, we can share the links and headlines with the sales team, who can then use the momentum to get more books into stores. Authors are expected to support these efforts with their social media accounts, making themselves available for media interviews, and either hiring a freelance publicist or finding other specific ways to help with publicity efforts. I always tell my authors that the more brainstorming they do and the more time they invest in the process of publicity, the better the sales will be.

Even if we collaborate and work really hard, we can't match the size of the big five machinery. We don't have the deep financial backing or the high staffing counts to do what a big press can do for its books. We don't have special media days for major reviewers and reporters to interview our authors months before publication. We're not equipped to manufacture fame or call in favors from glossy magazines. We don't have the money to spend hundreds of thousands of dollars on advertising.

PENGUIN RANDOM HOUSE CALLS THE books they choose to push toward bestseller status their "make books." Marketing executives spoke to us at the Yale Publishing Course in August 2018 and shared the specifics of two case studies. The staff explained that they pick one book a year to focus bestseller-creation efforts on, and they push lots of time, money, and other resources toward promoting that title. *Educated* by Tara Westover was one of the examples they cited. *Lilac Girls* by Martha Hall Kelly was the other. Both became instant *New York Times* bestsellers.

I wrote *5,000 galleys* in my Yale notebook—that's five thousand copies given away free before publication! That talk came before Covid pushed a lot of publishers to circulate e-galleys—because that avoids the cost of printing and shipping physical books—but still. There's no way Forest Ave could compete on that scale; small press authors are considered rock stars if they can *sell* a thousand. Giving away *thousands* of freebies is unimaginable to me—even if they're digital galleys! That's five thousand readers who won't need to buy the book. I wonder: giving five thousand away must have been calculated alongside a corresponding number of sales needed to make the effort and cost worthwhile. Is double that in sales—10,000—enough to be considered a success? Or 50,000? Or 100,000 copies?

Other books get major attention and full-tilt campaigns from the major houses, but there's only one "make book" a year in the PRH business model, or at least that's how it was in 2018 when I had access to that kind of information.

So, as you might imagine, if your publisher gives away five thousand copies of your book and invests six figures in your advance, then chances are they're going to invest a hell of a lot of money in publicity and marketing efforts so their up-front investments pay off in sales traction once the book comes out. In addition to bookstores and libraries, your book will be in Target and other big-box stores, gift stores, airports, and grocery stores—everywhere books are sold.

If you sign a contract with a major house and you're not selected for top-tier efforts, you won't get all the bells and whistles from publicity and marketing, and that's okay. It just means that you need to be vigilant about measuring your sales against a book that *has* been chosen, because it's like comparing millimeters to inches. It takes a lot more millimeters—a lot more small publicity hits, legwork, guts, and luck—to make up a foot, let alone a yard. Your experience as a midlist author at a big house might be more similar to an author who signs with a small press that has distribution. You'll get publicity support, but authors whose books are expected to sell better will get *more*.

MIDLIST: The authors in the middle of the pack. It's a term usually used for describing the big five hierarchy; I don't know anyone in the small press world who thinks of their authors as midlist.

Forest Ave isn't set up to compete with the biggest titles—the "make books" or the next in a series by authors who always hit bestseller status—but we can compete with debuts and midlist authors. When I search BookScan for sales numbers of midlist big five titles to compare them to Forest Avenue's projected and actual sales numbers, we're often competitive.

Maybe someday we'll hit a major success, a big-league home run of a book, but we still won't have the staffing or the money to invest in *making* that book as big as a big five "make book." Instead of measuring ourselves against those standards, we look at which books are big for us, and what we can do to publish more of them.

City of Weird: 30 Otherworldly Portland Tales is our biggest title to date; it keeps selling and selling, in part because of Powell's Books keeping it displayed on their Portland shelves. Editor Gigi Little tuned in to the buzzy excitement around our city as a place of weirdness, and her octopus monster cover art grabs readers. We've since produced several other anthologies—featuring a mix of science fiction, fantasy, fabulism, and horror—to build on that success and hopefully replicate it. Still, *City of Weird,* which we call COW internally, sits at the top of our list.

Big five books sell hundreds of thousands, even millions of copies. Their best-sellers are a league away from ours. Which is why agents focus on those submissions. If you want to make money as an author, if you want to build a career, the agent-to-publisher route might be your top choice.

CASE STUDY #8: A Leg in the Door

MY PUBLISHING ROUTE HAS BEEN a complex, slower-than-heck one, mostly because I kept choosing the agent route and then my books didn't sell. A lot of writers have this experience—adjusting their publishing path based on market forces, rejections, and / or understanding more about ourselves and what we want.

My first two books weren't ready for prime time. I didn't know enough about plot and editing. I didn't know what I wanted to say either. Or what my strengths are as a writer.

If those novels had come out, they would have been markers for growth, to measure future work against, and there's nothing wrong with that, but I'm long past the attachment I once had to them. If you let go of or abandon old manuscripts, I hope you can get to this point with them.

Sometimes it feels good to know you're not alone, that you haven't fallen behind.

I'VE WANTED TO BE A novelist since grade school. I've written and read and studied books with an eye toward publishing since those early years. My teachers praised my voice and my vocabulary, and I clung to their words.

My first professional author breakthrough came in

my late twenties when I received a garbled, signal-broken voicemail on my cell phone.

"Wonderful submission."

"If you are still looking."

"Hard copy if possible."

At first—this was 2004, and I think I still had my very first cell phone—I thought a local person was calling about a story idea for the coastal newspaper where I worked as the managing editor. But then I realized it might be a literary agent calling about my novel. I had been submitting and keeping track of each query.

Could an agent have called me? On the phone?

Maybe?

At that time the literary advice I had access to (primarily print magazines like *Poets & Writers*) made me believe that agents were *the* way to get a book published. So that's who I was querying. And I had never been called by any of them. Still uncertain, I begged my features editor Karen to help me decode the garbled voicemail. We huddled by the dumpster in the parking lot of a building that would be razed a few years later, and we listened over and over. Again, again, again. Eventually we deciphered enough of the words to agree it might be an offer of representation.

(*Maybe?*)

I studied my spreadsheet using the phone number area code—a city in California—until I decided who probably wanted to reach me. I had two possibilities but felt surer of one than the other. I wrote that agent the most awkward email, something like *if* you were trying to reach me and *if* you are interested in my novel, then I'd love to chat.

My cheeks flame hot even thinking about how scared I was to hit send. In case it wasn't her. In case I was inconveniencing her.

Then she emailed me right back and confirmed my hunch. She said: "I called earlier, right after reading the terrific pages you sent from your novel. I love the writing and the voice and the quirkiness and wonder of it all."

I couldn't contain my excitement. This agent not only understood my writing and sensibilities but wanted to read more. She asked for an exclusive. I said yes. (And I took notes so I could prove it to myself, as many times as I needed to.)

When we had our first and only phone call and she offered representation, I probably didn't ask one question because my heart was pounding so fast. *It's happening!* I told myself. *This is it!*

I didn't know if I'd get the New York luncheon I had always imagined or a deal written up in Publishers Marketplace. But I felt sure that being represented by someone powerful with a strong track record, someone who understood the wonder of it all, would launch my career in fiction.

When I called my mentor Stevan Allred to tell him the good news, he gave me a compliment that completely frustrated me. "You don't just have a foot in the door," he said. "You have a leg in the door!" Stevan was genuinely happy for me, but when I hung up, I growled to myself, *It's not just a leg. You are* in *the door. That's what having an agent means!* I desperately wanted Stevan to be wrong. Turns out, though, he was right. That agent never sold my novel.

Despite revising for her after the first two rounds of rejections, euphemistically called *passes*, my agent didn't send my book out again. I'm not sure if she got busy or if my changes didn't solve enough of the project's problems. Probably both? I spent a lot of time stewing over what had gone wrong.

Did I make a wrong turn?

Did I change too much?

Should I have been more aggressive with my edits?

Maybe she didn't like me anymore!

I didn't have the guts to ask if she had lost interest in the novel, so I quit futzing with it and turned my attention to a new book set in—surprise—a coastal newspaper office. My energy and excitement started bubbling back up. The disappointment healed.

Four years later, I submitted this new novel to my agent. After all, she loved my work. We had a signed contract saying she represented me. I had sent her holiday cards and sample chapters and kept her updated on my progress. But it was 2008—the Great Recession. I recall my agent explaining that this was a much better book, but she couldn't sell it at this time.

I had to, very embarrassingly, ask for clarification. I knew I'd lose my nerve if I didn't ask immediately. *Are you freeing me from my contract?*

Yes, that's what she meant. I was free to seek other representation. She added, "You are a talented writer and I have high hopes that you have a great future ahead of you."

But I didn't have high hopes.

I'd had a leg in the door! And then the door closed.

Now I had nothing at all. If she didn't think she could sell my work—this champion of mine, this advocate—then I was truly alone. Washed up before I even got my first book deal.

I WAS SUCH A SAD writer after that experience.

I grieved the relationship I thought I had with my agent. I had kept writing novels because she believed in me. Now she didn't.

She wasn't even *my* agent anymore.

What did I have left?

Where could I possibly go?

AGENTS AREN'T INTERESTED IN REPRESENTING books that have been submitted widely to editors; that really limits where *they* can send it. Luckily, in rejecting me before the submissions stage, my agent left me with a viable product. A way to knock on the door. *Hello?*

I revised the journalism novel again, then queried two or three other agents; one wanted to see more pages, then passed with feedback. I queried a local small press and got similar feedback. My protagonist seemed too young for her age. Maybe her story would work better if it was set in high school?

But that won't work at all! I shouted to myself. *And aren't there other people who feel awkward in social situations? Who try to mimic their peers and it all goes wrong?*

I didn't know to call myself neurodivergent or to name my character autistic, if only in my query letter. If I had framed my story through that lens, or if there had been more autistic protagonists in books and movies, maybe my novel would have made more sense to neurotypical editors. Instead, I quit that book too.

I DIDN'T START A NEW project.

I LEFT MY NEWSPAPER JOB and got pregnant. I entered a long, sluggish pause, a creative fallow time, my brain foggy with grief over my literary career that never really started while my body expanded. How could I sit down and write instead of, say, making dinner, when nobody cared if I ever wrote again? When I didn't have *representation*?

Slowly, in conversation with writing friends, I realized this shift in fortune had given me freedom. Nobody was waiting for my next book. I could write whatever I wanted between baby feedings and naps. Without thinking of an agent's sensibilities or guessing at the New York market or trying to imagine what editors might want in another five years.

Maybe, instead of pinning my hopes on publishing professionals, I could pull back and find motivation within. Count on myself.

What might writing for fun look like?

My style loosened up. Lightened up. Imagination and delight became my motivation. I quit yearning for external praise from my agent and her contacts in New York. If a sentence made me happy, I wrote another like it.

Without an audience, without expectations, I began to play on the page.

An original sound emerged. With an unusual story.

My leg in the door was just a leg after all. But that first taste of *maybe*, of someone believing in my storytelling, kept me working.

The book that developed from my time between agents became my debut novel. Eventually. By eventually, I mean fifteen years after I started making notes about a family of barrel organ makers in nineteenth-century France, my novel appeared on shelves.

Of course, as can be the case when you're eager to pursue your one true destiny, I thought I was done ages before I really was. I started querying the novel in 2014 with the certainty that the right agent would appreciate the concept enough to want to work with me, even if the pages weren't perfect yet. Even if it didn't fit into a pre-existing industry genre. Even if it was a little long. An agent meant the chance of real money and prestige. I still thought of New York deals as the best possible path.

I received interest from agents, which told me my query letter and concept were working. But each time after submitting the first fifty pages or the first hundred pages or the full manuscript, I received personal feedback about what wasn't right yet.

Being an editor, I went to work with these notes in hand. *I can do that!* I said to myself. Then I revised for months or a year, finally sending the updated draft back to whichever agent had offered to take another look.

Who then—you can guess—rejected it. I got responses like *that didn't work the way I expected it would*, or *thanks, but it's still not for me*. Now, being a publisher myself, I understand what those comments meant. I didn't slow down long enough to think about the *why* behind the revision suggestions. Or if those ideas matched my intent for the book. I spent months and *years* trying to adjust my vision of the novel to meet other people's expectations. And none of those drafts worked.

By the time I met my second agent over coffee in Berkeley, I had followed so many trails of possibility that I lost sight of what I wanted for my book. I was in town representing Forest Avenue Press titles to our sales team at Publishers Group West. Laurie Fox of the Linda Chester Literary Agency and I decided to meet, around 2016, because we knew people in common and because I wanted to interview her for this book. It took a few years of meetups and emails before I even mentioned working on a novel. Which is kind of hilarious to me now. It seems like an extreme overabundance of caution. But at the time, I intended to connect with her as a publisher, not an author. I had an earlier iteration of this very writing book in progress, too, and thought she might be a great person to quote as a resource.

When I finally mentioned my music box manuscript a few years later, she wanted to know more. But she cautioned me that fiction is very personal, and she accepts very few new clients. She didn't want her curiosity to get my hopes up or to wreck our relationship by considering my work. I reassured her: *This is a business, I get it.* I had finally understood, by then, that my novel was unusual and different, not to everyone's taste. Then I told her about serinettes and canary training. I recall it was less a formal pitch than a few sentences of sharing my wonder with her. *Look at this weird barrel organ! This is at the center of the world I'm creating.*

Laurie asked for a taste of my manuscript, and I sent a handful of pages, worried she wouldn't resonate with them and also sure something was wrong with the latest draft. I hadn't figured out (yet) that incorporating all the feedback led me in too many wrong directions. Instead of following my joy, or my vision for the book, I had been listening to outside voices that had no stake in the outcome of my manuscript. And when it didn't work, I was on my own with a bigger mess than ever.

Laurie loved my pages, so a few months later, I submitted a larger chunk. She confirmed it *still* wasn't working. So I revised. Eventually I submitted a new draft to her, and Laurie decided she wanted to represent me.

Proximity and people in common got us into the same room together, but a professional working relationship occurred because of her response to my work. Laurie could articulate my novel's flaws and messes in a way that made sense to me, and her goals for the project aligned with mine.

WHILE I WAS WRITING THIS book, Laurie and I parted ways. We've always appreciated each other as friends and industry colleagues, and she's been a key cheerleader for my fiction over the years. She even supported my decision to publish this book through Forest Avenue. From a financial standpoint, keeping the book with my press meant earning way more per book than if I/we sold it to another press and I earned only royalties. And I'm at the stage in my career where dreams don't earn dollars, and I could use another steady selling title in my catalog.

If writers take to this book and recommend it to other writers, the profits will help Forest Avenue continue. I expect to sell copies direct to writers at conferences where I'm speaking—another reason to DIY it. If a bookstore takes 40 percent of the cover price as a fee for selling it on my behalf, then my business gets the other 60 percent (minus my royalties). If I sold it to another press, given current royalty structures, I'd likely earn less than a dollar per copy for a paperback if the press supplied the merchandise—and those payments would show up in annual or semiannual royalty statements. If I brought books myself to consign for an event, I'd have to buy them from the press and pay for shipping them. Standard author discount is 50 percent. If the conference bookstore took 40 percent, I'd earn 10 percent net. Twenty books sold at a conference is fantastic. But if it earned me only fifteen or twenty dollars total? That wouldn't feel quite so fantastic.

Better to do it myself.

Besides, that decision gave me another one of my

dreams: having Gigi Little, Forest Avenue's cover designer, make a cover for one of my books.

I WISHED FOR YEARS ON every coin and every candle, and I read all the interviews and attended lots of events, writing down wisdom from authors who *made it,* and I revised scrupulously based on agent feedback.

But I didn't get a major deal with a big five house.

I didn't even get a small deal with a major house.

Or a major deal with a small house.

So far in my career, I've given up on two completed novels and abandoned a half dozen others. I had two agents who gave me feedback and believed in me, but I found the publisher for my debut novel through an open call on Submittable. *Singing Lessons for the Stylish Canary* sold to Lanternfish Press in 2021 for a small advance, during the pandemic, because collectively as a culture we needed hope, and my book is uplifting and joyful. I think timing can absolutely help a manuscript sell, but it's not possible to predict what might sell two or five or ten years in the future. We can only write what we want to write, in the current moment, and hope that we finish at a time when our words offer clarity or relief from the present.

Now, looking back, I realize that my novel was always a small press book. It doesn't have a tight, sharp arc. It doesn't fit neatly into a genre category. It's historical and fantastical, literary and funny, old-fashioned and pluckily modern. It's, in places, much too big for its britches. As a neurodivergent writer, I'm terrible at guessing what readers will think of a plot twist or an extra-frothy line of description. Mostly I try to get away with as much as I can and then an editor can pull me back. That's definitely more of a niche way of writing than, say, knowing when to place a grand gesture within the plot of a romance novel or understanding how to set up the crime scene in a cozy mystery. And, in case you didn't notice, I am a small press fanatic. I love them. I love *us*, being a publisher. I especially love the surprise of books that come from independent presses—interesting conceits, voices that have been spoken over by mainstream culture, risk-taking language.

You likely have different reasons for loving to write and a different style than me. You probably read deeply in specific genres, or find yourself gravitating toward books published by a particular press or imprint. Those pieces of information might inform your decision on how to focus your career.

Now I'm back to the fork in the road:

Agent?

Small press?

Which way is right for me?

SMALL PRESS TYPES

I LOVE SMALL PRESSES. PUBLISHING with a small press can be faster—depending on the press, their backlog of titles, and how many projects they publish a season. There's no second round of hoops to jump through; once you get an agent, you need to revise according to your agent's notes and then your agent will take up querying on your behalf. In other words, the book still needs to sell. News flash: even if your agent tells you it's going to be big, there's no guarantee anything will happen.

IT MIGHT NOT SELL.

Getting an agent is a step in your career, not a deal. I've heard from writers whose agents overpromised fame and fortune and then couldn't sell their books to anyone. It happens.

If you sign with a small press, though, it's all systems go. Your manuscript—as long as everything goes according to plan (and the press doesn't fold)—is going to become a book! Soon you'll be editing! And looking at cover options! Go you!

HERE'S AN IMPORTANT SUBJECT: NOT all small presses can get your books into bookstores. We, as writers new to the field, tend to conflate being published with having our books available in brick-and-mortar stores, as well as online ones, but that isn't necessarily true.

While agents all operate in similar ways—on commission—presses have wildly different business models. It's important to understand the mechanics of how a press gets books into customers' hands *before* you submit your work. That's because all presses say good things about the way they operate, especially when they're courting a new author. You might sign a contract, commit your work to a company, and then find out no bookstore will carry your book because of how the press is set up.

That's a disappointing scenario that happens over and over again in small-press-ville because of a lack of transparency and communication more than any ill intent. Authors want to do their best for their presses, so we're willing to go along with whatever is presented; the publishing staff members want to impress the potential author, so any gaps or downsides to their business models *aren't* exactly conversation fodder for a get-to-know-you phone call.

Plus: everyone in publishing is busy working on existing books. When a publisher says, *Yes, we will make your book available to bookstores,* they don't always add, *but it's likely bookstores won't stock your book unless you personally reach out to ask them.* It's an important distinction.

I USE *INDEPENDENT* AND *SMALL* to describe Forest Avenue, but I lean toward *small* because I take pride in our size.

In her 2023–24 Publishing Pathways chart, publishing industry expert Jane Friedman defines small presses as those that "avoid advances and print runs," meaning that they use print on demand to get books to readers instead of printing a bulk run of copies ahead of the publication date. By her definition, Forest Avenue is a traditional press because we do print runs. We pay token advances, though, usually $500 or less, which fits into her "small press" category. Jane, a true beacon in a complicated publishing environment, updates her Publishing Pathways chart each year. I recommend looking at her site for more information on any industry topic, because she's always adding new content, including essays by guest authors.

All this to say, publishing language usage comes down to who is doing the defining. Who is doing the labeling. Which is usually the press itself.

A hybrid press, where the author agrees to invest financially, might call itself indie or independent. (Although they should tack on the word hybrid to be clear with the payment expectations.)

An author who starts a press to publish their own work would be correct in calling that press an independent or indie press or a small press.

Self-publishing authors often refer to themselves as indie authors.

A traditional press might call itself small or independent because it doesn't rake in millions in sales per year. Or because it doesn't give New York–sized advances. Or because they can't afford more than a handful of staff members.

A micropress might call itself small because it has distribution, meaning the books are available widely, unlike micropresses that have more of a punk zine, DIY approach and no distribution.

Some of these term usages are interchangeable and acceptable, except for one hard rule: If money flows from the author *to* the publisher, it's not a traditional model. It's a hybrid or a self-publishing company or an author services company. If a press requires authors to pay for services, it's not traditional. Authors should never be obligated to pay for cover design or editing, which should be part of the press's commitment to you. Not all presses have their own in-house publicity team, which means that authors are sometimes encouraged to hire their own publicists. But that money should go from the author to the publicity team, not through the press's coffers, unless it's a hybrid.

Authors at traditional presses can buy copies of their books at a discounted rate from their publishers (best practice is 50 percent), but that's the *only* time money should flow away from the authors and into the press. There's plenty authors can spend money on—if their contract allows them to hire their own cover designer, for instance, or if they choose to hire a publicist or social media strategist. Contest entry fees may be paid by the press or the author or a combination. Those are all expenses that can help a book's chances, but they aren't being paid *to* the press. I'll say it again: with the exception of buying significantly discounted stock to give away or resell, an author should never send money to their press; funds should flow *from* the publisher *to* the author if it's a traditional deal. Presses that charge their authors for editing and design services or expect an investment of any sort, are hybrid.

TRADITIONAL: These presses operate like the big New York presses and can compete on the same level in terms of distribution, sales, and publicity. Most of them only accept manuscripts through agents. They have lots of titles per season, much like the big five. Many traditional independents can compete with the major houses in terms of professionalism and earning accolades and bestseller status for their books. Examples of these independents include Chronicle, Sourcebooks, and Kensington. I'm always and ever a fan of Microcosm Publishing, a fast-growing independent with out-of-the-box ideas and its own distribution.

 **SMALL**: Industry wisdom says small presses should produce six to twelve titles a year to be financially viable. They can have more or less titles than this, but for the sake of helping you differentiate between the "traditional" and "small" tiers, six to twelve is as good a benchmark as any. Some small presses run as collectives, where authors take up the mantle of publisher after their book comes out, so everyone is supporting everyone else. University presses, run by an educational institution, fall in this category.

 **MICRO**: I technically run a micropress, releasing one to three titles per year. Micropresses publish fewer than six to twelve titles per year. They are often run by one person plus some freelancers, as Forest Avenue is.

 **HYBRID**: Presses that expect authors to pay for part or all of the publishing process are considered hybrid. The author takes on some or all of the expenses relating to editing, design, printing copies for reviewers,

and/or printing the whole run of books. Many small presses expect authors to chip in on publicity, like paying for their own book tours, but hybrid presses detail what the author's costs will be in the contract. It's important to understand this up front before signing; hybrid can mean the press is more financially viable than a traditional model and there's less chance of the company shutting down abruptly three months before your publication date, but you don't want to sign a contract and only later realize you can't comfortably afford what's expected of you. While many hybrids honor the author's financial commitment with a higher-than-usual royalty rate, not all do so.

AUTHOR SERVICES: This is a category of service providers who can help you get published. Some author services companies do publish their clients under their own brand. Others offer packages and options to help authors move their projects to completion and into print via self-publishing. While hybrid presses are publishing houses, author services offer professional options like developmental editing, copyediting, layout, cover design, indexing, and business setup help. By using these services you, as the client, get to make choices and decide. I've set this category between hybrid and self-publishing because it's related to both—and can be used for either.

SELF-PUBLISHING: A lot of authors, fed up with the broken system of publishing or unwilling to wait for someone to pay attention, start their own presses. Some of these eventually publish other people's work and migrate into a micro-, small press, or hybrid category. Self-publishing can be done by yourself with hired freelancers filling in the skills you don't have, or through an author services company. A successful self-publishing experience can't necessarily be judged by profit and loss sheets; a lot of labor goes into making a book, and paying market rates for that support can cost more money than you'll earn from ebook and paperback sales. So just be aware, same as with hybrids: don't put money in that you can't afford to spend. If you come out in the black after the first year of sales, awesome! But be ready to measure success in specifics just in case: that your great-aunt loved your book, or that you got to send a copy to your first sweetheart or your grade school English teacher.

THE PUBLISHING TIMELINE WILL DEPEND on what kind of small press you work with; author services and hybrid presses may be able to accelerate the schedule on your request, while a traditional small press will need ample lead time to give the sales team a chance to sell your book into stores. Forest Avenue starts sending out the cover, metadata, and advance reader copies nine months before pub date. That means we have nine months to gather momentum for each book with booksellers and reviewers, not to mention organic preorders as those first reviews trickle in. Many independent presses operate on a four- or six-month lead time schedule, sometimes less; if you are considering a press with a condensed schedule, know the tighter the schedule, the less likely you'll get trade reviews or significant media coverage.

My preferred timeline from signing to publication is eighteen months; I used to acquire projects two or even three years out, especially while I was still learning the ropes and with manuscripts that needed significant developmental editing. There's nothing *wrong* with scheduling that far out, or a press trying to jam a book out in twelve months, which is on the short side. I've done both. *Chicano Frankenstein*, one of our best-selling titles to-date, had a twelve-month turnaround, in large part because Daniel had published multiple books and I didn't need to teach him the ropes. We signed our agreement on March 4, 2023, and the book came out March 5, 2024.

It's not necessarily a red flag if the lead time is longer or shorter than average, if the acquiring editor explains why up front and if that schedule works for you. You can also ask how many other titles are in the works for the same season and how many are in the pipeline ahead of yours. If a press is publishing ten books a season, that's a different experience than two books a season, or ten books a month. One isn't objectively better than the other, but knowing how your project fits the press schedule will help you have patience and understanding when the process feels like it's moving slowly.

INDEPENDENT PRESSES OF ALL SIZES are different from the big presses—we're smaller! We generally have lower budgets, fewer staff members, and less in-house publicity muscle. That doesn't mean we're inferior; we're just different.

Bigger independent presses have multiple staff members, allowing for more titles per season than micropresses, and often a workflow that is similar to what you'd see at a big five press. With smaller publishing houses, the founders are deeply involved in day-to-day operations, doing the accounting and acquisitions and everything in between.

At Forest Avenue it's me, my amazing volunteer advisory board, and contractors I hire on a freelance basis for editing, design, and other essential tasks. We gather volunteer readers when we're open for unsolicited submissions, which usually happens once a year. Everything else I do in-house. And by in-house, I mean on the couch, at my kitchen table (especially when it's too cold to work at my basement desk), or in the hammock out back.

Sometimes writers call me—don't do this!—and pitch their work over the phone, expecting to find a publisher at their desk. But they catch me out on a dog walk or in the middle of baking. A lot of us work from home. Keeping the overhead low means we can afford to make books and take risks on debut authors who don't have track records yet. But critical to this model is that writers must respect personal boundaries, knowing small press publishers have their own lives apart from book-making.

So what do small press books look like? It depends.

As a distributed press, we want our books to look like Forest Avenue books, but we also want them to compete with books from major houses. To have the same professionalism. To adhere to the same industry standards. That means eye-catching covers and blurbs from major authors. Most readers don't think about *who* published the book; they reach for what looks good.

Many small presses have recognizable aesthetics that aren't necessarily mainstream. Check out The 3rd Thing for a great example of this philosophy; the press works with different artists to create eye-catching covers.

Forest Avenue, like lots of other small presses, specializes in paperback originals; big five presses often publish a hardcover edition, see how it sells, and then commit to a paperback if the numbers make it worthwhile. Paperbacks are less expensive to print and more affordable for readers; it's an easier splurge to spend sixteen or even eighteen dollars on a debut novelist versus shelling out thirty for a hardcover. Hardcovers do remain the preferred choice for library acquisitions, but libraries buy paperbacks too.

Many paperback publishers use special design features, like matte covers, French flaps, deckled edges, or printing inside the cover to make their paperbacks stand out.

FRENCH FLAPS: When a softcover is cut wider than the trim size, some of it folds inside the book. It's a style reminiscent of a hardcover book jacket, with space for the book description (front flap) and author bio (back flap). The folded part can be almost as wide as the cover, but I often see them cut to a third of the size of the cover.

DECKLED EDGES: These are when a book's edges are rough cut instead of smooth and uniform. It's an artistic choice that can make a book stand out as an object in a sea of other books.

Most small presses create ebook versions of their products; some also record audiobook editions or sell the rights to an audiobook maker. Forest Avenue has sold our audio rights to Blackstone Publishing and Tantor Media, which we love, because that means getting an advance and royalties for our authors *and* we don't have to become audio specialists ourselves. We leave the narrator choosing, recording, file editing, and production to the experts.

Small presses definitely *like* to make projects that sell, but they don't have such high sales needs as presses with bigger infrastructure and salaried employees. We can take risks. We can make covers that look like *ours*, not someone else's, and we can ignore trends or a popular color.

Many of us run presses on the edge of our everyday lives in addition to full-time jobs, freelance careers, and/or being full-time caregivers. Many of us don't have infrastructure like staff members or office space, which keeps costs down.

If I sell three thousand copies of a debut author's book, I'm thrilled. That's success! But if that same author was signed by a bigger press, which would mean a bigger advance and more money spent on marketing, three thousand copies would be a bummer. Years ago, I heard that a large independent press needed to sell three to five thousand copies of each title to support their staff, office, and infrastructure. They couldn't afford to sell fewer books than that, so they avoided debut authors; they were looking for successful sales track records, for building on midlist authors' existing reputations by publishing more of their work. That's a legitimate, logical choice and probably good business.

Debut novels can earn splashy coverage, if they break out, but they are also a risk. Just because a debut novel with similar themes got a mention in the *New York Times* doesn't mean that achievement will be replicable, even by the same press or publicity team.

AUTHORS WHO CHOOSE THE SMALL press route often feel like they are deeply connected to the process. They work directly with the publishing staff who are doing the hands-on work of making their books. Your developmental editor may also be the publisher or your publicist or all three. Ideally, whoever does your developmental editing will *not* be the same person as your copyeditor or proofreader, because a fresh set of eyes (or several sets) is so important.

As Forest Avenue has received more direct submissions from well-known authors, I can acknowledge that how we operate appeals to authors. I've dropped books off at my authors' houses and given them handmade cards. My authors call and email and text me when they have questions. Some have even sat with me in the kitchen, working over edits with pencils in hand. It's rather romantic—with an old-school vibe like F. Scott Fitzgerald and Maxwell Perkins—but also practical; coffee shops can be loud when you're trying to have a conversation about commas!

On a practical level, small presses can maneuver and adjust quickly, unlike the behemoth presses with all their departments, staff members, and organized workflows. We're willing to take creative risks and to find a place for titles that do the unexpected and foment surprises in their pages, because we need fewer sales to call a book a success than presses with more overhead costs. With a small press, it's more likely that the staff can take your needs and wishes into consideration—including cover design, editorial work, and ways of promoting the project, including disability and health-related limitations.

Of course, with fewer titles per year and a smaller budget, independents risk losing money and going under, so you should always talk to some current authors and look for signs of instability before you sign a contract. Here are a few things to consider:

If authors return to a press with their next book(s), that's a good indicator of quality. The press might not be perfect, but it must have been a good-enough experience.

If the editor or publisher is making doom-and-gloom statements about the industry on social media, consider steering clear, especially if you are averse to drama. Transparency is great; bitterness on social media means proceed with caution. When a publisher is venting publicly about book sales or questioning their authors' loyalty, chances are the business model isn't working.

Crowdfunding doesn't necessarily tell you the financial standing of a press; many successful houses use Kickstarter or a similar platform instead of a preorder campaign. Not only does crowdfunding bring in money up front to pay for the print run, it gives the publisher insight into demand and may help the staff decide on a realistic first print run.

If you see a press that's recently expanded from a handful of titles to say twelve or twenty per year, try to figure out how that's being financed. Did an angel investor come along? Does one book just sell and sell and sell, keeping the rest afloat? I've seen so many presses try to supersize themselves as a way to become financially viable, only to run out of money faster than if they had stayed cautious.

The more frontlist heavy a press is, the more vulnerable it is to poor sales. Presses with sturdy backlists have regular income that they can count on.

Presses should be willing to connect authors they are wooing with their existing authors. If you ask and they refuse, do some more research.

If publication dates keep getting moved back—if you can identify that as a pattern at a press—then beware. Likely there's a resource crisis. Not enough staff or not enough money. Or both.

You'll want to do as much research as you can before signing with a press, especially if you're agentless. It's awful to sign a contract and then hear . . . crickets. And that happens when there are too many projects in the pipeline all at once. It's even worse to find out at your launch party that your publisher never actually finished and printed your novel. That happened to a friend of mine. As promises get broken, so do writers' hearts.

LIKE FOREST AVENUE, UNIVERSITY OF Hell Press centers the author's experience. Founder Greg Gerding told me:

> We have been an "author-first" operation in the sense that an author's involvement is up to them. Other presses do not operate this way and instead enforce, for example, the number of public readings/appearances an author needs to commit to each year. We haven't operated this way, but we do provide tools outlining how to make a book successful. And it has been proven that the authors who are driven to have a book release party (at the very least), tour their book (however far), connect with their local booksellers and get their books on those shelves, and are active in the social media sphere are successful and sell the most books.

Greg said University of Hell encourages writers to submit their next manuscripts and create a long-term home at the press. "As long as the writing is something we are interested in publishing and representing, we will continue to do so. However, the more complete of a package you are and are motivated with all aspects of your book, the better the relationship will be with the press."

Keith Rosson and Meerkat are a great example of staying

with a press for multiple books. Small press contracts may have clauses asking for the right of first refusal on the next project—if a press wants to have a long-term relationship and publish multiple books by the same author. Lanternfish included that line in the contract I signed, but they rejected my second novel, cutting ties either because the material didn't match their sensibilities, they had just acquired a batch of new authors, or some other factor. I wish I knew! This kind of unknowing is where the self-doubt creeps in.

Was my enthusiasm too annoying?

Does my new book stink?

Are they glad to be rid of me?

In Forest Avenue's early years I urged my authors to submit to another press with their next novel because I had so few slots available, plus I felt more confident in launching writers than sustaining them and growing their audiences. That shifted when I published Stevan Allred's second book, *The Alehouse at the End of the World,* which became one of our bestsellers. In more recent years I've become a home for authors who have multiple titles out with various small presses. They like what I've built, they like that we have distribution, and they like our commitment to a handful of titles a year, which means they get a lot of attention. Daniel A. Olivas and Scott Nadelson, both 2024 authors, fit in this category.

One of my touchstone friends in the business, Liz Prato, has three titles out with small presses—a story collection, *Baby's on Fire* with Press 53; an essay collection, *Volcanoes, Palm Trees, and Privilege,* out with Overcup Press; and *Kids in America,* another essay collection, with Santa Fe Writers Project. She also is the editor of Forest Avenue's first fiction anthology, *The Night, and the Rain, and the River,* and she is Forest Avenue's editor at large.

Liz and I used to have the same agent, years ago. While I was dropped by that agent, Liz ended the relationship on her own terms. She had decided to find a small press. *Baby's on Fire*—her first book—was a finalist for a Press 53 contest, and the publisher offered her a contract.

With her next book, an essay collection, she knew she wanted a small press. She told me:

> When I set out to find a publisher for *Volcanoes, Palm Trees, and Privilege,* I *started* with small presses. They were the first tier for me. I knew I'd written a book that the biggies probably weren't interested in. I suspected they'd prefer a book with a single through line, not a collection of essays, and that they wouldn't dig the way I mixed narrative journalism, history, and memoir. It's easier to market if it's just one concrete genre. My suspicions did bear out at one point: I was contacted by a big-time agent who read my work in a literary magazine and asked to see what I was working on. I sent it to him, and he responded that he thought I should turn the essays into chapters, and I should get rid of all the stuff about history and culture of Hawai'i and have it just be a memoir about me. That's what would make it "commercially viable."

Liz stuck to her vision for the project, sold it to Overcup Books, and *Volcanoes, Palm Trees, and Privilege* earned coverage in the *New York Times*—a huge coup.

FOREST AVENUE PUBLISHED RENEE MACALINO Rutledge's debut novel, *The Hour of Daydreams,* a novel based on a Filipino folktale about a woman with wings, in 2017. She was my first out-of-state author—all the way in California!—and she has gone on to publish several wonderful children's books with bigger presses. I interviewed her in the early days of publication of her debut and she said:

> From the start I've felt like I'm already ahead of the game—just getting a book contract when so many deserving writers struggle to get published. I'm ever an optimist—I'm hopeful this book will sell the same way I believe it deserves to be read, but if it doesn't happen it will be difficult for me to view that as a defeat. I'm already seeing that the book is a different experience for every reader. My brothers were the first two people to read the final draft. One said he wanted to stay up all night reading, the other took much longer to finish as he tackled the various themes. I know the book won't be for everyone, and I also know that if it were, it would not be the book I wanted to write.

Renee's perspective is a great example of holding the good things close and acknowledging that being there, in the moment of publication, is incredible all by itself. She listened to her heart, wrote the book she wanted to write, and it got published.

OFTEN SMALL PRESSES HAVE SMALL budgets. We can't compete financially or in terms of staff numbers with the big five or the larger independents. But one of the things I love about the small press community is that we support each other. We're not in competition with each other, trying to outsell each other; we're really in competition with everything that pulls people away from reading. TV shows, streaming devices, YouTube, social media, and other flashy media pull on people's time and attention, leading to questions like, *How do you have time to read?*

We can pool our resources, knowledge, and talent and answer each other's questions like a brain trust. Some small presses, like Airlie Press and First Matter Press, both poetry focused, work on the co-op model. Authors become part of the publishing house, helping to shepherd the next slate of authors through the process.

My earliest mentors in the Portland publishing scene included Rhonda Hughes of Hawthorne Books, Kevin Sampsell of Future Tense Books, Rose O'Keefe of Eraserhead Press, and Joe Biel of Microcosm Publishing. I learned so much from them and decided to pay back their kindness by helping authors and new presses understand the industry so they wouldn't feel like outsiders. But also, as my networks and circles grew, everything became more cyclical, asking and receiving and passing along information as a way of building our collective business acumen.

When a weird question comes up, something that seems confusing or insurmountable as a newer press, it's not a time to panic; it's a reason to contact some other presses and see if they have any experience with the issue. We may lack the financial resources that bigger presses have, but we can share information and buoy each other.

Often presses share tables at more expensive book festivals and conferences, making the price of exhibiting more affordable. It's easier to sell enough books to justify your appearance if you're sharing—and presses can draw different crowds of readers to each other's wares. I've often partnered with Michael Heald of Perfect Day because he publishes nonfiction and I do mostly fiction. Our catalogs complement each other.

Recently I reached out to Christina Vega, founder of Blue Cactus Press, for help with my business practices. They, in turn, tapped into my project management background to help with one of their titles during its reprint cycle. They explained the importance of our collaboration this way:

> So much of the work we do in publishing and bookselling happens alone. As publishers, editors, booksellers, designers, and project managers, we often write, edit, design, and sell and ship books by ourselves. And we definitely struggle in business and writing ALONE. But what does that get us at the end of the day? Mostly overworked, lonely, and in an information silo. But what if we stepped into community spaces and offered our skill sets and capacity to each other? We could lighten each other's load by exchanging services, offering reciprocal mentorship, and teaching each other valuable skills. Learning to build and nourish relationships, barter, and exchange services with other publishing professionals has been one of the most beneficial practices of my career.

UNIVERSITY PRESSES

UNIVERSITY PRESSES ARE SMALL PRESSES with financial backing and staffing through their institutions. That can be a great relief to authors who worry about a small press folding during or soon after the publication process. Some university presses focus on academic texts that will be marketed to other academic institutions. Others publish books for a general audience, known as *for the trade*. There's usually a rigorous acceptance policy at university presses involving faculty and peer reviews.

A university press can be an excellent choice for historical nonfiction, regional stories (fiction and nonfiction), poetry collections, and essay collections. University presses' editorial missions are impacted by the educational institution that funds and houses them, just like micro- and small presses have their own personalities. Some institutions prioritize regional content, which can be helpful to know when you're making submissions lists. If you have a novel set in the Midwest, for instance, I'd encourage you to research Midwest university presses.

Many university presses are distributed by the Chicago Distribution Center (under the auspices of the University of

Chicago Press), ensuring availability of your book to wholesalers, libraries, and individual customers.

I ASKED DANIEL A. OLIVAS, whose novel *Chicano Frankenstein* came out in 2024 with Forest Avenue, to talk about his experience publishing multiple books with university presses. He began by telling me the story of his father's love of writing.

> Unlike the vast majority of writers I know, I do not have an MFA in writing. I majored in English literature in college, but going into the arts for a living made little sense to me. My father had dreams of being a published writer as a young man, the son of Mexican immigrants. In the mid-1950s and early sixties, after marrying and starting a family, Pop worked the night shift at a factory in Los Angeles. By day, he clicked away on a Royal Quiet Deluxe that was Ernest Hemingway's typewriter of choice. He wrote a novel and poetry, but received only rejections from publishers. He eventually burned it all and focused on getting educated and improving his family's life. I inherited that gorgeous manual typewriter when Pop passed in 2020. I believe I harbored those same fears of rejection, so I made the logical career choice and went to law school. I've now practiced law for over three decades and have a deeply fulfilling career as a government attorney.

Twenty-five years ago, Daniel decided to write fiction inspired by his grandparents' migration from Mexico to Los Angeles in the twenties.

> It would be a love story, pure and simple, that celebrated the immigrant experience. I felt there was

> a void in the literary canon, and I certainly did not see such books on my high school and college curriculum of the 1960s and '70s. But I was also trying to find a way to deal with grief arising from my wife's fifth of what would be seven miscarriages. I worked with all my soul to help my wife and our young son with their pain, but I did not know how to handle my own. Writing became my way of making sense of my grief while celebrating the great joy that comes from loving someone deeply and making a life together.

That process turned into a novella, *The Courtship of María Rivera Peña*.

> Of course agents and major presses either rejected or ignored my submissions, but at the time, I didn't know about university presses. A small (and now defunct) press in Pennsylvania eventually published my little book. It received a few nice online reviews, but not much attention from "mainstream" newspapers and magazines. But I was bitten by the literary bug and started to write short stories and poems that ended up in print and online journals. Eventually, when I had enough stories for a collection, I submitted a manuscript to a New York agent who said that I had "writing chops" and talent, but my stories were not commercial enough. She wondered if I could write a Chicano version of *Waiting to Exhale*. I asked her what she meant, and she explained that if I wrote a novel with young, good-looking, middle-class Chicano characters, she'd be able to sell that especially since it would have "movie potential." I told her that if I ever wrote that book, I'd send it to her. Of course, I had no intention of writing such a book, so I needed to find a publisher.

Daniel submitted his short story manuscript, *Assumption and Other Stories*, to Bilingual Review Press, affiliated with Arizona State University, after reading some of its titles and being impressed by the content and design. It was accepted and published in 2003, and Daniel's career has continued to grow in scope and number of titles from there. *Chicano Frankenstein* is his eleventh book.

> All of my books have found homes without an agent because of the vibrant and daring small presses that are not afraid to publish quality literature even if it is not "commercial" enough—whatever that means. When I am invited to guest lecture, I often speak to students who are the first in their families to go to college. One of the things I tell them is that if they don't tell their stories, someone else will, and they will get it wrong. I also tell them that our stories matter, and not to listen to those who say otherwise. And I truly believe that without independent and university presses, most of our stories would not be in print today.

Portland State University runs Ooligan Press—kind of an outlier in the university press world because it's an independent press, acquiring books for the trade, but Ooligan is also a teaching press with university funding. Students in the master's in publishing program work on acquisitions, design, marketing, and so forth, shepherding titles to market. It's a great place for an author to feel very supported—not just by one assigned designer or one assigned publicist but by teams of master's degree students led by instructors with real-world publishing experience.

Jason Tanamor had a wonderful experience publishing his debut YA novel, *Love, Dance & Egg Rolls*, with Ooligan. He said:

> Although students, each person I worked with was professional, open-minded, and dedicated to putting out the best story. Their ideas, input, and criticism were so top-notch, I often forgot that they were students at all. What attracted me to the press was its rich history in Portland and the Pacific Northwest, and with the backing and reputation of Portland State University, I knew that the book would be successful. When *Love, Dance & Egg Rolls* was released in May 2022, it was immediately named a May "Pick of the Month" by Powell's City of Books. It also was featured in various festivals, including the Portland Book Festival (Portland, Oregon) and the Filipino American International Book Festival (San Francisco, California).

Jason had one concern about working with a teaching press: how the transition between semesters, with different students cycling in and out, would impact the consistency of the experience. He said he quickly learned that wasn't an issue. "The program is so well put-together, designed, and managed that its students ingrained the principles and values wholeheartedly and applied them to the novel. I always hear that the publishing industry is struggling. I can assure you that it's not with book publishing programs like PSU's master's in publishing program. I have so much reverence for Ooligan as a publisher, I'm doing another YA book with them."

Especially if you're anxious about small presses running out of money or energy, or if you've been burned by a press closing after acquiring your project, it's worth putting university presses on your submissions list. If your book takes place in a region of the US, research university presses in that area first; many prioritize local content. As you build your query list, pay attention to submissions guidelines, the kinds of projects each press has published in the last two years, and whether you could see your book on a shelf next to them.

HYBRID AND SELF-PUBLISHING

IF YOU HAVE THE FUNDS and are interested in investing financially in your career, you might want to consider hybrid or self-publishing. With the technology available today, either method can create a physical product that competes with traditionally published books.

Bigger investments up front generally equal bigger shares of the profit compared to a more traditional deal. But remember to budget for potential publicity and marketing expenses as you're adding up the cost of printing and shipping the actual product. Self-publishing and hybrid services don't always include those expenses in their contracts; you'll need to spend some cash to get review copies into the hands of people who will, well, *review* them. That's why it's so important to be realistic about your finances and only commit what you can afford to spend. (Or, if you're a realist, what you can afford to lose if you don't earn back the money in sales.)

With self-publishing, you pay for services, either working with freelancers for what you can't do yourself or hiring help. Here are a few business models that support the self-publishing author.

FREELANCERS: Freelancers offer services on a limited basis. A freelance editor might offer multiple kinds of editing: developmental, copyediting, and proofreading. Or they might offer just one: their favorite kind. A designer might specialize in covers or interior page layout or both. Sensitivity readers can be hired freelance to look at your manuscript from the perspective of an identity you don't have. You might find a freelancer to produce your audiobook. Usually freelancers are single-person entrepreneurs providing author services. Publicists often work on a freelance basis, and they're hired by traditional press authors as well as self-publishing ones.

AUTHOR SERVICES: I've defined this already, but if you want to self-publish but don't know what you need help with or where to start, you can contract with an author services company. These businesses offer a full menu of options for authors who want to get their books out, need pro support, and want to retain control over the project and the timeline. Services might include, in addition to editing and layout, securing your ISBNs, and/or an imprint name, producing ebooks, and recording audiobooks.

HYBRID: This is a publishing house that requires authors to bear some or all of the financial responsibility for producing their book. There's an acquisition process to get through—not all projects are chosen. The authors whose manuscripts are picked sign

> contracts that should explicitly include what financial outlays will be expected and when. Sometimes hybrids request multiple payments spread out over the months of the project. Others expect payment for specific items: editing and/or design, galleys, and the actual print run. Hybrid press staff may not consider their work under the self-publishing umbrella. I mention them here because of the financial commitment. They often operate like traditional presses, except money moves from the author to the hybrid press. In traditional publishing, money moves from the press to the author.

There are overlaps between these business models. You might hire a freelancer directly, on a friend's recommendation, and that person may also work with an author services company. When you pay for services to produce your book, the profits are yours to keep. Under the hybrid model, after the press reviews your manuscript and offers you a contract, you pay for the work up front and then you earn a higher-than-average royalty when your book comes out. A hybrid press can do everything a traditional press does; you just have to pay for some or all of those services. Hybrid presses are also more likely to do things *their* way, based on their experiences and preferences, since you're participating in their business model, not paying them to carry out your vision like an author services company. Having that experience and input can be helpful in putting out a quality product, especially if you're new to publishing. Self-publishing with the support of professionals offers the most control, but you have to know how to proceed on your own and when to hire help or ask for feedback.

Hybrid presses are a great option for writers who are on a timeline; by putting your money into the project, you're their author but also a paying client. Like other small presses, signing with a hybrid means your book is going to get published (if nothing goes catastrophically wrong), versus the agent route, where getting an agent doesn't always lead to a deal. Hybrid presses may have mission statements that explain their clients get chosen by traditional means (i.e., a manuscript has to be accepted). That's one way to differentiate between them and companies that exist to help their authors self-publish.

When asked at an Oregon Writers Colony presentation to define hybrid presses, I said the author is expected to take on the cost of *making* the book. Publicity often falls to the author, no matter the size of the press, so those expectations aren't clear-cut enough to be a marker of *hybrid* or *traditional*.

A small press that insists you pay for your own editing and cover design *isn't* actually traditional. They're not being transparent if they call themselves anything other than hybrid. A small press that encourages you to enter contests or hire a publicist on your own dime *is* traditional. It's rare that a publisher would ask an author to pay for advance reader copy printing; I'd consider that hybrid.

It makes for a confusing landscape. If a small press contract says you have an option to pay for a cover design, if you don't like their offered cover or if you really want to work with a certain freelance designer, paying out of pocket might be an option. That's usually spelled out in the contract. But if a small press contract says you must pay for the cost of cover creation, that's hybrid, not traditional.

The reason I want to spell that out, to expand on the definitions on pages 265–268, is I've been surprised recently how many hybrid presses skirt the word *hybrid*; they talk in these sideways terms about partnerships between the author and the publisher. Or they talk about you, the writer, investing in your career. It's a legit business model with some advantages—for one thing, you know there's regular funding for the press, so it's less likely bankruptcy will halt the production of your book—but you need to know what those expectations are up front. And you need to be clear with yourself that you can afford them *assuming you won't earn back your investment in book sales.*

LIKE ALL SMALL PRESSES, HYBRIDS must decide how they're going to get their books from idea to marketplace, particularly the (heavy) physical objects. A few have full-service distribution, but most do print on demand. Like any other POD press, you have to understand whether your local bookstore will be able to order copies for an event, or if you'll have to buy your own books to consign them. Knowing how it works will help you make sure you can get your title on brick-and-mortar bookstore shelves, if that's one of your goals, before you commit and submit the first payment.

One more cautionary note: if you sign with a hybrid press, be sure to understand what's included in the package and what isn't. Often there are extra costs ahead—paying for the actual print run or shipping costs for those copies. You'll want to sit down and write out a budget and look at your savings. Can you really afford to work with this company? What about if you need a second print run? Or extra advance copies to send out to reviewers because there's buzz? If there's any question of not being able to pay your rent or your water bill, don't risk it. There's almost never a chance to earn your money back, let alone earn a profit, especially at the higher-tier hybrids that require up-front payments as well as specific service payments. You may have flashes of brilliance and glory lighting up your brain, and of course you believe in yourself and your story, but remember lots of parties take pieces of the earned income from books and your share will depend on how many books sell.

You can also do some math ahead of time. If you pay for a print run of 500 or 1,000 books, and they all sell, how much money will you earn back based on the press's royalty structure and the expected cover price of your title? Is it possible to earn enough to cover the cost of the hybrid services, any editing services you've paid for, and any event travel? If not, know that going in.

THE SAME QUESTIONS APPLY TO self-publishing and working with freelancers or an author services provider. When we invest in ourselves, it's empowering, but as an outsider to the industry, you are at risk of underestimating what it's going to cost you.

Author services companies can do everything that's needed to put out a high-quality book, including editing, design, offering ISBNs and copyright filing, and marketing and publicity. Many use print on demand to produce copies of the books. Two I recommend regularly because they're local to me are Indigo: Editing, Design, and More, founded by Ali Shaw, and Yellow Bike Press, founded by Andrew Durkin. Ali and Andrew are members of the Portland literary community, so I've met them and watched them (and many of Indigo's team members) interact with writers and share great information.

"Some companies have whole packages so you can just pay a lump sum and they'll take care of everything related for your book to be published," Ali said. "Other companies offer à la carte services, so you can pick and choose what works best for you. No matter what, make sure the company you go with will let you retain all your rights and royalties. Also make sure they pair you with publishing professionals who are experienced with your genre and understand your goals. Not all author services companies are the same, but if you do your homework and team up with a really great one, you'll be glad you did!"

Kesha Ajose-Fisher self-published her debut story collection, *No God Like the Mother,* with Inkwater Press in 2019 and it won the 2020 Oregon Book Award for fiction. Andrew was her editor at Inkwater before that company folded. *No God Like the Mother* is only the second self-published title to win the prestigious statewide fiction award, following Joyce Cherry Cresswell's *A Great Length of Time* in 2017. Joyce worked with Indigo: Editing, Design, and More to publish hers.

I asked Kesha to share some insights as to why the self-publishing path was for her. She said:

> When I was young, I told someone I trusted that I wanted to be a storyteller. She encouraged me to chase my dream and share it with the world. The world continuously pointed out the obstacles ahead until rejection, or the idea of it, grew into a debilitating monster. Though content with creating, I dreamed of possibilities too, grand ones, like walking on the moon and dancing with the stars, things that should have quelled my determination. The dream, however, would not die, so I decided to bet on what I knew for certain, me. I would self-publish.
>
> After I held my finished book for the first time, I realized the monster had only lived inside my head. Believing in myself had always been the only path to consider. The satisfaction of meeting this moment was sufficient, more fulfilling than I had ever expected, then the world flung open its doors. I won the Oregon Book Award in fiction, I got an agent, I'm working on a second book,

> and most importantly, I get to share this journey with others. I'll never know how things might have turned out had I taken the traditional route first, but I know getting here could not have happened without first believing in myself, so now, I do.

If you choose to self-publish on your own, without hiring a company that knows the business, try to learn as much as you can about the market, your genre, and price points.

After Inkwater closed up shop, I worked with Kesha and her agent to buy the rights so Forest Avenue could issue an updated edition in 2023. We decided on a new cover, an updated glossary, a bonus essay, and readers' guide questions, adding value for anyone who already had a copy and for university use. If Kesha had published with a distributed press, I'm not sure it would have made sense for me to do a new edition. But because the first version didn't go out to bookstores nationwide *and* it earned strong regional favor, I could build on what had been achieved and still expand her debut's reach.

Who's an Expert?

A WHOLE LITERARY SERVICE INDUSTRY has sprung up around writers seeking to break into print. Some service providers are intensely useful, legitimate, and can make a huge difference in the trajectory of your manuscript. These editorial services can be career changing. I swear by hiring a developmental editor (or two!) in the course of working on a full-length book.

But some services overpromise and underdeliver. Some are run by people who claim expertise but haven't actually published anything or worked in publishing. Before you say yes, pay attention to credentials, testimonials, and the business owner's experience. If you want a big five deal, make sure the editor you hire has worked on projects that have sold to that market. If you are struggling with thorny issues in your memoir, confirm the editor you want to hire has experience in that genre.

I am currently offering consulting and metadata support through Forest Avenue to increase revenue and keep my business healthy. My focus is working with small presses and authors wanting to get published by small presses. Can I edit a query letter for an agent or a big five editor? You betcha. But I don't work as an agent or at a major press, so there are other editors who might be a better fit. With metadata, I have to write my own for Forest Avenue titles and I can use my knowledge of best practices to help other distributed publishers.

If you want to hire a developmental editor to help you with a revision plan, a writing coach to keep you focused, or a consultant to demystify the submissions options, here are some questions to consider:

- Does this consultant have a track record of working with authors whose books sell to presses you'd like your book to sell?
- Can the coach you're interested in working with share an estimated timeline or workflow pattern so you have a sense of the commitment? Can you pause working together if life gets busy and then come back later?

- Are there testimonials on the business website? Look some of the clients up, especially if you haven't heard of them.
- Is the social media presence of the person or the company a professional, kind, connected presence? Do people *other* than clients interact with the professional, or are their socials full of me-me-me? Do they offer advice and encouragement?
- There are industry expectations for specific genres. What are the expectations for your genre? Are you clear on how your book fits into the marketplace?

It's important to tap into your community to see what others have heard about these services. That's a great way to leverage your connections. And it's much more likely in asking around that you'll find and work with the fabulous teacher of memoir who has written multiple memoirs, or a writing coach who focuses on the kinds of challenges you're facing (i.e., a neurodivergence-friendly coach to help you hit word count goals).

All this to say: not everyone who hangs out a shingle and insists they can help you get an agent/editor/publisher/book deal knows how to do those things. A higher-cost consultant isn't necessarily a better consultant; it depends on what they know and what you need. Some people pay more than they can afford for services, and they still don't (can't) sell their books, which makes the heartbreak harder.

INTRO TO DISTRIBUTION

DISTRIBUTION WILL IMPACT YOUR BOOK more than any other factor; it's also the biggest difference between small presses. I teach workshops on distribution because despite its importance, most writers don't know how it works or what it is. In fact, many small publishers don't understand it either!

Many honest, well-meaning publishers call their books "distributed" not because they are but because they've never had access to full-service distribution, so they don't know the difference, which means they give misinformation to submitting authors. This gets especially ugly around whether bookstores can order copies easily; not all print-on-demand (POD) presses have bookstore-friendly discounts. Imagine going into your favorite bookstore, proud of your long-awaited debut and certain the bookstore will carry it, and getting turned down for an event because your publisher hasn't been transparent with you about how they do business.

So before exploring all the kinds of distribution, I'm going to explain this misconception.

If a POD publisher doesn't accept returns, bookstores won't

want to take the risk of ordering the book. Why would they, when they can order books that can be sent back to the warehouse for a full refund if they don't sell?

Likewise, if a POD publisher sets up a smaller-than-normal discount, known as a "short" discount, then bookstores won't order the book. Anything less than 55 percent is considered short. There are financial reasons behind presses choosing not to accept returns—they increase the financial risk and each return accrues a processing fee. Short discounts are also appealing, because the publisher keeps more money, which means the author earns more. Win-win, right? Not exactly. If your book is $20, a 55 percent discount means $11. That leaves $9 heading back to the publisher, only with print on demand, the price of printing the book gets subtracted from that $9 too. If the book costs $6 to print—an arbitrary number, just as an example—the publisher's max earning is $3 per copy. Royalties still have to come out of that. Ouch.

If you know in advance that a POD publisher doesn't accept returns or has chosen a short discount, there are workarounds like consignment. Many bookstores are willing to do the extra paperwork needed for consignment, but not all of them do. It costs staff time to work with authors, track the time those consigned books are on the shelf, and pay authors after their books sell. If a local author's book sells well and needs to be restocked, that takes additional staff time.

If you don't know that your publisher has bookstore-unfriendly policies, and your local bookstore says no to stocking your book, it can be a devastating surprise. Over and over again, I hear from authors who expect bookstore placement and then don't understand what has gone wrong when a bookstore refuses them. Is it *their* book? Are they not a good enough customer? Did the blurbs not impress the buyer enough? Chances are, it's distribution—something that's out of the author's control.

Distributed by Ingram is a hint that the press is not distributed; usually print-on-demand presses and self-publishing authors use this phrase to tell people that their book's metadata is available through the Ingram catalog. The books, physically, aren't waiting in a warehouse to be shipped out. There's no sales team telling bookstores and other retailers about why they should order these books. All it means is that data about the book, including its price and cover image, exists in the system, so someone who is seeking out that particular book has the option to buy it.

Every author, before they sign a contract, should understand how the press that wants to acquire their work will push that work into the marketplace. *We operate this way,* I want all presses to tell their prospective authors. *Here's how your books will get to readers. Here's how they will get to bookstores.*

Big five presses and the major independents all have top-notch distribution, which is why they're able to make the bestseller lists with the titles they choose to push hardest. It's also why those presses reign over wish lists. Sell a book to one of these houses and it'll be available, truly, *wherever books are sold*. The major houses can make authors' careers because they can get their books into Targets, airports, grocery stores, garden stores, museum gift shops, and anywhere else that might possibly sell books *in addition to bookstores*.

Small presses and micropresses can approach this level of visibility—and compete effectively—*if* they have actual full-service distribution with hands-on support from the distribution staff. (We'll get deeper into that in a few pages.) That being said, many presses use print-on-demand technology. So if POD isn't distribution, then what is it? It's printing and order fulfillment.

It's up to you to know the difference between distribution models before you start submitting to independent presses.

BEFORE I GET INTO THE specifics of distribution, I want to share something very important: how a press is distributed is part of its identity, and arguably the part that will impact sales the most. But there are a lot of other reasons to choose a press. Those reasons are all valid and can include:

You received an acceptance! Yay!

You love what the editor said about your work.

The acquisitions letter suggested edits that feel right and will make your story better.

You don't want to keep looking.

You have more books to write and just want to get this one out.

The staff impresses you; you believe they want what's best for your book.

You don't have other options at the moment; saying no feels like a risk.

Once I got distribution for Forest Avenue, I started telling writers, *You need a press with distribution and here's why*. I can still make that case, but I'm aware of how many great presses are not meeting the metrics needed for distribution deals.

Right now, I'm trying to decide the future of a finished novel I've been keeping under my dresser for two years—the one Lanternfish passed on. Does distribution matter to me? Yes, *and*. Timeliness matters—moving this project forward so I can go back to focusing on new work. A publisher with a community focus is important to me, perhaps as much or more so than distribution. With these thoughts in mind, I started my search by submitting to four presses, only one with traditional distribution. I chose the other three for a specific reason:

- The call for submissions matched my sensibilities.
- The press is located in the Pacific Northwest.
- The deadline was coming up.

For this novel, I'm not working in order from most prestigious to least. I'm working across categories, seeing (and seeking) the good. The process feels organic and joyful. If I had opted for a valued tier system, I probably would have spent a year or more querying agents. I didn't want to jump through those hoops this time, so I'm approaching small presses. Getting my own creative work out there is more important to me, at this stage in my career, than *how* it goes into the world.

"When is your next novel coming out?" is a question I want to answer.

HERE ARE THE POSSIBLE KINDS of distribution, roughly in order of size and scope from biggest to smallest:

- **The big five.** The major New York publishing houses all have their own in-house distribution systems. That's what makes the top presses so effective in moving books onto the bestseller lists. They have a mechanism. They have sales teams in-house, not to mention teams of marketing and publicity people and access to data about what's selling and why that they can factor into acquisitions, marketing, and every other facet of their businesses. They're immense and not replicable by a small press. Some of these major houses take on outside presses to distribute, like Simon & Schuster distributing She Writes Press or Penguin Random House's DK division taking on the wildly successful Rebel Girls books. The major houses can also afford to take big risks or throw crazy money at a hot new author because there's an excellent mechanism for getting the physical products onto shelves. They also tend to have deep backlists—lots of titles that keep selling, earning income because they're available long after pub date.

- **Full-service distribution.** These publishers have signed on as clients of businesses with sales teams. Forest Avenue, my press, is in this category. I think of it as a high-touch model, able to compete on a title basis with what the big New York presses can do, albeit with scrappy, independent spirit. The sales reps sell clients' books into bookstores, libraries, gift shops, and big-box stores like Target and WalMart. Basically, anywhere you might find a book for sale is an outlet a distributed publisher can theoretically reach. Publishers with distribution will participate in regular sales conference meetings to promote their next season's titles and help the reps understand how to sell them. These publishers generally print a run of books on a traditional offset press. Most offset presses start at runs of a thousand and the numbers go up from there; anything under would be more cost-effective to order from a digital printer. An example of a full-service distribution company is Consortium, which is owned by Ingram, same as Publishers Group West, my distributor.
- **No-frills distribution.** There's a tier of distribution that moves books from warehouse to customer on behalf of publishing clients without as much hands-on support as full-service distribution. There might be some marketing and sales support, but that's from a core group of employees, not a whole sales force. For lack of an agreed-upon industry term to use, I'm calling it *no-frills*.

This option is great for a press that isn't big enough to afford or maintain full-service distribution but is headed in that direction. Having distribution makes bookstores happy and it opens possibilities of trade reviews and major awards; Small Press United client Atelier26 published Margaret Malone's *People Like You*, a story collection that won the the Balcones Fiction Prize and was a finalist for the PEN/Hemingway Award. With this model, books may be printed in shorter digital runs or bigger offset runs. Some distributors offer warehousing, others don't. Like full-service distribution, there are bonus opportunities for presses to connect with fellow distribution clients to learn more about the industry and create efficiently. The March 2024 closure of Small Press Distribution, founded in 1969, was a recent major change to this category—one that left many small presses scrambling to get their stock back and find alternatives. Asterism, a new distributor run by independent presses, has helped fill that gap.

- **Fulfillment.** Fulfillment companies bridge the gap between full-service distribution and self-distribution or print on demand. A publisher that prints a run of books, whether digital or offset, sends copies to the fulfillment company's warehouse, and then that company is tasked with sending out orders and accepting returns as they come in. The publisher, like with the other two tiers, prints a run of books and ships it to the fulfillment company. It's a stepping stone to full distribution and can help a press create an attractive sales record and determine if they're really ready for leveling up. Like distribution deals, signing a contract with a fulfillment company includes paying a percentage of sales for the services the company will provide.

- **Self-distribution.** A publishing house can print a run of books, pick it up from the printer (or have it shipped), take orders from their website, and then ship those orders out. This involves having space at home to warehouse copies until they are needed. It also involves willingness to go to the post office (to take advantage of media-rate mailings) or to create mailing labels at home. To make this model work, the publishing house needs to build personal connections with bookstores and individual customers because there is no online metadata being sent to all the bookselling websites. The staff also needs the time to search for copies, box them up, and keep the website updated so payments are smooth. Some successful independent presses, like Pomegranate Books and Microcosm Publishing, have their own warehouses, sales reps, and fulfillment staff, which can compete with and/or exceed the traditional outsourced distribution model; those businesses fall more under the full-service distribution category. They just do it all themselves instead of contracting with another business.
- **Print on demand (POD).** This is a key option that has helped level the playing field for new publishers, but it's also much discussed and often misunderstood as "distribution." In this business model, publishers submit their book files to companies that will print them when copies are ordered. The publisher might decide to bring fifty or a hundred copies into their office for sales—known as a *bulk order*—but the rest are printed only when ordered. The metadata for each title gets sent out to the book catalogs, and if someone wants a copy, they click through the shopping cart, confirm the order, and then that order is printed and shipped. This can get very tricky for bookstores, which need a significant discount

> on cover price to be able to carry titles. Amazon owns a popular POD service that virtually guarantees independent bookstores will refuse to sell your work, as Amazon is actively trying to put all bookstores out of business. Even if you (the author) are the publisher, not Amazon, if Amazon stands to make money from the transaction, bookstores won't touch it. Many POD presses prefer to use an Ingram service, either IngramSpark or its sibling Lightning Source. They're two portals to the same book printing technology.

I encourage you to think of the differences between these distribution tiers not as better or worse but as high touch (full-service distribution), less high touch (no-frills and fulfillment), and mostly automated (print on demand). Some ways are less expensive and less labor-intensive, which lowers the barrier to access for new publishers and self-publishing authors. Those ways might also make it harder to reach your author dreams if they include bookstore events and it may mean your preorder links go live closer to publication date than your friends' books. (But it might be fine! And usually you can work around any systematic disadvantages! And chances are, your friends who aren't writers won't even notice!)

LET'S CONSIDER A DIFFERENT ARTISTIC product. If you make greeting cards and sell them off your personal website, you'll get orders from people who stumble on your website. Your sales will depend on people finding you there.

If you join a site like Etsy, your discoverability skyrockets because now you can reach anyone who's shopping for cards on an already popular platform. Likewise, if you create a wholesale program so gift shops and bookstores can stock your cards, you'll increase your reach. But now you're beholden to the fee structures of these other outlets. The DIY option lets you keep all the money—but you are dependent on your own audience reach. Working with other parties or platforms means a decrease in income—you have to pay fees and/or percentages—but your work gets shown to a broader customer base. There's also greater risk, because you'll have to make more product to keep ahead of demand—and what if it doesn't sell?

It's common wisdom that the more times someone sees a product (or a mention of it), the more likely they are to buy it. If your book is available at lots of stores, it will probably sell better than books carried by three stores. Of course other factors like publicity, marketing, and your publisher's budget all matter too, but those factors are also influenced by the quality and scope of a press's distribution. If many copies of one title are being sent out, then there better be sizeable publicity and marketing spending behind that title to make sure readers find out about it and buy it. Your efforts to promote your book will build off its availability and visibility.

Now that you know why distribution matters, let's look more closely at each type.

FULL SERVICE

FULL DISTRIBUTION IS AN ELITE option. As mentioned, the big five publishers have their own in-house distribution, as do some independent presses. Other presses work with distributors; Forest Avenue is distributed by Publishers Group West. An independent press needs solid financial footing and a demonstrated track record of sales to be eligible for consideration.

If a book is *going to be everywhere*, because a distributed press picked it up, it's much more likely to earn magazine coverage, newspaper coverage, and trade reviews than a book that exists primarily as a set of data on a website. A book picked up by a distributed press has an automatic advantage, right from signing the contract through the sales campaign. When a book sells for six figures (*Publishers Marketplace* calls this "a major deal") or at auction with multiple imprints competing to buy it, that title gets earmarked as a special one. It's more likely, when that kind of money and attention show up at the start of a book's life, that it *will* be everywhere. Distribution is the mechanism that makes it happen, while publicity and marketing and industry news coverage all combine to fuel demand.

Some independent presses reach a certain sales volume or reputation that they are invited to be distributed by one of the big houses. Good Night Books, for instance, is distributed by Penguin Random House. You've probably seen their titles in bookstores, libraries, airports, museums, and toy stores—anywhere the kid market is. The titles are brightly colored children's board books for ages zero to five that explore cities, states, and specific topics. I met Mark Jasper of Good Night Books a few years ago when we had the same distribution team at Ingram, Legato Publishers Group, which later folded into Publishers Group West. Good Night Books was founded in 2005 by Adam Gamble and their first two titles were *Good Night Cape Cod* and *Good Night Boston*.

"All the books in the beginning were regional, and then we branched out into more general, universal books, such as *Good Night Beach* and *Good Night Ocean*," Mark told me when I was doing initial interviews for this project.

The Good Night Books market is what the industry calls *gift* because these titles make great gifts for parents, grandparents, tourists, and baby showers. Even with the huge success of the business and a catalog full of comp titles, Mark said it's difficult to predict sales patterns for new titles. "When I write a book, I never know. Even if I love the idea, I don't know. Is the public going to love it?" Mark said. "Books we think are going to be bestsellers aren't. I've learned that we put it out and do the best we can do with it, and let the public decide what the successful books are going to be."

I believe in knowing how books move into the marketplace, but if you have an agent and you get a book deal with the big five, you probably won't get much of a view inside the process. A lot of that will happen automatically, without your knowledge. What you will have, for sure, is sales reps bringing your books to trade shows and conferences and meetings with book buyers.

IF YOU'VE DREAMED ABOUT A big five deal but are tired of looking for an agent, or if your agent couldn't sell your book, a press with full-service distribution might be able to meet your goals.

Small presses with full-service distribution can compete with big five titles—*Braiding Sweetgrass* by Robin Wall Kimmerer (Milkweed Editions) and *The Hidden Life of Trees* by Peter Wohlleben (Greystone) are two best-sellers by small presses distributed in the US by Publishers Group West, which also distributes Forest Avenue Press. PGW also distributes Europa Editions, which published the *New York Times* number-one best book of the twenty-first century, *My Brilliant Friend* by Elena Ferrante, translated by Ann Goldstein. It only takes one title like that to sustain a press financially for the long term.

As a distributed press I prepare metadata and advance reader copies of our upcoming titles beginning at least nine months before pub date. PGW wants the information early so they can make suggestions, help us tweak the price point, the cover, and anything else they feel might increase the book's chances in the marketplace. Then I mail print advance reader copies (also known as galleys) to the sales team so the reps can become familiar with the material. The field sales reps, who handle independent stores, get extra copies so they can hand them to buyers when they make their rounds. It's expensive and cumbersome to circulate physical objects—but it's effective to place a physical book in front of a potential reader. And it works. Because of PGW, our titles land on shelves across the world, with our strongest representation in US independent bookstores (not Amazon).

Independent presses with full-service distribution have a sales team of book lovers to spread the word about all the awesome new titles. That means real people talking to buyers about *your book*. I get invited to sales conferences twice a year—once online and once in person in Berkeley—to tell the reps about our new titles. While the in-person costs can be prohibitive, going allows me to share my enthusiasm about our catalog and give the reps quick, easy handles to use to pitch to buyers. My job is to help them talk about our projects.

In other words: I can give authors the dream of seeing their books on bookstore shelves. Not just on consignment at their local stores, but also in all sorts of places—Santa Fe, New York City, Boston, San Francisco, and Oxford, Mississippi. Lots of presses that *say* they're distributed don't actually have the ability to make that kind of multicity placement happen.

David Ciminello's book tour for *The Queen of Steeplechase Park* started in Oregon and included Massachusetts, New York, New Jersey, and San Francisco. He emailed several stores ahead of time to see if they were carrying his book and offered to come in and sign copies. A few times, he popped into a store he hadn't contacted and found his book there too. "While on tour, finding my book on the shelves of East End Books in the Boston Seaport and Provincetown, and Books Are Magic and the Center for Fiction in Brooklyn, as well as City Lights in San Francisco was thrilling and proof that independent publishers do make writers' dreams come true!"

Sometimes a bookstore buys only one or two copies, but that's okay. The availability is what matters. If the book sells because it's on the shelf, then the buyer can order another one or two.

WITH PHYSICAL BOOKS, DISTRIBUTION IS a process of printing copies and sending them from wherever they are warehoused to where the customer is. These customers can be consumer-facing businesses like independent bookstores, which will then try to sell the title to their patrons, or they can be individuals purchasing a copy for their personal use. When we choose a printer to work with, and the printer ships our books out, they get sent to an Ingram warehouse in Tennessee. Each case (or box) must be labeled appropriately with the title, author name, quantity per case, price, and ISBN. From there, once they're received, the books get *distributed* to the accounts that have pre-purchased copies in advance of the launch due to the sales reps' pitches, reading reviews of the book, and/or customer preorders.

Reorders—a key to a successful title, selling what's in stock and needing more—also go through the warehouse.

With ebooks, distribution happens through digital means. The ebook file is sent into the world coupled with metadata. Both physical and ebook copies can be searched for and found online thanks to keywords in their titles, subtitles, descriptions, review quotes, and so forth. Presses that have distribution can add much more metadata to their titles—sales and marketing information, comparison titles and to date sales numbers, past books by the same author, awards the author has won, places the author has lived, lists of cities where the author might speak about their book. There are pages of categories and guides to best practices for each. We also receive regular emails about metadata updates and have the option to attend metadata training sessions during sales conferences.

Distribution is about getting books to their audiences, but it's also about discoverability. And making books discoverable, in a global economy, has to do with metadata. The more information I can create about each title, the more likely it'll get seen by potential buyers when they're scrolling online. Edelweiss is an online sales tool that industry professionals use to buy (booksellers) and sell (sales reps) new titles. There are lots of fields we can populate to help our sales teams sell our books. Edelweiss shows a lot of categories that consumer-facing websites don't; the difference is invisible to authors who aren't in publishing, because it's not something you can see on Bookshop.org or Amazon. Presses that can provide metadata like promotional plans and sales tips in Edelweiss have a significant advantage; we can make lists for buyers about why they should buy our titles and make that information available.

And like I said, in a sea of books being produced each year, *discoverability* is key.

We know a good cover helps, and covers are considered part of metadata, but all these other pieces of information add to the buyer's understanding of a new book. We even have the option to ingest actual page spreads, examples of what the laid-out book looks like, which is essential for illustrated or picture books.

Besides Edelweiss, the more robust a listing, the more metadata is attached to it, the more likely it'll show up in a search engine. Keywords help that discoverability, even though they aren't visible on most sites. To use an analogy, basic metadata walks around the block once a day. It's out there, doing something, and that's great! *Go metadata! You rock!* But full-service distribution clients have access to a metadata portal that's like a whole gym's worth of equipment, plus there are coaches to explain how they work. We have tools that, if we use them correctly, give us some significant advantages.

Metadata can be evaluated regularly and updated as the market changes, as staff members take feedback from client publishers, and as new information about the industry circulates. Our distribution team checks our listings to make sure we've used the data fields correctly. Moreover, there are staff members to ask when information isn't populating correctly. That hands-on help and training is huge for adjusting to the market, changing your metadata when best practices change, and keeping competitive with bigger presses.

HOW DO YOU KNOW IF a press has a distributor? If you look on a press website under their About section, or if they have a Booksellers or Trade tab, and you see a company named as a distributor, you can do a quick search to confirm it's true distribution (versus, say, a fulfillment company or print on demand). Full-service distributors include Publishers Group West, Consortium, Independent Publishers Group, Baker & Taylor, and SCB Distributors. University presses usually have full-service distribution through the University of Chicago.

Some presses list subsidiary rights agents on their site for publishers from other countries who are looking to buy rights for publication or translation.

What to ask a publisher with distribution:

- What's the expected print run?
- How fast can you reprint? (Some publishers have gap strategies that involve print-on-demand solutions.)
- Does your distributor have sales reps actively selling books into their accounts, and/or are they listed in a catalog? (In other words, is it full-service distribution?)
- Are there sales conferences? Does your press go to those? Do you get to chat with the reps so they get a sense of your press's personality?
- What's the average return rate?
- How far ahead do you prepare galleys, metadata, and marketing language for your distributor, and how does that affect author deadlines?
- What happens if an author misses a deadline? (This is

especially important if you are disabled or a caretaker of a disabled person; you might be able to push back your pub date and extend deadlines if your health or the health of a loved one might impact your ability to meet expectations.)

- How many ARCs or galleys do you expect to print for this title?

NO-FRILLS AND FULFILLMENT

SO WHERE DO NO-FRILLS DISTRIBUTION and fulfillment companies come in? *No-frills* is my term for distribution services that don't actively have sales teams meeting with buyers but do represent publishers and take order requests from wholesalers, bookstores, universities, and individual customers. Similarly, fulfillment companies hold warehouse space for publishers' books, and they *fulfill* orders that come in. I put these two in the same category because they don't include the same face-to-face sales time as full-service distribution, but they *do* offer some of the same advantages.

Many presses use one of these options to get books as an alternative to selling out of their houses or using print on demand as a circulation tool. Any distributor, no matter what the cost or the service level, helps an independent press earn reviews and coverage. That's true of no-frills and fulfillment—and a huge reason why presses might want to work with one of these kinds of companies.

Rosalie Morales Kearns, founder and publisher of Shade Mountain Press, signed with Small Press Distribution, which is now defunct. When I interviewed Rosalie in 2016, she said, "For a new, small press, having a distributor is crucial. There are bookstores and libraries that simply won't order a book that's print on demand, and / or won't order directly from publishers. They want to go through a distributor or wholesaler. There are also literary awards that won't consider books that are print on demand. Small Press Distribution was a good fit for us because they work solely with literary presses and they have a solid reputation among booksellers and librarians."

Often these smaller distribution and fulfillment companies are stepping stones before a publishing house is big enough to sustain full-service distribution. If a press starts out at Small Press United, a part of Independent Publishers Group, and then they grow their catalog and sales, they might move up to the IPG full-service tier.

Before I signed with Lanternfish Press, which used a fulfillment company for distribution, I asked questions. I wanted to know how my novel would reach readers.

Does the bulk of the print run get sent to the fulfillment company? (Yes.)

Is there staff you can reach via phone or email if you have questions or want advice? (Yes.)

Is there a way to add lots of metadata? (Yes, but the fulfillment company updates the listings—i.e., when a new review or blurb comes in—instead of the publishing company.)

What worked really well?

Having fulfillment gave Lanternfish an advantage compared

to the small presses that don't have any sort of distribution. Bookstores that wanted my book could order it easily. My books were printed offset and sent to the fulfillment company's warehouse, which avoided the quality issues that can come with printing one book at a time, as they're ordered.

I knew lots of stores would order my book because of my connections to booksellers from my publishing work. If I hadn't had those connections, I would have had a much smaller reach. So fulfillment, from that angle, worked great for me. I might have sold better nationally with a distributed press because more bookstores would have heard about my novel from their regional sales reps and decided to order it. But I sold well for a debut and especially well in the Pacific Northwest Booksellers Association territories.

What did I miss out on?

I got a lot of reviews for my novel, which tells me that fulfillment (instead of another kind of distribution) isn't a minus. But the review quotes never made it into the metadata, which means we lost a huge sales opportunity. Reviews are meant to sell books. They are seen by people who read trade journals, but that's a limited, niche audience, and there are always new reviews coming out. When quotes from trade reviews get added to a book's description, and that information populates on websites, those bits of praise and keywords all help your title get discovered by browsers. (Remember: more metadata = more likelihood of your book being seen online.) If trade journal reviews are not added to metadata, they aren't going to do anything besides bolster the author's ego and maybe (hopefully) help sell her next book.

As an author not wanting to be pushy or damage my relationships, I asked once or twice if the reviews could be added, and they weren't. I made up stories in my head about why—was

I asking for too much? Had I said something wrong? Did I come across as pushy because of my publishing insider status? Or maybe there were practical factors. Maybe the staff was in the middle of acquiring new books and they didn't have time to update my metadata. Or maybe the fulfillment company charged a fee every time updates were requested.

This is the kind of insider info that happy authors who love their presses are reluctant to share publicly. I know, intellectually, this metadata issue was a very small cog in the great machine of publishing, and that most authors wouldn't notice. But anytime communication breaks down, there's hurt there, and the hurt can fester if not addressed. In a book about being honest about publishing, it would feel disingenuous not to mention this small example of a communication breakdown and how it led me to self-blame.

Overall I had a great experience with Lanternfish and the resulting product made me proud. I didn't need distribution to feel cared for. Lanternfish has also since started distribution with Consortium, an Ingram branch—and at press time for this book they had even added three trade reviews to the *Singing Lessons* metadata. Hurray!

Now: Would my sales have been better with a full-service distribution press? Yes. Emphatically yes. My book would have been available on more shelves (at bookstores and in libraries), leading to more browsers picking it up. My appearance at the American Library Association conference would have especially impacted library sales more than it did. And online browsers would have found *Singing Lessons* more readily if all those reviews, keywords, and other categories were visible to buyers as part of the title metadata. If those things had happened, I'd also have a stronger sales record, important for future acquiring editors, who might not take into account how fulfillment impacts sales. I can see that in the distance between sales numbers of our debut novels at Forest Avenue and my own. The difference is *full-service distribution.*

What to ask a publisher with no-frills distribution or fulfillment:

- What's the expected print run?
- Do you sell books from the press website or do all orders go through the fulfillment company?
- Can you update the metadata or do you have to ask a staff member to do it for you? If the latter, is there a fee per change?
- Do your books get into libraries?
- How about bookstores? Is that something the distributor takes care of or do authors generally consign copies?

PRINT ON DEMAND

SOME PUBLISHERS SAY THAT PRINT on demand is too expensive because of the per-copy price point being higher than a book printed as part of an offset run. Others say it's the least expensive option because they don't have to hand over thousands of dollars up front to get a print run done.

Traditional offset printing uses printing plates; any quantity under a thousand is best suited to digital printing, which distributes ink or toner directly onto the paper just like a home printer. POD printing is digital printing. With advances in POD technology, most readers don't notice the difference in quality.

So let's look at both scenarios. Printing a few thousand copies of a book costs more out of pocket than POD, but it also costs way less *per book*. That savings is feasible only if the publisher can afford to print a few thousand copies up front or if they can get a line of credit to help them afford that expense. If, just to put arbitrary numbers on it, a POD paperback costs $6 to print per book, and the same book printed offset costs $3, that's half price! But to get to that $3 number, the publisher might have to commit to two thousand copies. Now we're looking at the difference between one $6 payment and putting $6,000 down for printing plus more money for shipping. Both sides of this debate are right: It *is* more expensive to do POD. Per book cost goes up when you print one at a time. It is also *less* expensive because you're paying a small amount up front, not thousands of dollars months ahead of when the book goes on sale.

It's also true that print on demand is less consistent product-wise. While quality has increased substantially over the years, one book being printed at a time introduces a potential for errors. Most readers can't tell a POD book from an offset one, but sometimes there are inconsistencies or errors.

Joe Biel of Microcosm has long been a vocal advocate for traditional printing:

> Years ago, an author contacted me to say publishers should pay her a better royalty because publishers don't have to pay for printing anymore. I tried to explain that POD is four times the price and ebooks are 1% of our sales. But it sent me on a deeper dive as a bookseller and distributor: I started paying attention to turn times on POD titles vs. offset printed titles.
>
> During the pandemic POD titles began coming with a disclaimer "X is a print-on-demand title so processing will be delayed," which continues to this day. Some distributors just began canceling POD titles from our orders immediately. In about 32% of cases, the POD books never arrived before the 90 day cancellation window. In 27% of cases the books took over two months to arrive. In 30% of cases the books took over a month. In only 11% of cases did the books arrive within the first month.
>
> For comparison, offset printing usually takes 12 days, door to door. These timelines are critical

> for booksellers as they are often desperate to restock a hot title while there is sales activity before it cools. So 1–3 months isn't an acceptable timeline and it shows that POD is not only four times the price for the publisher, but it fails to deliver on the basic value proposition of the service. Publishers frequently ask "Why don't you just use POD for some titles?" and as a publisher, I feel like I can only see its shortcomings. So instead, we built a software system for publishers to manage inventory, print runs, and reprints, which achieves the alleged benefits of POD without the costs.

While it's true that there can be catastrophic delays for print on demand especially during the holiday season, I've found an advantage in setting my popular titles up for quick POD restock, via Lightning Source, in case we run out of copies before a full offset run can be started, shipped, and stocked at the warehouse. Only after all those steps can the books be sent back out to fulfill orders.

The most frequently discussed POD companies are IngramSpark and Kindle Direct Publishing (owned by Amazon; formerly called CreateSpace). Lightning Source is also an Ingram company, but it's geared toward bigger publishers. Bookmobile is another popular choice; it has its own distribution and fulfillment company, Itasca Books. Some traditional printers are now advertising digital and print-on-demand services to compete in this market in addition to their offset options.

POD companies have digital portals where authors or publishers can input information about their books (the metadata), set the trim size and page count, and upload their files. Submitted files are checked by the printer before they can be approved by the publisher; it's not instant turnaround. Once those steps are completed, the book becomes available to print.

If the publisher uses print on demand for distribution, the metadata will feed out to book catalogs.

TRIM SIZE: The length and width of your finished book. I usually use 6″ × 9″ for Forest Avenue paperbacks, in other words, six inches horizontally and nine inches vertically. Other presses do 5.5″ × 8.5″ for their standard paperbacks. When a book is printed, the excess paper gets trimmed off, leaving it the correct size.

SPINE WIDTH: This is actually the depth of your book, how thick it is based on the number of pages and the thickness of the paper. The printer dictates the number for you, or with Ingram, there's a spine width calculator, where you plug in your variables and the system gives you a number to use.

Getting books to individual customers is a cinch with POD. If you decide to write and publish a family cookbook, let's say, and you want to send one copy to each of your aunts. Once the title is set up, you create an order for each aunt and input each address, click all the approval buttons, and huzzah! Your book will print and ship like magic. No post office runs! No handwriting addresses or making your own set of labels! You just plug and play, set the number of copies to go to each location, and go. There's no need to keep cases of books in your garage because you don't have to print five hundred or a thousand or five thousand at one time.

The advent of print-on-demand technology has been a boon to small presses and DIY authors—especially with the increases in quality, the option of printing in color and hardcover, and additional trim sizes. It's way better now than even a decade ago, when I first was using the technology, though it seemed remarkable at the time.

Do you know how to spot a print-on-demand book? Flip to the very last page of text. If there's a barcode there, it's printed on demand. If there's no barcode, the publisher printed a run of books, either offset or digitally.

Offset is best at runs of a thousand or more; they're the books that *smell* like books, if you are a book smeller. The process involves setting up printing plates and transferring ink from the plates onto the pages. Digital printing is when ink or toner gets printed directly on paper; print on demand is a type of digital printing. A traditional publisher might print three hundred copies of a book using a digital printer. Using digital printing doesn't necessarily mean it's a print-on-demand operation. In the early days of Forest Avenue, I used to print runs of five hundred copies at Gorham Printing in Centralia, Washington. I self-distributed those copies, making for a traditional model, even though my books were printed digitally.

Print-on-demand books get shipped to whoever orders them, saving costs on warehousing, but the higher cost per copy impacts profit. A print-on-demand publisher might print and ship a hundred copies for their own in-house use: tabling at events, giving copies to reviewers, fulfilling pre-orders, and for author use. Then from there, orders can be printed one at a time as needed.

Greg Gerding, founder of University of Hell Press, began with traditional print runs in part because of quality issues in the early days of print-on-demand technology. "The glue binding was sloppy and would melt apart," he said. "Pages would spill out. The covers looked horrible. Everything was done glossy and just looked wrong. They didn't look or feel like a real book."

By the time he decided to expand his press, the technology

had gotten way better. Gerding realized he could make books available to a larger audience through print on demand. "Their quality is now on par and competes with traditional printing. Some of the options are limiting, but you have to be creative to work around those limitations," Gerding said. "Working with a POD [company] enables us to print books only as needed. We're not motivated to commit to a bigger print run like with traditional printing that not only ends up costing more, but also shackles you with inventory."

IN POD LAND YOUR BOOK is a data point in a digital catalog.

Can bookstores order it? Absolutely, if the publisher has agreed to accept returns and if they set their discount percentage to include Ingram's cost *and* still give booksellers the 40 percent cover price discount they need. If a publishing house that uses Ingram print on demand lists a 40 percent discount in their metadata, that's not enough for a bookstore, because Ingram takes a cut too. The "correct" discount for getting books into stores is 55 percent. Anything less is termed a *short discount* by bookstores and gives buyers an obvious reason to say no to stocking a title.

Let's break that down. First, there's no reason for a bookstore to choose *your book* out of all the other books. It's words on a list—the title, your name, pub date, and ISBN. The book description and hopefully some early reviews get pushed from the print-on-demand portal onto this digital list, known as a catalog. Booksellers' standard catalog is—have you noticed a trend here?—another product from Ingram.

Without a sales rep talking it up or without major publicity hits or an effective publicity team—all of which are keys to POD presses earning traction in the market—the potential for sales is severely diminished.

Small presses that use POD often find a niche where they can be competitive—whether that's in a particular genre or style, a particular region, or some combination.

Even without publicity, if you sign with a POD press you'll likely get your title into local bookstores if you've built community and if your publisher sets the bookstore discounts and return policy correctly. If the press has set short discounts—less than what the bookstore wants to see—and / or decided to make your book *not* returnable, bookstores will probably refuse to order copies.

If that happens you'll have to consign copies. Consigning is at no cost or obligation to the bookstore. You'll get paid at some point after copies sell—and that could be months away. If you're successful, the bookstore might ask you to bring in additional copies after the first batch sells. Or you might get an email asking you to pick up your books because they aren't selling.

The following scenario happens too often. An author signs a press that says they're "distributed" by Ingram. They're so excited—this is a dream come true at last! When it comes time to ask a bookstore for an event, though, the staff turns it down. If it's a big enough store, you probably won't hear why. Smaller stores may say: *This book isn't returnable.* Or: *This book has a short discount. Short* means not a standard discount, it's like short-sheeting or shortcutting: not good for the bookstore.

Bookstores need a 40 percent discount per book to be able to bring a title into the store. Otherwise there's not enough margin to make it worthwhile. After all, brick-and-mortar stores have rent, electricity, heat, and staff members as costs in addition to purchasing all that inventory. And books do need to be returnable for a store to feel financially secure enough to order an event-sized batch: stores want to be able to ship copies back that don't sell, then apply those refunds to bringing in new stock.

If either of those variables is wrong and you're a local author, the events coordinator may offer a consignment deal. The standard is 40 percent of cover price. Which means you can bring copies to the store, sign a piece of paper, and then take back whatever doesn't sell after an allotted time period passes. That's more work—physically bringing a box to the bookstore can be challenging for disabled bodies—but it solves the problem.

Unless.

And this is where it gets tricky.

Unless your author discount on copies you buy from your press is less than 50 percent.

(I know, math.)

If you buy copies at a 40 percent discount and consign them to the bookstore at a 40 percent discount, the bookstore and the press make money on the deal. And you, the author, make zero dollars. A 50 percent author discount, though, works out okay. Your book costs $18, then you pay $9 to the publisher per copy. The bookseller takes 40 percent—$7.20. So that'd leave you with $1.80 profit; most royalty structures lead to earnings of a dollar or less per copy, so that's fine. What about shipping costs though? If you are responsible for those, as is common, you might see more of that $1.80 profit disappear.

What if you already signed a contract that only allows you to buy stock at 40 percent off? You might be able to negotiate with your press to buy a certain number of copies at a 50 percent discount just for consignment purposes and so you can get your events booked. After all, your press wants you to sell books! But they may say no. And if you only figure this out after signing a contract agreeing to a 40 percent discount, you don't have any recourse. You'll have to focus your event schedule on house parties, libraries, and other non-bookstore places—or maybe you'll do a bookstore event anyway, with the free copies your publisher gives you, and just accept that you'll make zero dollars on those sales.

It feels awful to find yourself in that situation. You're upset, and rightly so, but what to do is not exactly clear. You can tell the publisher and possibly explode that relationship if you let your anger drive the conversation. Or you can sit quietly and wish someone had told you sooner. I've counseled so many writers who have landed in this spot. Publishing is expensive; I get why presses would refuse returns or offer a 40 percent discount to their authors. But I also get the limits those numbers put on an author's ability to see their books in stores. And authors who expect bookstore sales have every right to be frustrated if and when they discover bookstores don't want to carry their work because of how the publishing house is set up. If you know this in advance, you'll be in a better place to make all the variables work out for bookstores, your publisher, and yourself.

What to ask a print-on-demand publisher:

- Are you focusing exclusively on online sales? Or are you setting your per-copy discount at the recommended rate to encourage booksellers to bring titles in?
- Are your books returnable?
- If your terms are unfavorable to booksellers, can I get a 50 percent discount on author copies, then consign them to my local bookstores at 40 percent?
- What company are you using for print on demand? Independent bookstores will not carry titles printed through Kindle Direct Publishing because of Amazon's business practices.
- What's your sales goal for this title?
- What marketing and publicity are you doing to help bookstores, libraries, and readers find your books?

- Do you print a run of stock to use for promotions, consignment, and/or direct sales, or is it all one at a time?
- How do you handle preorders? IngramSpark, in particular, expects finished files to be uploaded, which means the final cover, blurbs, and edits must all be ready. This can lead to short preorder windows compared to other presses. A six-month preorder campaign will look very different from a one-month one, and it's good to know what you'll be working with.

PRINTING GALLEYS

PRINT-ON-DEMAND SERVICES ARE GREAT FOR printing advance reader copies, also known as ARCs and galleys and promotional copies. These terms are mostly interchangeable. I use *galleys* to refer to the earliest print copies, usually before they have cover art, which I send out to get blurbs. ARCs are what I call the more professional ones—copyedited, with blurbs, a finished front cover, and a back cover that describes the book and lists sales and marketing information. At Forest Ave we use Lightning Source for these.

Advance reader copies are printed months in advance and sent out to reviewers as soon as possible. Most trade journals want four months lead time or longer, which means if your book is coming out in May, you'll need your ARCs printing in January at the latest to even have a chance at a *Publishers Weekly*, *Kirkus*, *Booklist*, *Foreword*, or *Library Journal* review.

We use ARCs at Forest Ave for pitching trade

reviews, magazine coverage, library reach-outs, bookstore connections, and sometimes as submissions for awards programs (although I prefer to use finished copies when possible). For those uses, I send a few cases to my home office. I also print ARCs to send directly to the sales team at Publishers Group West; they go out from the Tennessee warehouse instead of routing through Oregon first. POD allows me to print and ship without having to buy boxes and print labels—and I get better shipping rates doing it direct.

Some publishers print nine months early and then sticker those books NOT FOR SALE instead of printing a run of ARCs. Making ARCs buys me time and a few more editorial passes; if I went to press nine months early and then used the finished copies to promote the book, stickering them as review copies, I'd be stuck with the "finished" edition even if we spotted typos or if something major changed in the world that impacted the information in the book. As it is, we usually go to press with finished files before trade reviews come out, but every once in a while the stars align and we can include those quotes on the finished book jacket.

SELF-DISTRIBUTION

ANOTHER OPTION THAT'S HIGH TOUCH—and a lot of work but potentially very effective—is when a press decides to distribute its own books.

For the sake of clarity, there are some big independent presses that have their own sales teams and warehouses; Microcosm and Pomegranate are two that come to mind because they're local to me. These presses can match the power of the full-service distribution model, but they do it on their own terms. They aren't contracting with another company to warehouse products and fulfill orders.

Since we've already covered the advantages of full-service, for this section we'll be talking about presses that self-distribute on a micro level.

This can be done on a very small scale—out of your car, suitcase, or perhaps even a trench coat. (*Psst, buddy, over here. Wanna buy a book?*)

When Jacob Weisman founded Tacyhon Publications in 1995, he set distribution up as a mail-order business. "It's an old model—you can't really do that anymore," he said. "You used to put the new book out, send out 300 postcards, and get 180 orders right away, and no bookstore discount for those orders. I knew our market really well so the return on the postcard investment was huge. More than half we sent it to would buy the book."

Back then, Tachyon titles were available in some specialty stores. "At some point they would order one of our books and they would just keep ordering," Jacob said. He added that he would produce a run of a thousand books, and the goal was to sell that thousand.

Now Tachyon is distributed by Baker & Taylor. They are best known as a wholesaler to the library market, but they have a full-service distribution arm as well with sales reps who meet with buyers and encourage them to carry their publishers' latest titles.

Michael Heald, publisher of Perfect Day Publishing, self-distributes his titles, in part because of his decision not to sell books on Amazon. Michael's press averages one book per year and relies on bookseller relationships. Sometimes he cultivates those connections by walking into the store with books, and other times by asking the store to host an event featuring a Perfect Day author, which opens the channel for future titles.

"What I have found is that some of the very best bookstores around—Elliott Bay in Seattle, McNally Jackson in NY, Verbatim in San Diego, Skylight Books in LA, Green Apple in SF, and of course Powell's here in Portland, to name a few—have been willing to feature our books prominently because they've become fans of Perfect Day," Michael said. "It's an imperfect system (it creates extra paperwork for the stores, and I'm not always great at keeping tabs on inventory), but the payoff is huge: getting our books in the hands of readers who live in the cultural centers of our country. And for people who want to buy their books online, but not directly off our website, Powell's ends up being the go-to option, which is great for a lifelong Powell's customer like myself."

While authors are often eager to know what the first print run of their title will be, with self-distributing publishers who don't have their own warehouses, that number may not be tied to sales goals because they need to print what they can afford and safely store.

What to ask a micro-scale, self-distributing publisher:

- What happens if the first run sells out?
- Do you have a suitable warehouse space for cases of books (a basement? A garage?) and the capability to fulfill orders on a timely basis?
- Do you have strong bookseller relationships? Do you sell direct or consign to independent bookstores, and are you able to offer the necessary 40 percent discount bookstores need to bring books into their store on a nondistributed basis?
- How long does it take to get a check from your key bookstore accounts once a copy sells off the shelf?
- Does the press have a presence at any writing festivals or trade shows or other direct-from-publisher sales events in addition to bookstore sales?
- Are authors encouraged to buy their own books at a discount and sell them direct to customers, and if so, what is that author discount?
- Can readers order titles online? If so, is that through a bookstore or direct through the press?
- What is the author's responsibility in terms of continuing or growing bookstore relationships? Would I be expected to hand-deliver my books to my local store?

CASE STUDY #9: Forest Avenue Press's Distribution Journey

I STARTED FOREST AVENUE PRESS'S fiction catalog by combining two options. I printed a short run—250 copies for starters—of Stevan Allred's *A Simplified Map of the Real World,* and I also put the data online for print on demand through Ingram's Lightning Source. (Now the smallest presses are slotted into IngramSpark, another Ingram business, but in 2013 it was all Lightning Source.)

The online piece of my business model meant when readers or booksellers wanted to get copies, the data was present on multiple bookselling platforms. The book, therefore, was available. With the print-on-demand model, copies get printed when they are ordered and not before, which helped me avoid the up-front expense of paying a printer.

The copies from the short run went into my house (boxes of books are called *cases* in the industry). From there I consigned handfuls of copies to bookstores, sold them directly to readers at events, and shared copies with Stevan. Wherever I drove my minivan, I had a case of books in the back, just in case I needed to deliver some.

At the time I thought setting up an account at Lightning Source meant I was distributed by Ingram. After all, I paid Ingram a setup fee. I gave Ingram my data. Ingram sent the data out on behalf of my press. I even typed that statement on the copyright page of our earliest titles: *Distributed by Ingram*! But I was wrong. Print on demand is a technology that allows many presses to operate with minimal overhead, lowering a major barrier to access (money) and inviting more would-be publishers to jump into the industry and make good-looking, professional books.

But it's not distribution, because distribution is *not* just making data available on a network. It's for presses that print actual runs of books and house them at the distributor's warehouse.

Ingram, through their Lightning Source branch, moved my data through an online system. No people, save me, were involved in telling other people about our books. I didn't have any advisors telling me my prices were too low or too high or that a black-and-white cover would scratch more—and mean more potential returns—than other colors.

Available through the Ingram catalog would have been more correct.

Print on demand was a great starter business model for me. I wouldn't have been able to launch Forest Avenue Press if I had to pay to print a thousand books my first time out; doing 250 was feasible, a safe and reasonable quantity.

When I first started trying to get trade reviews for Forest Avenue Press titles, the publisher of one of the top journals told me to get distribution first and then I'd have a shot at coverage. Print on demand was holding me back, this expert said. That blew my mind. I had been thinking that the journals didn't pick us up because we weren't *good enough yet*. Because I wasn't *good enough*. But quality had nothing to do with it. Wanting to be eligible for more reviews spurred me to get distribution. So did having an author who wanted to go on a national tour. I realized bookstores outside of the Pacific Northwest were more likely to invite an out-of-state author if their regional sales rep could vouch for the book and the press.

I was probably too small to level up that fast, but I went for it, and we're still hanging in there. Stevan's debut came out in September 2013 and we began distribution in December 2014. Working with Publishers Group West gives me the potential to sell thousands of books and keep selling them beyond the first three months post-publication. I have to pick the right books, and they need incredibly powerful covers, and publicity and marketing efforts need to pay off . . . but I can do it. And as the years go by, books from past seasons that keep selling have become financial backbones for our company.

BACKLIST: Books that have been published in the past. The more backlist titles a press has, ones that are still selling, the better likelihood that the press has a steady passive income to sustain its next projects. Backlist is something I heard about a lot when I first started publishing; I kept being told that publishing more titles, putting money in now for earnings later, would be an important strategy. I'd add that a book that doesn't do well out of the gate isn't likely to contribute much to backlist earnings. A book that "backlists well" is publishing gold.

 **FRONTLIST**: Books that haven't come out yet or are newly published. "New" might be within the first three months or within the first year since publication. These are the flashy books that are being pushed to the media, usually starting nine months before pub date. Once they are out in the world, it gets harder to earn media attention. The better a frontlist book does in sales in the first three months of publication, the more likely it'll be a strong backlist candidate, although sometimes old books find new life (like when one gets turned into a TV series or gets rediscovered by a celebrity book club).

Having distribution also allows me to be emphatically pro–independent bookstores, which was a major reason I created a press: to bring readers and writers together inside independent bookstores. PGW makes my books available (easily!) to stores. They're why we get yeses when we ask for events. They're why we can say, *Find this title wherever books are sold*. They're why we can urge people to shop local. We know our books are available.

I don't miss the old days of lugging cases in and out of my minivan, but without the print-on-demand model I wouldn't have been able to start my own company. I wouldn't have had the money or the knowledge necessary to jump right into distribution. I get to run my business my way: by making independent bookstores the center of my publishing world, like the stars they are. *Live and learn* has allowed Forest Avenue and its authors to thrive and earn.

TELLING PRESSES APART

WHILE DISTRIBUTION DIFFERENTIATES INDEPENDENT PRESSES more than any other characteristic, there are other factors to consider.

Covers

You can get a sense for the personality of a press by the covers they produce. I fell in love with Lanternfish's covers and that was a big reason I went with them. Kimberly Glyder created the *Singing Lessons for the Stylish Canary* cover, and I couldn't love it more. Likewise, if a press has covers that look sloppy, too dark, or unprofessional, you might not want to submit. Or submit and, if you get accepted, prepare a conversation about design before signing. Some presses are okay with an author paying a freelancer for cover design if they reject the in-house options. Go a step further and look inside books published by the presses you're researching. Do they look professional? Are there lots of pages where lines of text are squished too close or spread too far? Does the title page include the press logo and location, as per Library of Congress requirements? Is the font too small for you to read clearly?

Staff

Who's on the masthead? Are there editors of color? Queer editors? Disabled editors? Do you see someone who identifies in a similar way as you? You can check out the author list for more demographic information as well. Most micropresses are one-person operations.

I work at my kitchen table and don't plan to grow. But my masthead includes advisors and regular freelance contractors. I hope that if someone doesn't see themselves in my masthead, they'll find a book of ours that speaks to them in terms of its themes and representation.

Awards

Are the press's books earning praise? Is there a news page or information on social media about their latest coups? If there are awards listed, are they legitimate ones or are they pay-to-play? This can tell you whether the products being created by this press are professional enough to catch the eyes of judges.

Publicity

Not all presses have in-house publicists; many put the onus of that onto their authors. I'm the publisher of Forest Avenue but also the developmental editor, accountant, project manager, and publicist. But you'll want to see some movement around new books—an article here, an interview there—to confirm that the press puts at least some time and money into spreading the word about books.

Many responsibilities rest on the author's shoulders, but it's a promising sign if you see the press chipping in—sharing new content and promoting the book beyond its first three months. Even (especially) if the publisher is piggybacking off an outside publicist's efforts, you'll want to see them sharing, sharing, sharing.

Blurbs

Are there blurbs by famous writers decorating some of the books in their catalog? If yes, and authors at this press have a track record that's impressive, that's a great sign. If not, think about why. It might be that the press doesn't send out print advance copies; digital versions are easier to say no to, I've found, because they're exchanged with a few clicks. When a publisher or author sends me a print book, I have a stronger feeling of obligation, of wanting to make that small investment pay off for the people who sent it to me.

Authors talking online

You can check out the publisher's social media accounts, for sure, and get a good idea of what's going on, but their authors' accounts are more revealing. Are they squeeing about their publisher? Are they openly sharing submissions windows and encouraging others to query? Are they interacting positively with their pressmates and/or editors? If there's an absence of information about the publisher on the authors' accounts, then consider digging deeper. A lack of excitement can mean something has gone wrong or hard feelings have developed during the publishing process. Often if an author is dissatisfied or fighting with their publisher, you'll see a steep drop in interactions with their press. It's when author mentions of a press disappear that I start wondering if things are *really* bad and if the conversation has moved offline between authors who are trying to get restitution or a response of some kind from their press. When publishers stop being transparent with their authors, there's an eerie pressure that builds, and usually news comes out later, when the tension gets high enough.

Memberships

Does the press you're studying belong to any organizations?

The Community of Literary Magazines and Presses, the Independent Book Publishers Association, and PubWest are a few of the publishing-centric nonprofits. CLMP has a code of conduct for its members particularly relevant to contest protocol. Belonging to a group means the press has other publishers to learn from, access to skill-building classes and conferences, and an understanding of best practices. If there are no memberships, don't panic; maybe it's a new press, or maybe memberships are one expense the leaders decided not to pay for this year. If you see affiliations, though, that means the press has support from peers, and that's a good sign.

Social media

I run Forest Avenue's accounts by posting occasionally, as I have time and interest. I don't have any apps or services that help me position my content at key times or on certain days of the week. My personal newsletter, which includes Forest Ave content occasionally, ebbs more than flows. If you want to get a sense of my press from our social media, you might see long stretches of postless time.

Maybe these things would be yellow flags (*caution!*) to a social media–savvy Gen Z author, and maybe they'd decide not to submit. But I do what I can, and there are other things people can learn from our accounts. We celebrate other presses and authors, not just our own. We say *we* a lot. We like colorful images and post original photographs and designed graphics (not Canva backgrounds). Reshares are generally links to content featuring our authors or event signup information. Everything else is original content. That speaks to our brand. So does, honestly, my lackluster posting schedule. I'd much rather text an author or make heirloom bean soup than create another online post just to feed a soulless algorithm.

CASE STUDY #11: Making the Ask

BLURBS ARE MOST OFTEN A topic for after you get your book deal, but getting great ones can depend on the press, so it's worth going over the material in a before-signing context. Suzy Vitello, author of *Bitterroot* (Sibylline) and a freelance developmental editor, shared this insight: "I'm always impressed/intrigued by a given press's outreach regarding endorsements. Who gets them? How to get them? Etiquette? I know it's mostly on the author to leverage relationships and ask for blurbs, but I think a potential blurb-giver would also rather align themselves with a well-thought-of press?"

She's absolutely right. If a press has a good reputation, a query for an endorsement already has an edge over one for a book from a press that author hasn't heard of. Here are a few other things to think about.

Are the press's covers professional?

This will help potential endorsers feel good about the quality of the books the press puts out, especially if they haven't heard of the press. Pay special attention to whether the press's covers match genre expectations. Does a fantasy book *look* like other books in that category?

Does the press regularly get review coverage?

Again, this is something a potential blurber can check pretty quickly. If nobody's talking about a press out in the world, then maybe it's not worth an author's time unless the material really resonates or there's already a personal connection in the mix.

Do you like the jacket copy of existing books in the catalog?

This will tell you if the staff knows how to describe their books in effective ways. Good jacket copy—also known as flap copy or book descriptions—should grip the potential reader without giving too many spoilers.

Does the press have distribution?

I don't actually know how many authors care, but as a distributed press, I like to include that information in my ask letters. The stakes feel higher if the book is going to be on shelves across the country and worldwide, especially if the author being asked for blurbs is famous. Their words can actually make a major difference in readers picking a book up when the book is available in brick-and-mortar stores. I suspect that small press authors are more clued in to this question than six-figure-advance-earning authors at big presses.

Does the press website seem active or defunct?

Website trends come and go, and not everyone can afford a professional designer, but if a press you're interested in has a page that seems, well, outdated, that's not a great look.

If you query successfully and you're offered a deal, either before signing or during the onboarding process, you should ask how much the press (or its publicist) might help with blurbs. Can someone review your ask letter and give you feedback? What did they love about your query letter? Maybe you can recycle some of that language into a blurb request. Does the press send out requests for endorsements on behalf of their authors, or is it the authors' responsibility? Are there authors in their catalog who might be good matches for your book—and might they be willing to blurb? I love it when prospective authors want to know my ideas for blurb outreach—who I know, who I see as a good fit, and who I would feel comfortable reaching out to.

I asked Joyce Cherry Cresswell, author of the Oregon Book Award–winning debut novel *A Great Length of Time,* about her experience getting blurbs. She decided to ask Molly Gloss. "Molly's prose is somehow both tight and lilting," Joyce said. "Reading a Molly Gloss story is like wrapping a homemade quilt around your shoulders and settling in with a good cup of tea. You want to adopt her characters."

On the advice of a mentor, Joyce attended one of Molly's readings with her two-page prologue in her pocket. "Before the reading, as she introduced herself to the attendees, I screwed up my courage and handed it to her," Joyce said. "I said I was a new writer and asked if she had time for a cup of coffee to discuss publishing options. She graciously accepted the envelope. I followed up with an email a few weeks later. When we met I asked about publishing options. I did not ask for a blurb. That came six months later, in an email in which I reminded her of who I was and attached an even-more-polished version of the prologue. She replied that she would be happy to read my full manuscript, with no guarantees, which was all I could ask. A few months later, I received the blurb of my dreams."

Joyce's experiences running a nonprofit for more than a decade, volunteering for the PTA, and working on political campaigns all came in handy when she had to summon her courage to ask Molly Gloss to read her work. Here are Joyce's six tips for getting blurbs:

> Rule Number 1: Know your donor. If you haven't read and loved the blurber's work, don't ask. You don't have to write in the same genre, but it helps. Molly Gloss and I both write historical literary fiction. Her expertise in the field is what makes her endorsement so powerful. But most importantly, this is a matter of respect. You hope it is the beginning of a long and productive professional relationship. Do your homework.
>
> Rule Number 2: Cultivate your donor. Molly knew nothing about me. My first ask could not be, "How-do-you-do, and by the way, will you read and blurb my novel?" I needed to introduce myself and let her know I was qualified to ask for her support. I chose to ask for a cup of coffee. My novel has a convenient, two-page prologue that is long enough to prove I could write, but which could be read in two minutes. I started there; it was a very small ask, but a necessary first step.
>
> Rule Number 3: There should be something in it for them. The blurb should benefit both parties. An author puts his or her professional reputation on the line with an endorsement. It is not a casual favor. When someone blurbs your book, your names will be linked forever. Show them only material that has been thoroughly vetted and polished, so they will be proud to be associated with you and your work. This way they do not have to disappoint you, which they should

and will do if they think your book will taint their own brand.

Rule Number 4: Respect their time. These folks are just as busy as you are. Busier. Give your blurbing author enough time to get his or her head around your material. On a dark December day, Molly and I met for an hour over coffee. By then she had read my two-page prologue. The following summer, five months before my publishing deadline, I requested the blurb. She was in the middle of a project, but was willing to read my full manuscript if she could have two or three months. Perfect.

Rule Number 5: Believe in your product. The sweet spot in asking is that moment when the donor sees a vision of a better future, and the part they played in making it come true. They will never get there if you show hesitation. Why should they believe if you don't? Of course you believe in your story, but is it your best possible writing? Get feedback from others, listen to it and polish, polish, polish. You must believe totally in what you are offering the other person. It's hard, given the stew of self-doubt we all swim in as writers. But you know. Deep down, you know. Believe.

Rule Number 6: Be brave. At some point, you just have to ask—if possible, in person. I have always found it helpful to pre-plan what I will say and practice it ahead of time. It never goes exactly as I have planned, but there is comfort beforehand in having a plan. And remember that writers are a generous bunch. As long as you do your part by preparing properly, they are almost always happy to help.

WHEN PRESSES FOLD

Sometimes small presses overinvest or acquire more titles than they can afford, which leads to them closing without completing their contractual agreements.

Other times, presses run by one person or a small group can decide the financial picture isn't rosy enough to keep going. Or the publisher can decide to retire, work in a different field, or take a job with a bigger press. It's an incredibly exhausting business, especially for those of us who handle many roles to keep overhead low.

Whatever the reason, authors have to scramble for alternatives. They should get their rights back, automatically, which allows them to consider ways to give their work new life.

After Inkwater Press ceased operation, as I mentioned earlier, Forest Avenue bought the rights to Kesha's *No God Like the Mother*. I knew we'd be able to reach a wider audience than the original because we have distribution. Forest Avenue rereleased the collection in spring 2023 with a new cover, an updated glossary, book club questions, and an author's note. I felt strongly that Kesha's debut needed to stay in print. We even got to use the Oregon Book Award seal on the cover! Most of the time, though, once a book is out in the world, it's hard to get another publisher to pick it up. So it's better to talk to existing authors before signing a contract and make sure that the business is fulfilling its obligations.

Often conversations about a press's financial health start out quietly, between existing authors, before they spill into public view on social media or are reported in trade journals.

In 2016 I interviewed novelist Paula Coomer, who had five books published with Booktrope and worked for the company for a few years. She shared her thoughts on the end of the press—and what happened to her books afterward: "Part of what killed Booktrope was the exact same thing that kills many small presses: book returns. Publishing is the only industry in the world where retailers are not responsible for what happens to their inventory. If a book doesn't sell, it can be returned to the publisher. A store owner can't do that with shoes or cartons of yogurt or tires. A retailer is expected to take some risk."

There are cases where publishers have the best intentions and work really hard for their authors, but the business model doesn't work and eventually they have to fold. Often this is because of a torrent of returns, or from handling returns over a number of years and not getting ahead on earnings to balance the deficits out.

Sometimes this happens seemingly out of the blue with little notice—from the author side, it's almost always a surprise, unless someone at the press gives you a heads-up. Best case in these situations, the press makes a good faith effort to help their authors find new homes. Black Lawrence Press stepped up in 2023 to acquire titles by more than a hundred authors when Nomadic Press announced its closure. I was one of many publishers that received information from Nomadic about their frontlist titles and their backlist catalog; the publisher didn't want their existing and future books to disappear. I thought that was so classy and smart—to ask for help, to reach out to community instead of shutting down in a void, cutting off communication, and letting the authors figure out their own paths forward.

DECISION TIME

HERE'S THE BEST THING ABOUT knowing how presses move metadata and products around: you can decide who you might trust with your story, consider whether an offer is right for you, and help your friends who haven't read this book. It's also a great reminder that publishing is a business, and your words are the product. As you establish relationships with your agent and/or editor, you can start from a place of understanding the system.

Whatever path you choose, know how it works. Know why you've chosen it. Ask questions if you get an offer from a press that doesn't explicitly explain its distribution methods. Be willing to change paths if the one you want turns out to be blocked by a skull and crossbones TURN AROUND sign. Don't take the detours personally. The industry isn't out to get you. Publishers aren't intentionally blocking your access. There's just a lot of work circulating out there, and it's a labor-heavy (almost always unpaid) task to evaluate a manuscript.

It's okay to start pitching in one direction and then change your mind.

It's okay to get rejected and try another path.

It's okay to reevaluate the commerciality of your book after you talk to more writers and learn more about their experiences in publishing.

It's okay to abandon a book that isn't selling because you have an amazing new idea.

It's okay to work on two or three or four projects at once if that's how your brain works. I have two novels started, neither going very fast, but my brain is happy!

There's no one correct path, no matter what other people try to tell you.

The reason to write is to write.

Writing so you can say you've written isn't quite as fulfilling as slowing down and appreciating the actual making, the building of sentences and stanzas, the way writing allows us to sit quietly with ourselves.

Setbacks and roadblocks are part of finding your way in the door. What happens next depends on lots of factors; your manuscript is only one of those. Your future success is bound up in the economy, whether publishers are expanding or shrinking their workforces, and what trends are on the rise during the period when you're querying. When you have to adjust your goals, don't fold in on yourself or berate yourself or decide *you* are the problem. The industry is opaque, fickle, and hard to predict. Lots of people who used to read constantly now prefer to watch streaming content or play games on their phones.

Remember, creative writing is an art form. A no from an agent or a publisher is more likely a referendum on their busy schedules or a reflection of their individual preferences than a total rebuke of your art. That's why so many rejections say *not for us* or *not at this time*. It may feel like a cop-out to receive such a statement, but often it's truer than anything else we can say about your work.

If you're struggling with mental health around submissions, talk to other authors who are a few steps ahead of you. Attend workshops and classes on publishing. Read Jane Friedman's website. Reread the opening chapters of this book to recenter yourself on your work. Create your own community of writers who are at similar stages so you can brainstorm and laugh and worry together.

And also? Take a few deep breaths. By reading this and considering what you want from your publishing experience, you're crafting tools you can use to plan your career.

And that in and of itself is something to celebrate.

You're figuring it all out. *Go you!*

SAYING YES TO THE YES!

WHAT IF YOU GET ONE offer? One choice? One door opening?

It's easy to say you can *choose* to say yes, or you can *choose* to look for other options, but that doesn't feel like an affirming, author-centric choice. It can be a tough call if the yes comes from a place you aren't that excited about. You're choosing between the offer on the table and the possibility of not getting another offer. Walking away from someone who opens their door to your work, to your story, feels like a huge risk. And it is. You can wait, hold out for something else—more advance money, better distribution, or more aligned with your goals—but there's no guarantee anyone else will say yes.

This is where centering your path and who you want to be in the world as an author might help. If you want to write and publish multiple books, how does saying yes to this offer help your career? Are there any ways saying yes might *harm* your future? For instance, signing with a nondistributed press means less impressive sales numbers, which could cause a future agent or editor to look away from your next manuscript.

What are you most worried about?

What can you work around?

If you've read all this operational information and decided you want a publisher with distribution for the sales reach, or a big five for the potential advance, or a micropress for the individual attention, and your offer comes from another type of press, can you work with that? Can you let your expectations reshuffle? Can you adjust and be happy with it?

Sometimes it feels good to say yes to someone who believes in you. Then you have to make the most of what you have, reframe your journey based on who said yes, and work with any limitations and drawbacks.

I definitely see tiers in the industry because we have full-service distribution and know the potential that comes from having a sales team actively pushing a book into the world. But that's just one rating system—and one I'm bypassing in my current search for a novel publisher. Would I choose an editor who takes great care of me at a micropress over an editor who ignores me at a major house? Today, absolutely. Next year or five years from now? I'm not sure.

What other ways can you look at the options and see the potential in what you are being offered?

The people behind each press are just as much a part of the experience of being published as the mechanics of how the system works. Maybe even more so. When Lanternfish offered me a contract, I said yes because I loved the acquisitions editor's feedback and vision. I felt like she really *got it*. My concern about going with a fulfillment-only publishing house melted away because I felt this deep connection. And Lanternfish also had a publicist, which many small presses don't.

Another good way to think about an offer on the table is this: What's your next step if you say no?

Or if you want to say yes, will you always regret saying yes?

If it's not an ideal offer, can you step up to the challenge and make it work for you? I think that's a whole other book—how to manage publishing with all the misinformation and missed opportunities and unfulfilled expectations. Probably, with whatever press you sign with, you'll have some regrets, but hopefully a lot of wins too.

Remember, we are living in an age where books are still revered, but they're competing for leisure time against quick-burst, bright, loud distractions.

Bottom line: most readers—especially those who aren't also writers—don't pay attention to what press publishes what book. They look at covers, book descriptions, blurbs, and the author bio. Those things mean more than the publisher's identity or the imprint name, unless you're in the business. A book published by a micropress absolutely can hold space on a shelf next to a Penguin Random House book if the micropress makes it easy for the bookstore to carry their books and if they are professional in making their products.

Which is, truly, great news. Especially if you're like me and you root for the independent businesses, the risk-takers, the visionaries and creatives who decide to do something good for other writers.

YOUR PART IN PROMOTION

WHEN WE HAVE A MANUSCRIPT we want to sell, it's deliciously satisfying to flash forward to thinking about the future—the contract signing, the advance money, the book tour, and all those autographs.

It's important, though, to really think about each element of the journey and whether it's what you really want. You may not get a choice, you may only get one offer, but why not organize your querying process around what your hopes, strengths, and deficits are? Now that you know your way around distribution types, the answers to these questions can help you understand which path—agent, editor, hybrid, or self-publishing—might fit best with your goals and personality. If you know what you've written and where the readers are, you can get a few steps closer to seeking a publishing trajectory that makes sense for *you*.

Small presses without publicity staff may encourage their authors to hire freelance publicists, who can cost upward of $20,000 for a several-month commitment. If you can afford that, then choosing a press without an in-house publicist is an option that's open to you.

If you don't have thousands of dollars set aside to invest in publicity, that's okay—most of us don't! We're artists. We can band together and share ideas. The more honest you are with yourself about your abilities and challenges, the more likely you'll rewrite your author dream into something you can actually accomplish. Here are a few things to consider.

Can you do an event at a bookstore?

Do you have the physical strength and stamina to stand for an hour? To travel to a store that's thirty minutes away? How about two hours? How about three events, standing for an hour each? How about five? Can you afford to travel to bookstores outside your area if your expenses aren't paid by your publisher? (Few pay to tour their authors these days, and even the biggest authors are getting smaller tours after COVID-19.) Be sure to factor in whether you'll have to take time off work and/or arrange child- or elder care. Can you do it, physically, and can you afford to do it, timewise and financially?

Do you want to take the microphone and speak to big crowds of people about your ideas?

If that's your jam, publication is a great way to get yourself into high school auditoriums, college theaters, and fancy lecture halls. Getting those placements might mean working with a speakers' bureau, and there are many independent ones if your press isn't big enough to have its own. Or maybe that sounds terrifying. Maybe you'd rather meet with small groups of people to have real conversations about the topics in your book. That could include book club visits (virtual or in person), leading workshops in your field, or participating in a conference. Writing classes and conferences often invite authors, but you can also explore events that center themes in your book or the kinds of research you did.

Do you like writing essays and doing written interviews?

Or does that feel like unpaid busywork? How do you feel about pitching major news outlets? Trying to, say, get into *HuffPost* or *Newsweek* with an opinion piece? Often this kind of publicity can lead to book sales, but even if it doesn't, it feels good to land a byline that includes your book title.

How do you feel about podcasts?

Are you a natural with a microphone or do you panic and stammer? Would you want to be on one podcast? Five? Twenty? If anxiety flares when you think about this, consider skipping this option, doing a practice recording with a friend, or taking a public speaking class. Don't sign up for all the scary things and expect yourself to just deal with it.

TAKE CARE OF YOURSELF SO you can do all the other things on your list. Otherwise you'll risk a physical or emotional crash. That's the bottom line of this self-inventory exercise. If that means saying no to something your publisher wants you to do, then that's important to understand about yourself.

If you're immunocompromised and speaking in person at bookstores will use too much of your valuable energy, or feels unsafe even if you're wearing a mask, then listen to your body. Maybe your publicist will insist on events and you'll have to have some hard conversations about focusing on online formats. Or maybe your press will figure out a way to create a low-energy, low-risk alternative.

If you do this kind of thinking long before you hold a

contract in your hands, you'll be more likely to stick with what works for you personally, instead of agreeing to do everything because you feel obligated. It's hard to say no to a publisher.

CASE STUDY #10: The Cost of Events

BEING A WRITER COSTS TIME and money—setting aside hours to write instead of, say, working more hours at your job, not to mention attending conferences, taking classes, creating a DIY retreat to finish a draft. It all adds up over the years.

We imagine, someday, we'll earn back this investment when we get published, but that's only true for the highest earners. And that's just in the *writing* of books. Being a *published author* also costs an incredible amount of time and money. Even if you have a press with a publicist, there are still tasks and related expenses that will fall to you, the individual. Publishers almost never pay for tours, for instance, so it's best to understand these—and your publisher's expectations—up front.

Evan Morgan Williams, author of *Stories of the New West* (Main Street Rag) and *Thorn* (BkMk), shared this cost breakdown of one of his tour stops for *Thorn*: "A writer who publishes a book with a small press needs to be prepared to do hours of marketing. Setting up readings at bookstores and reading series, securing reviews . . . it's a ton of work. We all hear those words, but I learned that it's more true than one can possibly imagine. Also, the writer needs to be aware that all of that work will not be profitable. Here is one of my most successful outings: a combined junket to Sacramento (Stories on Stage) and San Francisco (Book Passage). Airfare: $200 round trip. Taxi: $40. Lodging: free (cousins!). Income: Stories on Stage gave me $100 from the admissions, plus sales of 16 books (50 people in attendance), and I have no idea how many books I sold at BP, but it was not many, surely. All in all, a successful weekend, especially the event at Stories on Stage. Does that pencil out? Of course not! Barring those rare cases where a small press book catches that rare momentum, the small press writer will not make a livelihood of it."

Adding on to Evan's point, if you have a sales goal in mind—a bestseller list, selling out your first run, or over a thousand copies because that's what many small presses consider the rock star number—think about where you got that idea from. Somebody's comment on social media? A well-regarded resource website like Jane Friedman's? A famous writer talking about the process during a lecture? Is it a reliable source? Is the information coming from the tiny percentage of writers who actually do make a livable wage from their work? And if they *are* making money as a writer, is that because of their speaking fees? Taking editorial clients? Teaching?

Talk to the people in your literary community and find out more about real-world writers and their career trajectories. Especially if you are setting your sights on the stars. There's nothing wrong with aiming high, as long as you don't deflate yourself entirely if your dream doesn't come true.

But also: you don't need to have the same dream as other writers.

You don't have to define your success by theirs.

Or by anyone else's measurement system than your own.

RETURNS VERSUS SALES

OKAY, SO YOU'VE DONE A self-inventory about your intent, your available time, your finances, and your health, and you're ready to figure out where you want to submit your manuscript. Hold up another moment. This is important to share *before* we go any further, because it's another layer of understanding the impact of putting your creative work into the business world.

When authors receive sales numbers from their publishers, there's always an emotional value attached. Usually that value is arbitrary and disconnected from reality. What authors expect versus what publishers expect is usually shrouded in secrecy and shame. Or everyone at the publishing house is too busy to explain, reassure, or clue in authors about what might be a good number.

Which means authors are left to imagine whether their publisher is happy or not. We're great at making up stories, after all!

And these are hard questions to ask: *Are my sales good enough?* is pretty much the same as asking, *Do you still like me? Did I fail? Do you regret choosing my book? Will you even want to look at my next book?*

Not asking doesn't do us any favors, though. We—sensitive

souls and even the hardened, realistic writers—worry, whatever the number is. In the absence of information, that worry can become debilitating.

Maybe we did something wrong.

Or we could have done something better. More events. More social media posts. More . . . anything! Here's where saying no, holding a boundary, is apt to resurface and scare you. (*If only I had said yes to that podcast . . .*)

But how we think, as writers desperately wanting to be loved, is different than how publishers think. Most of the time, the publisher is happy with the numbers, or more likely, is *prepared* for the numbers. Where your book is in its life cycle matters when it comes to sales reports; after the first three months returns start coming in, and seeing numbers subtracted from your balance sheet feels cruel. Often whoever is sending these bookkeeping updates doesn't have the time or energy to imagine your response to the numbers, so they send the email and move on to the next author. Which leaves you either elated—on the off chance the numbers are better than you dreamed of, which is great!—or morose.

This emotional response to accounting is one I've worked really hard to address in my publishing life. I used to get all panicky at royalty time. It's when I really have to focus on the numbers, to admit to myself whether something is selling or not.

And then I have to tell the author!

Almost always, I land on the side of imagining my authors are sad to hear the latest reports. We tend to hope for milestone numbers—like selling another thousand or maybe even another two hundred. When thirty copies of a three-year-old book sell in a six-month pay period, I'm excited for the author because that means the book is still alive. It's still finding readers. But thirty copies doesn't seem like much weighed against the years of work that went into the author's career, that brought these pages into the world. Thirty copies is . . . almost nothing. So even though I'm pleased, and appreciative of how books don't disappear after their first three months out, I am simultaneously holding space for the author's emotions. I know, in my heart, that feeling anxious about the numbers isn't going to make them grow or change because as a distributed press, the payments for sales come 120 days after the books actually sold or were returned. The sales and returns happened long ago. How I feel about the numbers in the present won't change what happened four months ago.

This sense of stakes around money only increases when we, as authors, start adding up all the hours of work that a project took to complete. Not to mention the cost of writing workshops, generative retreats, the MFA in creative writing, that several-night hotel stay you splurged on to finish the next-to-last draft. It's expensive to learn the craft of writing from top teachers, and it's expensive to get into classes that teach you how to navigate publishing. So much of the learning comes with barriers to access—a huge reason why I started this book in 2016 despite ongoing doubts and competing projects and raising kids and caretaking the elders in my life—I actually finished it and put it into the world.

Here's the other big thing that gets misunderstood or shoved aside when it comes to sales: returns.

RETURNS: Books that sell into stores but don't sell to customers and then are sent back to the distributor (or directly to the press).

This is why the traditional wisdom exists about the three-month window for new titles. If a book doesn't sell in three months, it's often shipped back to the warehouse or wherever it came from. Gone! *Returned.*

The cost of the return to a press is more than just having the cost of the product flow back to the buyer. There are fees for handling returns. I'm not sure about shipping, if that's a buyer thing or if it's folded into the press side of the cost, or if it depends on the bookstore's contract with the distributor. So a press can actually *lose money* on a book and royalty reports can *turn negative*. It's pretty common, especially a year after the book comes out. That doesn't mean the book is dead; it just means the initial stock outlay was overexuberant, or overestimated, in relation the publicity and marketing efforts, and therefore books got sent back. Some books, instead of being returned to the warehouse, are marked DESTROY, which saves shipping and restocking fees, but feels harsh.

Always, unless it's a bestseller and copies sell out and more runs are printed and those copies get sent out, there are returns. Even with big-name books, after the early surges, once the supply and demand numbers flatten out and become more predictable, there will be returns.

Here's something authors don't always hear about. Books sold in stores actually have to be sold twice: first to the store buyers and then to the customers. The store that decides to buy the book is actually kind of borrowing the book on a temporary basis. Let's say your local bookshop brings five copies of your novel into their store. If one sells, and the other four don't, the store will have the opportunity to send the remaining four back. To *return* them. And guess what? The store gets a refund! It's like, lease our product, pay us for it up front, and if nobody takes it home to keep, we'll pay you back and you can send us the product back. If a book is returned damaged, it goes into a HURTS category and the bookstore isn't refunded.

Consignment gets around this cycle. A bookstore that wants to bring in books from a micropress that doesn't have distribution might ask the author or publisher if they can bring copies to the store and fill out a consignment agreement. The bookstore standard is a 40 percent discount off the cover price. That means the author or publisher gets paid 60 percent of the cover price when the bookstore works on consignment accounts. That could be the night of an event—sending the speaker home with earnings and what's left of their book pile—or it could be done on the bookstore's timeline if they, say, keep five books in stock and want to write checks for all consigned titles at the end of the quarter. If you're consigning and counting on profits to help you print more copies of your book, you will want to confirm payment terms before handing your product over, just so you know what to expect.

Sales Data Without Details

Some presses handle authors' nerves around royalties and returns by overinflating sales numbers. They're using the correct numbers for their books—or at least we have to assume they are—but they aren't explaining what kind of numbers they are. This has to do with that double sell I mentioned, where books need to sell into stores and then they need to sell to customers to be actual point-of-sale sales that get counted toward your royalties.

A writer sent out a newsletter saying she had sold eight thousand copies of her small press book in the first six months. It was a great book, but she didn't get major media coverage to build momentum with readers. She did tour with her book but not extensively. I couldn't understand, as a publisher, how she could have hit that kind of sales traction given what

I knew about the situation. Eight thousand is *huge* for a small press—even a distributed one, which hers was! Maybe the press knew how to market ebooks better than me, and most sales were ebooks? I have access to BookScan, the industry standard reporting tool, so to understand this mystery, I looked her up. Her sold number there was less than a thousand.

Could ebooks have made up the difference? Or was something else going on? I can't see ebook sales for other presses, because BookScan doesn't report those, but the author's Amazon numbers weren't hugely inflated for digital sales, and I would have expected to see that if her ebooks were a cash cow. After some more consideration, I realized that the press must be sending the sales numbers of books that are selling *into* stores. Which is a much more optimistic number than the number of actual sales.

Bookstore sales aren't true sales until someone pays at the cash register and walks out with your book in their hands. Yes, a customer might return it to the store after that, depending on the store return policy, but that's an infrequent occurrence. More commonly, a bookstore overorders a title, fewer readers than expected buy it, and what's left goes back as returns to make space for new shiny inventory—the next batch of Tuesday releases.

It's also costly for bookstores to hold on to stock that's not selling; if they go to the trouble of returning it, they get their capital back and can invest it in books that *might* sell better. Local authors often get priority for having their titles on shelves longer. A perk of being an author who works at a bookstore, in case you're thinking of changing jobs or picking up a part-time gig at your local indie: your title will keep getting sold and reordered, prolonging its life even more!

One of the scary moments in publishing is when stock is running low in the three months before publication. Does the publisher go back for another print run? Or do we hold tight and wait to see if the books that sold into stores actually sell to customers?

If we overprint, feeling sure the book is going to fly off shelves, we can end up with thousands of dollars invested in unsold stock, which then accrues expensive fees. It also costs time and money to reprint, and starting a reprint order early is better than waiting too long and having stock run out. But if you don't go back to press, because you don't want to spend the money or you don't trust the numbers, and the books actually sell through, you run the risk of having a hot book and no stock. Print-on-demand technology can help fill the gap between printings—an option that's great to have if turnaround times are slow or if you aren't sure you really need another run.

Back to the newsletter author and her eight thousand copies. She went ahead and printed more copies, paying out of pocket on the request of her hybrid press, because she thought all of those had sold to readers, when they had only sold to bookstores. That's an expensive choice based on partial information, and I suspect it became a terrible heartbreak.

QUERYING

READY? SET?

BEFORE YOU START IDENTIFYING AGENTS and/or small presses to submit to, pause and think about your writing life.

Why do you write?

How do you feel after a good writing session?

Who needs to hear the story you're telling?

How might your words make someone's life better? Or *clearer*, if *better* feels fraught?

What are some of your strengths as a writer? List five:

Shore yourself up, best you can, before you start submitting. This is a great way to bolster your confidence and tap into what makes your work special. You'll need those insights soon, when we get to the mechanics of query letters.

Return to this exercise as often as you need.

UNLESS YOU HAVE CONTACTS IN publishing, chances are you're submitting to people who don't know you, throwing your work into the wind and hoping someone catches on and sees potential in what you've created. This is often referred to as the *slush pile*.

 **SLUSH PILE**: The group of manuscripts that have been sent to an agent or a press without being requested. I've made the decision to quit using this phrase because it conjures up dirty snow, a messy melting that's more nuisance than potential treasure. A submissions pile, to me, feels a bit brighter and neater. Who knows what might be in there? Still, because it's a phrase you'll probably see around, I've chosen to define it.

Whatever they're called, unsolicited queries end up waiting for attention in a file or a folder or an email inbox. Often more pressing tasks take precedence. Responding to an author's email. Finishing another editorial pass on a book that's due to the designer.

While we as writers throw our courage to the wind when we submit, and we sometimes obsess over who might be paying attention, the other side is very different. Nobody has been breathlessly waiting for your book (probably). Eventually an intern or editor or assistant might take a peek if they have a few minutes to read, or if the pile of unread work is starting to feel stressful. If the person dipping their toe into your pages likes what's there, that peek might turn into a partial read or a request for the full manuscript.

Your goal is to get someone's attention and hold it long enough to get sorted into the maybe pile. You won't get a yes for your book with a quick glance at this earliest stage, when your submission is hanging out waiting to be noticed, but you *can* successfully avoid the no pile. That's the best you can hope for in this first round of sorting.

WHEN DO YOU KNOW YOU'RE ready to submit?

Over and over again, I hear from writers who started sending out their manuscripts before they were truly ready. A door opens, they race through it, and a deal doesn't materialize. They have to walk backward along the path and try again. Sometimes it takes a few false starts. Other times the rejections pile up, and the best thing you can do is start a new book while waiting for the next round of responses.

Looking back, I feel sure my first novel—the one that earned me that agent phone call and representation—wasn't ready to go out on submission. At that time in the commercial publishing world, voice-driven literary fiction by West Coast authors was hot. Editors were buying a lot of it. Some new blockbuster names were emerging, and my agent felt like I could be one of them. She told me I was going to have a big career. I know she believed in me, perhaps even as much as I believed in her, but that didn't make a deal manifest because my novel didn't have enough of a plot. The voice was precocious, original, and urgent, but my characters stumbled around the pages not really propelling themselves forward. That was the point—that was what I wanted to write, a twentysomething small-town book. But I didn't have the language to describe myself as neurodivergent or the understanding of why I wrote this lonely young woman into being. Not knowing how to talk about it, or the why behind it, probably were signs that it wasn't ready for the world. I wish my agent hadn't told me I'd make it big because my daydreams took off from there, and when the rejections came in they felt like dream stabbings, one after the other. I wish I had listened to Stevan Allred—acknowledged, in my heart, that representation really was just a leg in the door.

My second novel never made the rounds. I was so ashamed and saddened about losing my agent over it that I submitted it to one agent and one small press and then gave up, even though both offered personalized feedback. I didn't have the courage or the energy to set out on the publishing path again. That's when I stepped away from trying to publish my own work and started publishing others' work. It felt like a heart balm to give authors what they had been working toward even though I hadn't achieved it for myself.

With the manuscript that became my debut novel, I also sent it out way too early. I earned revise and resubmit requests; agents were intrigued by the concept, my query letter was good, and they liked my writing, but the manuscript itself wasn't ready. I hadn't published a book so my sense of what *finished* meant wasn't accurate. It was based on me realizing that I could keep changing punctuation around until the end of time—that I wasn't changing anything substantial on my own. That's not a bad reason to send a manuscript out: realizing you're only making tiny edits. There's a point that's like standing on the diving board at the community pool. There's a line behind you and water in front of you. You have to jump or say excuse me and climb back down off the ladder. Both are brave.

If you go for it and get rejected, then you can reassess. I always like to submit to a few places at once—not too many in case my pages or my letter aren't working, but enough so I'm not focused on one person or agency. Others suggest five or ten at a time, and that's a matter of personal taste. Before you start submitting, it's easy to use that imaginative brain of yours to picture all the yeses rolling in. Which feels good but doesn't necessarily prepare you for the reality: a lot of no-response nos and form-letter nos. The key to unlocking your next steps is patience, especially after you get your first few rejections.

Dian Greenwood, author of the debut novel *About the Carleton Sisters* (She Writes), spent twenty-five years working on her manuscript, completing other books before she circled back to her first. She had an agent representing the novel for a while, but when it didn't sell she worked with a developmental editor to revise, and then she started submitting on her own.

"It's like a garden," she said. "The roots need time to take hold and the plant needs to mature. You don't pull up carrots the first time you see the little leafy top sit above the ground. You have to wait."

COULD AN EARLIER VERSION OF my debut novel have found a home if I had been searching for a small press from the start? What if I had identified it as a small press book because it's omniscient and unwieldy, a twirl of threads and thoughts? Maybe I would have gotten here—published—faster. Or at least more efficiently.

An editor who worked with me on an early draft said she felt it was "perfect" when she saw it years before its eventual publication. I loved it then, too, because I had achieved what I set out to do. In fact, I loved my novel at several overlooks and rest stops on the journey toward pub date, all those pauses when I took stock of what I had on the page and liked what was there. I would have been happy with a finished copy of any of those incarnations. It would have been a different book, but it might have been in the world sooner.

Deciding when to submit is one of those things that doesn't have one right answer. Starting to submit is exciting: there's possibility! Your career as a writer is just getting started! You might get a windfall of an offer!

Especially if you're dreaming big and trying ever so hard to believe in yourself and your art, getting that first rejection feels like a finger snap against a house of cards. All those hopes fall down. Repetition doesn't make those nos feel any easier, but they stop being such a surprise after a while.

Every time a rejection comes in, you have a choice: keep pitching or pull back and revise (or give up). The more time and editorial work you put into your manuscript before submitting, the more fuel you'll have to stay the course, to keep believing in what's on the page.

ONCE YOU GET THAT MAGIC first acceptance for your first book, you'll have this concrete experience, this perch on which you can rest for a moment and judge. Career hindsight. We can't anticipate how we'll feel when we do get a yes, which choices we'll regret making earlier (or not making). But now, while we wait for attention, we can ask ourselves, with everything we do know: *Will I be okay if ___________?*

If you wait to submit and your writing group friends get book deals before you?

If you submit now and get rejected?

If you banish a project you love to a digital drawer and never pick it up again?

If you get a yes from a press that doesn't have distribution?

Okay, I realize, is relative. But sometimes asking these questions helps me get clearer on what I ought to do next. If I can't figure out what will make me feel good, whether I'm really ready to submit, thinking about what I'll regret is another way to eye the options.

CASE STUDY #12: To Revise or Not?

Let's say I'm trying to decide whether to turn my novel into a YA book or keep it adult fiction and submit it, and if the latter, whether I want to look for an agent or not.

When I first started getting feedback from agents and editors, I didn't know that I could simply ask *myself*. I just listened to *them*. I'm also easily convinced by people who see something good in my work—but that doesn't mean their way is the correct way. So many of the wrong turns I took with my debut happened because I got carried away believing in someone else's vision for my work.

My questions for this particular book problem might look like this:

How will I feel if I submit now and get a no-response rejection? Will I wish I had done another revision?

I'll get frustrated with myself for rushing and burning through a chance, or five chances, say, if I query five people. I don't think a revision pass would take very long; it's a clean manuscript, and I've had two developmental edits so far, plus conversations about what I might change. There's no risk if I make myself wait a while longer, if I do another pass.

How is the "you should make it YA" advice feeling? Do you want to be a YA author?

My agent and an outside reader both encouraged me

to reevaluate the novel for younger readers. There are a lot of reasons they cited, and I agree with most of them. But I keep coming back to how there should be books for adults that aren't driven by trauma. Making the novel YA would help explain why my protagonist, Violet, is socially immature and young seeming, but so would labeling her as autistic. Normalizing and centering her experience in an adult book is what I set out to do.

You have a clear plan for making it YA, but will you regret changing the genre?

I'm starting to think so. I believe there are readers like me out there who are naïve and stuck because of grief or neurodivergence or PTSD. Violet has always been stuck, ever since I created her; it's like the last ten years of her life don't exist. That's why collapsing those years, cutting them and making her younger, came up as an option. If I changed her to be younger, though, I'd be making her more like her peers, less neurodivergent, *more relatable to neurotypical readers*. Perhaps then she'd be more marketable. But I'm not sure I want to do that. It feels like the easy way out—and not true to my original vision of writing an adult book featuring an adult woman whose whole journey isn't about getting a date or a spouse. She's content on her own, if mired in the past.

What could you do instead?

Lean into my protagonist's oddness and get her decade-long grieving on the page more, so we see that her life stopped ten years ago. So we see her, now, floundering. That she hasn't grown up; she's kind of like Snow

White, hidden in her father's house, living the rest of her days out as a spinster even though she's in her thirties in this version. I wonder if I could play with the fairy-tale magic of it too. Like she's been asleep or something. Or I could think about it being middle grade—my current genre obsession. If I age the neighbor girl down by a few years, she could be the protagonist. That feels smarter than trying to write for teenagers. I'm just not that cool.

Where is the energy right now?

I'm definitely interested in this fairy-tale idea, like Violet lost someone important in her life and that extinguished her relationship with the outside world. I haven't wanted to diagnose her on the page as autistic or agoraphobic, but she's a deeply shy person and has chosen loneliness and her father's company over having a social life, if not a suitable 1920s spinster job like being a seamstress or a teacher.

OBVIOUSLY, IF YOU'RE AT THIS part of the publishing journey with your manuscript, your questions will be different. But the technique is the same. You probably know a lot more about your book than you think, even if you haven't admitted it to yourself yet.

BEFORE QUERYING, CONSIDER WHETHER THIS is the book you set out to write. If you did what you set out to do, that's awesome.

It's also a great check mark in your READY column. But if you aren't sure, especially if you want to focus on a specific theme or plot arc and those elements aren't fully on the page, that's a check mark in the REVISE AGAIN column.

When a friend asks you about your book, can you answer with focus and certainty? Do you know what the book is about? If yes, and if you can describe the story with passion, that's great, but is there a disconnect between how you talk about it and what is actually on the page?

You know the drill: focus and certainty mean READY, a disconnect means REVISE AGAIN. You have to be honest with yourself.

One of my favorite tricks to see if I'm ready for submissions is imagining what feedback might come in. To find this information, quiet your mind. Imagine coming upon your story for the first time as an outsider. What sticks out as imperfect, as unpolished, as a possible problem an editor might want to fix? What are you most worried about, craft-wise? How is the pacing? Do you really need the first three pages from an artistic perspective? Or are you pretty sure the story starts on page four? Whatever you can access from holding your manuscript at arm's length will help you decide if you're in query territory yet. Or not. Yet.

If your list is full of craft issues, or if you know one character's arc isn't working as written, maybe that's a sign to do another round of revision. If you've taken creative risks and aren't sure if they work, maybe it's time to ask a writer friend to exchange drafts or look for a freelance developmental editor you can afford.

Or maybe these are the risks you set out to take, you've done everything you intended, and you want to plunge on ahead. You believe there's space in the world for a book like yours even if it breaks a few rules or doesn't sit neatly in one category. You can always query, get rejected, and step back to reassess. It's not okay to resubmit to an agent or editor after a rejection unless they specifically offer a revise and resubmit.

REVISE AND RESUBMIT: Also known as an R&R, these are the golden rejections, the ones that tell you you're on the right track, but something isn't working quite right, at least for this particular reader. You'll want to really think about if you want to follow the advice, and if so, don't turn it around in two weeks. Take your time. Rework what you have. Really dig in to the revision. If you turn it in too fast a second time and you haven't done the required work, that door will close.

As an example of this readiness question, I had always worried about the final third of my novel, which introduced a brothel madam and her workers in Five Points, New York. I had reasons for this, ones that I thought were okay at the time, but when submitting I was most worried about whether sex workers would feel like I got it wrong. Whether the humor was too thin or the girls' lives too casually drawn.

Did I get the human cost of selling pleasure on the page? *My hope, but also one of my biggest fears.*

Did I need that detour for my protagonist to understand his societal power as a cisgender white man? *I decided I had done this work throughout the novel and didn't need another hundred-plus pages to prove the same point.*

I loved the idea of this effeminate, naïve young man being in a brothel and having the women explain things to him, but at what cost? It wasn't my material, from lived experience, and I hadn't gone to a sensitivity reader, perhaps because I already knew it wasn't where the book wanted to land. Can manuscripts *want* something for themselves? I like looking at a story from the outside like that, imagining what it needs instead of trying to enforce my will on what's there. But maybe a better way of thinking about it is that introducing a whole houseful of new characters in the final act was a literary challenge better left to nineteenth-century novelists, when serials were more forgiving and final manuscripts could be longer than four hundred pages. It was okay for them to go on (and on), but now? Especially with rising costs and paper shortages? It's not the best idea.

Anyway, my agent and I went out on submission with the really long ending and didn't get any takers. After a while an editor who was interested in the original version said it felt like two books. When it came time to look at small presses, I listened to that editor and changed the ending. I was not just listening to her voice; I was listening to all these questions piling up inside my brain about whether my impulse to create found (female) family in New York was actually working.

My new ending felt thin but more satisfying, and a benefit was bringing my character to an established family for the conclusion. I received an offer from Lanternfish with the new iteration and my editor there had excellent suggestions for making the ending more robust and in line with the rest of the novel. It was a great experience to work with her to capitalize on the potential of those new, weaker-feeling, less robust scenes.

Part of me wishes I had been more honest with myself from the start. If I had listened to myself about those ending doubts, maybe I would have written a new version before we went out on submission. Or while we were still on sub with the major houses.

If you get an R&R for your novel because the agent thinks the point of view should be third person and not first, or third person close instead of omniscient, you can decide to revise or not. What do you think? How long will it take? Does the idea of changing POV open up scenes or character development? What are the drawbacks to doing this work? Do you feel a rapport with this agent or editor and want to be repped by them? If you have a phone call or an email with revision information, how enthusiastic about your book does this person seem? Are they *your* person? If they love and understand the rest of your book, that might be a vote for trying their suggestion. But maybe you love what you have and don't want to adjust your vision for the book. That's back to asking yourself if you did what you set out to accomplish.

There's no wrong answer. Often I advise that writers try what's asked because they might always regret not trying it—especially if it's not a huge change.

Are your side characters too one-dimensional? Would the book be better if you gave them more life and plot points? Then maybe you should go for it.

Is the present-tense point of view getting in the way of the story itself? Too loud for a reader? You might try changing a few chapters just to see how it feels.

Does your story start in the wrong place? There are so many wrong places a manuscript can start—and often people who read lots of unpublished manuscripts can pick those up quickly. You might want to think about where else it could start.

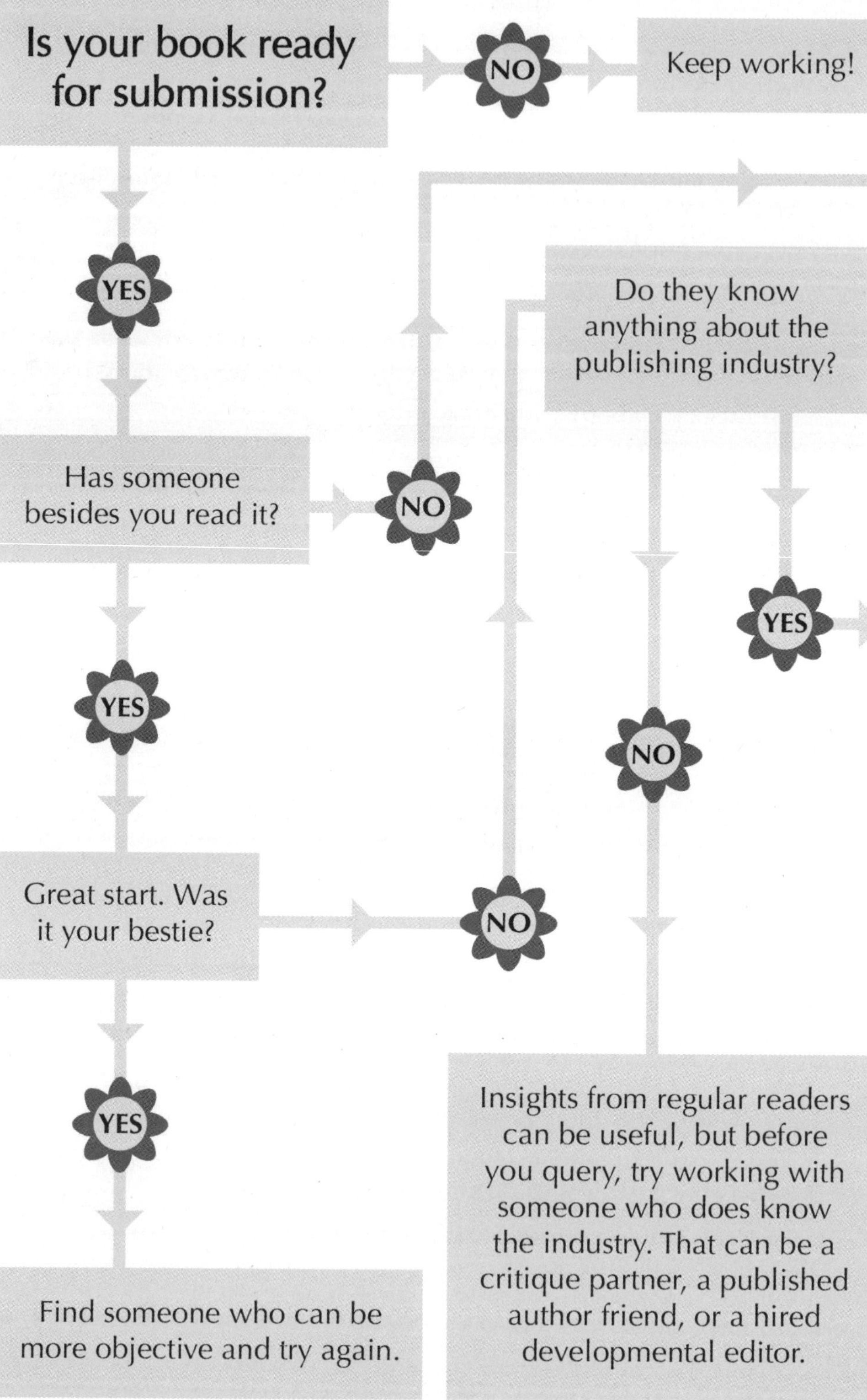

Is your book ready for submission?
NO
Keep working!
YES
Has someone besides you read it?
NO
Do they know anything about the publishing industry?
YES
YES
NO
Great start. Was it your bestie?
NO
YES
Find someone who can be more objective and try again.
Insights from regular readers can be useful, but before you query, try working with someone who does know the industry. That can be a critique partner, a published author friend, or a hired developmental editor.

Maybe you're ready, or maybe you are rushing things. Consider finding a reader or two or hiring a developmental editor who knows the industry and what's expected for your genre.

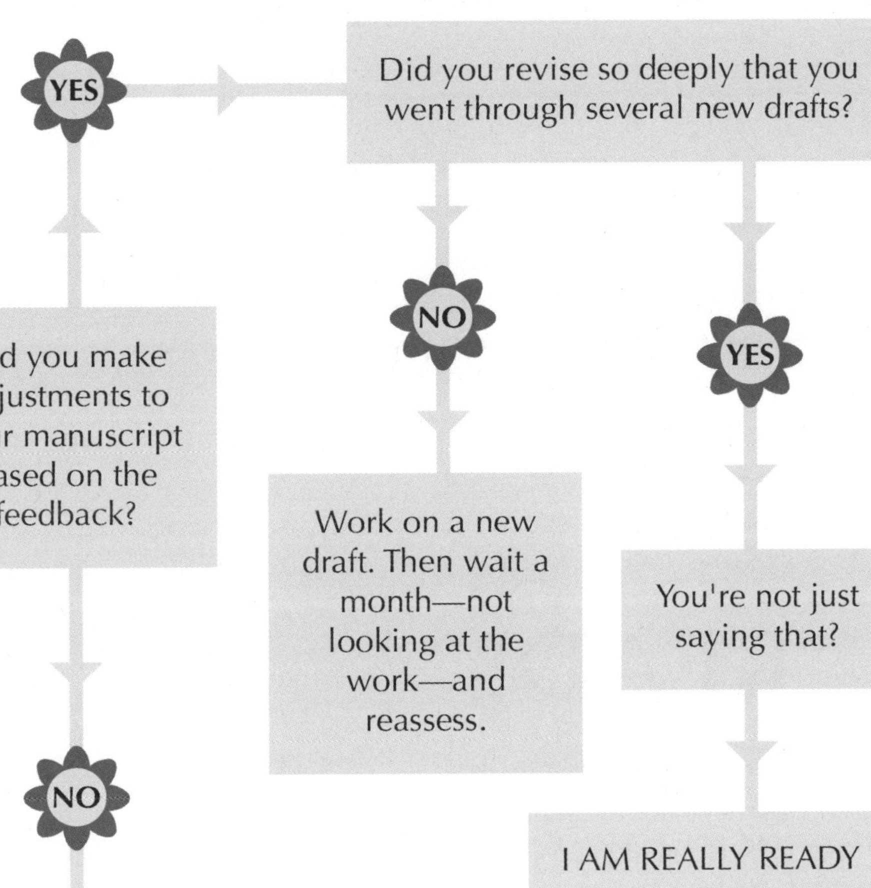

Find a few more readers and ask for notes. See what's consistent, what you agree with, and let go of the rest.

Query a handful of places. If your query gets interest, and the pages don't hold up, you'll find out soon enough. Then go back to the first question.

HOW DO YOU FIND A MATCH?

Read!

Read!

READ!

(Sorry, I got excited there.)

If you're not reading, especially if you're ignoring contemporary writing in your genre, you're missing out on an essential part of your publishing education. The more time you spend getting to know who is writing what, and which agents and presses are supporting those texts, the more you'll figure out your place in the ecosystem.

If you're interested in a particular press, or if your style or voice matches a particular author, seek those books out in your local library or bookstore. Acknowledgments are a great way to source information about who is behind the books you love.

Database resources include *Publishers Marketplace*, Duotrope, New Pages, Chill Subs, the *Poets & Writers* website, and Submittable. Manuscript Wish List is another fabulous resource for what agents are seeking. Some require joining the platform for the most useful information; Publishers Marketplace is a site you can join for a month just to research what agents are selling which books and what editors are buying them. You can sort the information by genre, by size of advance, and so forth.

Your local library and its staff are also great resources. Same with your local bookstore—but be aware it's a business, and staff aren't there as free reference guides: be respectful, offer to come back if the store is too busy, and buy at least one recommended book, especially if they've spent more than a minute or two helping you.

Writing conferences are great sources of information, even if you can't afford to attend. You can shop for agents and presses by studying conference websites to see who is actively seeking new clients. If an agent or small press editor is taking pitches at a conference, chances are they're looking for new authors.

In 2016 I asked Erin Harris, now the senior vice president at Folio Literary Management, how she shared her wish list with querying authors. She said:

> Finding a succinct way to describe my tastes and the kinds of submissions I'm seeking is always a bit of a challenge. In my bio, I want to be comprehensive, but also brief. Citing favorite authors, or recent books that have won my heart, has been a great way to talk about my interests in a kind of shorthand. When we pitch editors, we use comparison titles, or "comps" (i.e. this manuscript is like x book meets y book). So it feels very natural to use comps when I tell writers about the kinds of projects I'm looking for. For example,

> in the past when I've said, "I represent upmarket mysteries, thrillers, and suspense," I would receive submissions for very commercial novels with CIA agents and global terrorism plots that weren't the right fit for my list. When I qualify my interests by saying, "I want upmarket mysteries, thrillers, and suspense in the vein of Tana French, Gillian Flynn, Caroline Kepnes, or Ruth Ware," my hope is that authors will have a much clearer sense of what I'm actually representing. So far, this strategy has been effective.

Now that Erin has represented many more projects, her Folio bio is chock-full of successful titles she's worked on. I think it's so helpful when an agent can share specific titles, whether they are comps drawn from other agents' lists or their own clients' work.

I've noticed as Forest Avenue has increased the size of our catalog, our submissions periods have become more competitive because there's more information available about the kinds of manuscripts we love.

One thing to note about submitting to small presses is that many charge fees of $20 or more just to get your manuscript considered. A few years ago, contests with cash prizes cost money to submit, but regular submissions were often free. I used to urge authors to seek out the free opportunities.

These days, fees seem to be the norm. If you're focused on small presses, just know that your money will help the press continue to publish great books, even if your project isn't chosen. And, like always, don't spend what you can't afford in the hopes of recouping it. Be realistic in where you submit and how many fees you can afford.

AIM FOR THE MAYBE

YOUR GOAL IN SUBMITTING TO agents or editors is to get a yes, right?

Well, of course!

But how about we break that down and say your *first* step is to get sorted into the maybe pile.

When we're open for submissions at Forest Avenue Press, there are two categories at first—NO and MAYBE. On those first-look passes, we'd never jump over to YES because we haven't even read the whole manuscript yet. We may have read a dozen pages. Enough to feel like there's potential, but not enough to choose this one story over all the others.

Besides, once we start to winnow, we will have to look at manuscripts side by side. Does one fit our mission better than the others? Is one better written than the others? Do we know how to sell a book like this—or not? Is this familiar territory or does it feel fresh and new?

So really, your job as a writer is to get shuffled, at first, over into that MAYBE pile. Don't make it easy for us to say no. That means be nice, don't argue, don't threaten us, don't use gimmicky fonts, don't misgender us, don't claim we're bad at our jobs if we don't see your potential, and so forth. In other words: if you're kind and professional and if you research where you're submitting, you'll have the best chance to land in the middle pile, in the group of possibilities.

In the next few chapters we'll look at some components of your query journey and some common missteps so you can avoid them and increase your chances of MAYBE. Once you get there, into the possible acquisition pile, it's all about your manuscript: the writing, your characters, all the work you've done on it. We'll look at some of these specifics next.

TITLES

TITLES ARE A GREAT SALES tool, not just for publishers seeking readers' approval but for us as writers. A great title can move your project into the MAYBE category or get a few pages read ahead of a less notably titled manuscript.

But they're often underappreciated in the querying phase, since it's likely that a future agent or editor will change the title. In the early stages a title is a placeholder, but sometimes we get attached and don't question it before submissions. A great title can make your project stand out; a not-great one can make your query easier to pass over. You *should* think twice—three times—twenty times!—about your title before querying.

Here are some things to consider.

There's a lot of misinformation about this topic, so to clear it up: titles can't be copyrighted. That's something important that I didn't know until I became a publisher. Your title can bear resemblance to someone else's title—or it can be exactly the same as someone else's. That's legit and okay. That doesn't mean it's a good idea, though, especially if the other book has sold well. Chances are, if the established book has sold decently, naming your book the same thing may seriously harm your discoverability, confuse readers, and perhaps make an agent or editor gloss over your query. On the other hand, if there's a fantasy novel with your title that was published in the eighties, and you've written a cozy mystery with the same title, you'll probably be okay sticking with it. If you're writing a reimagining or fairy tale retelling, you might play with a version of the original title or go with something completely different and refer to the inspiration in your description.

I asked Dan Lazar of Writers House what makes a great title. "Great titles should be memorable. Sometimes that's short and punchy, like *Dork Diaries* by Rachel Renée Russell, *The Deviant's War* by Eric Cervini, or even a one-word like *Juliet* by Anne Fortier or *Mexikid* by Pedro Martin. Other times, longer and lyrical can work: *The Little Giant of Aberdeen County* by Tiffany Baker or *The Book of Madness and Cures* by Regina O'Melveny or *I Woke Up Dead at the Mall* by Judy Sheehan."

Novelist Tracy Manaster changed both her novels' starter titles with her agent's support. "There's a bend in the road between my home and my day job office where I came up with the two titles at the last minute before we sent them out to publishers," she said. "It's a good bend in the road! I could get superstitious about it, but I drive past that bend in the road four days a week. Like a pianist practicing scales, eventually you'll hit on something if you practice enough."

Tracy's debut novel, *You Could Be Home by Now* (Tyrus), first existed as *Slow News Week*. Perhaps the original would have been easier to abbreviate and turn into a hashtag, she said, but as a subplot gained strength and the book grew in scope, she worried it didn't fit the story anymore.

Enter the bend in the road, an epiphany, and a new title. "I do like titles that are sort of like a catchphrase, phrases familiar to you in everyday life that become more complicated, given the context of the book," Tracy said. "I think *You Could Be Home by Now* does that a little more aggressively than *Slow News Week*. To me, it's more evocative of the longing of the thing."

If you don't have an agent to weigh in on your title choice or a bend in the road that triggers literary epiphanies, then you need to get serious with yourself about how your title is working.

You may have chosen the perfect phrase to represent your work, but will it work on the shelf when a browser knows nothing about what's inside? Will it reach your intended readers?

Many titles don't make sense until the reader is partway through reading. They can be brilliant pieces of language or evocative phrases, but if they don't work without context, you'll be at a disadvantage not just in submitting but when your book is on a shelf. Readers like to be drawn in by titles, not mystified. When it arrived in my submissions inbox, poet Kate Gray's debut novel, an unblinking look at boarding school bullying, was known as *Skin Drag*. The physics concept of drag, deftly explained by one of Kate's two teacher protagonists, works really well with the novel's themes—but here's the catch—only *later*, when you get to the explanation.

My designer and I started worrying about how those words would work on the cover without one of us standing nearby to explain the physics. *Skin Drag* sounds like Kate Gray's voice, it launches a strong theme in the novel, and it wouldn't get confused with another book, but what would that title lead a reader to expect? Probably not two lonely teachers taking turns narrating.

Kate's wife Cheryl shared alternative options with friends and coworkers to get a broad overview, then accumulated the results in a spreadsheet. The options that scored best had the word *sky* in them, and after sitting with *Crack the Sky* for a while, Kate landed on *Carry the Sky*, which I loved as well.

"I also wanted to get the sense of Hercules in Jack's character, how heavy a world on one's shoulders can be, especially when you're the only one doing the lifting," Kate said. "He is the one with integrity in the end."

The beautiful cover art by Forest Ave designer Gigi Little features hand-folded origami cranes flying across the page, filling in the line between water and air with intricate precision. *Carry the Sky* is also more uplifting, as a piece of language, than the other options. Kate's book, while about the weight of being different in a world of uniformity, has moments of joy, humor, grace, and plenty of love.

Carry the Sky also evokes an undercurrent of responsibility, how we must carry the weight for others at certain times, when they cannot bend their own backs to such weight, and how we cannot possibly carry everything (the sky) on our own, but we need to try, to keep trying, no matter what, and to let others help us when we are feeling lost.

Singing Lessons for the Stylish Canary had many temporary titles—LOST NOTES, THE SERINETTE, and THE BRIGHT SIDE all stuck around for a few years. We sold it as THE BRIGHT SIDE, a reference to the always-sunny weather in the French village I imagined, but friends who had seen the movie with the same name really didn't like that. Plus it didn't sound whimsical enough. It might be that some of our rejections were because the working title didn't do enough work. Or maybe not. It's impossible to know unless an editor says the title was part of the decision.

The final title, chosen in conversation and with a lot of back-and-forth between me and the Lanternfish editorial team, has more rhythm and flavor than all of those early options. It's harder to remember, though, than some of my earlier versions. Readers often want to talk to me about my book and they get the words wrong or can only conjure a piece of the title. Which is fine; it's just another piece of information you can use to investigate your current title.

Title Assessment

IF YOU'RE DOUBTING YOUR TITLE, pick words and phrases out of the first fifty or a hundred pages. Make a big list—they don't all have to be viable options—then look at your list and spend some time thinking about what's on there. Perhaps a new (better) possibility will manifest.

With your working title or a short list of possibilities, ask yourself these questions:

- What does the phrase project about your book to someone who knows nothing about its contents?
- Does your title make sense without cover art? Without a description next to it?
- What kind of visual image does your title bring to mind? Does that image match the manuscript? Why or why not?
- Is your title an invitation?
- What kind of readers would think, *Ooh, that sounds interesting*, and are those the readers who would love your book?
- If you're a big social media user, think about using your title as a hashtag that other people could recognize and share. Does it work in that context?
- What other books have the same title, if any? How recently have they been published? Are they bestsellers? If so, consider steering clear,

or you'll never be at the top of the search results list.

- When you talk about your manuscript, do you say *my book* or use the title in conversation? If you're not using the title, maybe you are instinctively recognizing it's not doing enough work (or the right work). Or you're afraid that your friends will misunderstand your book because of how you have condensed its essence into a short phrase. Chances are, if you're reluctant to use your title in conversation, you should keep brainstorming.
- Think about doing informal title research and creating a spreadsheet. You can ask friends, coworkers, neighbors, family, or some combination of people. Which options get the most interest? Which words have the most resonance?
- Ask a favor from ten people who don't know what you're writing. Tell them your current title. What associations come to mind when they hear the phrase? Ask them to guess what your manuscript is about based on the title. See how close the results come to what you expect to hear. If nobody gets it, then maybe it's time to go back to the first fifty pages and hunt for new options. Your title isn't necessarily in the manuscript, but you might find words or concepts that lead you to a better one.

SHALL I COMPARE THEE . . .

COMP TITLES SELL BOOKS. THAT'S short for *comparison,* although some people say it's short for *competitive*. Mostly you'll hear the short version: *comps*.

Identifying books that are similar to yours serves several functions: it shows you've studied the literary landscape, it confirms that people buy books like yours, and the list itself can help agents or editors think about what kind of audiences might want to read your book.

There are a few ways comps can work to get your project some extra attention in the submissions pile. The most common is as shorthand about the unpublished manuscript. Sometimes it takes the form of an *X meets Y* comparison. For *The Remnants* by Robert Hill, about the last three near-centenarian residents in a town full of genetic oddities, I've used *Geek Love* meets *Tinkers,* which I find hilarious. And—more to the point—it works for the kind of literary fiction readers who might want to read *The Remnants*. But it didn't work at all when I pitched a movie executive who hadn't heard of either book.

After I presented a two-hour lecture on query letters, a

writer approached me to ask about her epic space fantasy novel. She had been stuck on this issue of comps for a while.

"There aren't any books out there like mine," she said. "What's your advice on finding a comp?"

While what she shared with me about her plot was indeed original, I redirected her to think about other epic fantasies, preferably but not necessarily also set in space; there should be a common theme or style she could mention.

I used *Olive Kitteridge* as a comp for *A Simplified Map of the Real World* because:

- They both have a small-town setting; Maine for *Olive* and Oregon for *Simplified Map*.
- Both linked short story collections have characters that come in and out of the different stories.
- *Olive Kitteridge* won the Pulitzer and was made into an HBO miniseries, so it was an extremely well-known example of that format, and more recent (and therefore relevant) than Sherwood Anderson's *Winesburg, Ohio*.

Of course the comp breaks down at a certain point. Olive is the protagonist of *Olive Kitteridge*; *Simplified Map* has several main characters. And if we're talking sales, *Olive Kitteridge* doesn't work as a comp because a big five title by an established, best-selling author will perform much differently than a small press title by a debut author.

That brings us to another way the industry uses comp titles. Small presses with distribution must push realistic comp title data to the sales reps so they can use it when pitching independent bookstores and other book-buying accounts. We're required to pick titles that are two years old or newer and will perform similarly in the marketplace as our new title. So *Olive Kitteridge* doesn't work because it's too old and definitely not a sales comp. A Random House book by an established author, which happened to win the Pulitzer and get made into a TV miniseries, will surely sell many, many more copies than a small press title by a debut author.

In more recent years the qualities of a comp title have narrowed even further. If you're publishing a trade paperback original, you need to use trade paperback originals for comps—not just the paperback release of a hardcover. So that's another reason *Olive Kitteridge* doesn't work; it first came out in hardcover, while Stevan's is a trade paperback original.

Finding comps for a sales team is different than pitching. If you're pitching an agent with the intent of seeking a deal with one of the major New York publishers, it's okay to go big with your comps as long as you can justify why they're a match.

If you're pitching a small press, though, you might want to consider offering reasonable comps—not famous, best-selling ones. If that press has published something similar in subject or theme, then point to that, even if it's on the older side. A book from a similar-sized press, listed as a comparison title in your query, shows you have understanding of the market and reasonable expectations. I once rejected a manuscript because the author had been previously published with a big press, and she wrote that she couldn't wait to be on NPR again. I knew I couldn't guarantee that! What the letter told me, though, was that I'd likely spend the next few years trying to fulfill near-impossible expectations, had I accepted the manuscript.

Of course, nobody wants to compare their book to a title that bombs in the marketplace, so don't pick too-obscure options or ones that only have five-star reviews (assumedly from the author's friends and family).

When it comes to this topic, I have a tactical advantage as a publisher: a subscription to BookScan. It's hugely powerful to be able to look up the sales stats of a book and confirm whether or not it will be a reasonable sales match given my predictions for the title I'm researching. I often do use novels from big five publishers because their sales stats are in line with what I expect ours to achieve. I'm always on the lookout for impressive debuts or midlist titles that fit my aesthetic so I can add them to the comp lists. It's another tool I can give the sales reps, as long as I'm accurate and thoughtful about choosing them.

Memoirs and creative, story-based nonfiction need similar comp title strategies as novels, but subject-oriented nonfiction comps can be found by looking up other titles with that same subject, comparing price points and page counts, and seeing which ones would sit nicely alongside yours.

Make Your List

- WHAT BOOKS ARE LIKE YOUR book? Think about style, voice, plot, theme, and genre. Split your comp list into blockbusters and more realistic choices so you can use them as needed.
- Make a list of ten agents (or editors if they're small press titles) who have worked on those books.
- Look those individuals up, see who is open to queries, and what they're currently seeking. Agents often share their wish lists on the platform formerly known as Twitter, especially with the #mswishlist hashtag, so that's a real-time resource that might be more relevant than whatever the agent's website page says.
- Go to the library. Study an industry journal,

like *Publishers Weekly, Booklist, Bookforum, Foreword Reviews,* or check out the online *Shelf Awareness* archives. What books are coming out in the next few months that are like yours? Mark down relevant comps and their pub dates. Then search online for reviews, interviews, features and conversations about those books, especially once their pub dates arrive and pass. That will be useful information for publicizing your own title down the road; in the meantime, if you decide to approach an agent attached to the project, you can in a sentence or two show that you've been engaged in how well X title is doing and show your savvy and willingness to learn.

- Decide how you're going to track your submissions before you send anything out, and then create that document or buy that notebook. Saying *I'll do it later* makes it easy to ignore when later rolls around.
- If you are interested in hybrid or self-publishing, find two or three friends who have done it to help you make your budget. Often paying a hybrid press an up-front fee sets your expectations (i.e., this project costs this much money). But the closer you get to pub date, the more cash outlays may pop up. Costs for advance reader copies, publicity efforts, mailing books to reviewers, the actual cost of the print run, the shipping costs for that print run, and—possibly, if your book sells well—a reprint. Even if you feel like you have control of the

numbers, these pieces can add unexpected price tags. When you're that far in, it's hard to back out without completely losing your initial investment. So ask all the questions to the company you're working with, people who have worked with them, and your literary friends.

YOUR HOOK

PART OF WHAT MAKES YOUR manuscript yours—and allows you to talk about it as marketable—is the *hook*. This has been defined and unpacked in countless how-to writing books by countless experts, often in conflicting terms, but in each case the definition gets at what makes your manuscript special. What gives it a spark? What gives it legs?

The hook is, in essence, your elevator pitch—the answer to the question, What is it about? that could be delivered in the time it takes to get to your hotel floor at a conference.

Some people define the hook as something that occurs in the first few pages of the novel, connecting it to the inciting incident that jump-starts the action. Others say it happens within the first fifty pages.

Middle grade author Rosanne Parry said, especially for a debut author trying to break in, "It's not just that you need something good. You need something distinctive that says, *here's somebody new on the scene who's right up there with the flavor of the day,* someone who has something distinctive to add to the conversation."

Sarah Cypher, freelance editor and author of *The Skin and Its Girl*, defines the hook as the first point of interest. "That point of interest can be an intriguing event, an unusual setting or situation, truly exceptional point-of-view writing, or anything else that promises the reader a journey."

I think of a hook as the sales handle—what short combination of words would get our press's sales reps nodding in recognition when I pitch a particular manuscript?

Your hook could be the inciting incident in the first few pages, or the first big turn in your novel where the plot really starts rolling, somewhere around page fifty. It could be the question at the heart of your story or an unforgettable setting. It's not necessarily the down and dirty distillation of your full pitch, but it might be. Or your hook might be a straight-up sales handle—a few words that might be found on the front cover (also known as a *reading line*) or at the top of a press release, something catchy, smart, and evocative. Whatever it is, your hook must grab the reader.

When I talk about Stevan Allred's *A Simplified Map of the Real World*, I'll often get a flash of understanding if I say it's like *Olive Kitteridge* but with more divorce. That is, to people who have read *Olive Kitteridge*. Otherwise the gimmick doesn't work; the hook has little allure. (And note here that I'm using it in conversation, not as a piece of metadata promising *Olive Kitteridge*–sized sales.) That can work better for a certain subset of audience than calling the book a linked short story collection set in a rural Oregon logging town.

It might seem too soon to consider your hook when you're in the early phases of a manuscript, dabbling with possible openings or creating your characters, but as a publisher, I see so many novels that are written well but don't grab our committee of readers. These usually languish, not earning any comments at all, because there's nothing wrong with them but they also aren't as gripping as other options. Those are often the hardest to decide on; we can't winnow them out easily because they look like the kind of thing we might like, but there's just something missing. If you do the work of figuring out your hook and how to articulate it, you'll create urgency. It'll be harder for an agent or editor to breeze past.

APPROPRIATE LENGTH

RESEARCH THE STANDARD WORD COUNT in your genre and, once you have a finished draft, see if your manuscript is in the acceptable zone. If not, it's not impossible to get a deal, but you are making it easier for an editor to shuffle you into the NO pile. Especially if your book is far longer than standard. Extra pages mean everything will cost more, from paying editors to sending out review copies.

Longer = Heavier = Higher postage

In a tight-margin business, this matters. Of course there are some epic, industry-dazzling books that are way longer (or shorter) than standard, and if you've written one, great! You can submit it and hope for the best. It's not *wrong*; just be aware if you get rejections right away that they may have to do with your word count, not your query letter or your protagonist's journey.

So how do you know what size manuscript yours should be? Lots of websites and genre-specific organizations offer this information; it's a great question to research online because word count preferences do change over time. Recently, for instance, there's been a trend of calling novella-sized books of forty thousand words *novels*, mostly because *novellas* are such a small category compared to novels. Shorter books mean less money to print, which means the price point can be lower, possibly stimulating more sales. Or the price point can be in line with other titles, leaving a higher margin for the publisher and making the book less of a risk to invest in.

None of this has to do with artistic merit or talent; it's business. And practicality. With TikTok, Instagram, YouTube Shorts, and other high-energy, quick-burst content, attention spans have been waning. I'm a huge reader, but I often catch myself scrolling through other people's content when I could turn my phone off and open a book.

Once you've done some basic research, look up books in your genre; if you don't have a copy on your bookshelf, check a site like Bookshop.org because price point and page count are listed in books' metadata. You'll likely have to scroll down below any descriptions and reviews to the data block that includes the ISBN, any relevant subject categories, and the pub date; that's where you'll find the publisher and page count. Then you'll want to figure out how to take your word count and turn it into an estimate of a finished book's page count. That depends on a lot of factors including font size, leading (how wide the spaces are between lines of text), page margin width, and whether all chapters start on the righthand (recto) side as tradition would have it, or if they start at the next blank page, which is more common now to save on paper. Usually our books are in Palatino font size 10.5 or 11 and have generous margins; an 80,000-word novel will land around 325 to 350 pages. Our 100,000-word books, which are rare but we do have some of them, go to 400 pages or even over. Shorter books, like a 65,000-word novel, will be shy of 300 pages.

Fifteen years ago, when I started down the path of being a

serious novelist, we aimed for 100,000 words. That was the standard acceptable word count. These days, with big New York houses folding into each other and social media competing for clicks and eyeballs, the standard word count for a literary novel is 80,000 or less. Worldbuilding novels, like sci-fi or historical, where the setting needs a lot of attention because it's vastly different from our present-day life on Earth, can have higher word counts to allow for the extra setting details.

It's true that some 150,000-word novels earn million-dollar advances and incredible buzz, and some 45,000-word ones earn prestigious awards and the same level of industry buzz.

Writers House agent Dan Lazar said an out-of-the ordinary word count shouldn't impact a title's chances with the big five, unless it's in a very prescribed category or genre, such as a romance novel or a children's picture book. "Or unless it is way, way shorter or way, way longer than most," he added. "But publishers are mindful of printing costs, and we see a range of word counts in successful books."

Keith Rosson, when he sold his horror novel *Fever House* to Penguin Random House, was asked by his editor to add 30,000 words to the project, landing it at 119,000.

The bigger the book, the more expensive it is to produce. This becomes especially important for small presses running on shoestring budgets, pouring prerelease dollars into publicity and bound galleys, hoping that in a year or two or three, those dollars will be earned back plus a bit of profit.

But what if it's art?

When I see a 167,000-word manuscript in my submission pile, the word *art* doesn't even cross my mind. That's nearly three times the size of our shorter novels. Production costs will skyrocket, including for advance review copies, and I'll be pouring a significant chunk of annual revenue into one book instead of several.

But—you say—what if it's unlike any other book?

Print costs depend on the paper being used, the current market cost of that paper (it fluctuates), whether the book is printed overseas or in the US, and whether there are any extra special touches, such as French flaps or deckled edges.

But—you say—what if I need all 167,000 words?

A longer book takes more hours and staff time to edit and lay out. It takes more of a reader's time to read and then review. It takes more dollars and energy from everyone who encounters it.

If your book is art, if it's unlike any other book, and it must be 167,000 words to achieve said brilliance, then best of luck to you in finding an editor who falls in love and can convince the marketing department to agree to the acquisition. It can happen.

Lazar also told me, "If your book is twenty percent longer than others in the genre, but you've edited til you're blue in the face and can't even think of changing a comma, that should be fine. But if your book is way, way longer—almost double!—then you really have to justify it. The book just needs to be extraordinary. Easy, right? Ha. Consider long books like *The Goldfinch, Wolf Hall, Jonathan Strange & Mr Norrell*; perhaps they could have been shorter, but it sure didn't matter in the end. Or books like *City of Thieves, Mothering Sunday, The Children Act*; perhaps they could have been longer, but their authors justified the form in spades."

Our shortest Forest Ave titles are in the 45,000 to 60,000 range—and they're pretty rare. They have to be stylistically fantastic to pack a huge punch in a short space. Some of our longest books—*The Alehouse at the End of the World* and the anthology *City of Weird*—are among our bestsellers. And one of our shortest, *Chicano Frankenstein*, is a top seller too.

AUDIENCE AND PLATFORM (SIGH)

YES, OKAY, *FINE*. SINCE WE'RE talking about querying, we have to address audience. As writers in the twenty-first century, we are expected to engage with the world beyond the page. We can't entirely ignore the prevailing wisdom about knowing your target market and understanding how to reach those folx.

Our audiences are out *there,* and to find those readers we have to figure out where they are, how to talk about our work in ways that persuade those readers to care, and how to consistently feed social media accounts so we *appear* vibrant and interesting.

Sometimes it feels absurd, this focus on identifying your readers as if they are sheep who all love, say, mayonnaise, or pigeons who prefer sesame seeds to sunflower seeds. SFF author Tina Connolly, author of the Seriously Wicked series (Tor Teen) and *Glitterpony Farm* (Chooseco), recently shared this with her writing friends on social media: "I dreamed we were all at a party complaining about the weird self-promo things we end up doing as writers and I was like 'ugh I had to hang-glide over the city yesterday' and one of you was like 'seriously, I had the toy company out here all this week because I agreed to be in the writers' dollhouse series where they make a miniature of you and your actual house.'"

There are some authors who succeed without having robust online presences—Julia Glass, Patrick DeWitt, and Elena Ferrante among them. But everyone else, prevailing wisdom says, need to engage or publishers won't see you as viable. Not just your sweated-over, revised a million times, tearstained pages: you, the person. Most of us don't sign up for public-facing lives when we decide to write a book, though. I'm Gen X and I grew up thinking of writing as a way to communicate without engaging with people directly. I wanted my words out there, not my *self*.

Of course, if you're going after a major deal or trying to get on the radar of a top-tier agent who expects certain follower counts, then go for it! Nonfiction agent Ted Weinstein puts it this way: "Major publishers and agents look for a high level of commercial potential to interest them in working with an author. Instead of 'If I get a book deal then I'll be famous,' the reality is 'Get famous first,' which gives an author the greatest chance for traditional publishing success. But for any author who just wants to write and get their work out into the world, there are many paths that don't require major publishers, major agents, or major public platforms."

If you are famous or you want to become famous, that's great—the social media part of your writing career might not cost you in existential angst. Maybe you have a successful business, and a book will help you sell your product or earn national acclaim. Maybe you have a concept or insight that will make people's lives more functional—if only you can get your message out widely. Maybe you have an award-winning podcast and know from your episodes exactly what kind of manuscript you want to write and who will read it. Those are all legitimate reasons to write a book—and if that's you, there are plenty of resources out there to help you leverage and grow your platform.

I wrote this book for those of us who write because we love it. Because we feel called to string words together on sentence chains, to bedazzle them with adjectives and metaphors, or to strip and twist them like bark into rough cords, spare but strong. We have stories to tell. Our love of language keeps us returning to the page. We survived something and what we know now might help someone else. We're compelled to put words down and pull them back up again, like setting wallpaper, until no wrinkles or seams show. Whether we want to shock, surprise, elucidate, or entertain, figuring out the *how* keeps our brains buzzing.

And eventually, when we get our words out in the world, we have to stand beside them. As ourselves, or a public-facing version of ourselves.

THERE CAN BE BITTERNESS, FRUSTRATION, and even rage when a writer finishes a book, lifts their head, and realizes that the self-imposed creative solitude is essential for creating a manuscript, but the opposite—a rah-rah, out-there presence online—is what you need to sell it. Many of the strategies for building followers require cash up front—like with digital book tours, hiring a publicist, or taking classes on social media—and *then* they cost a lot of hours making content, responding to feedback, and connecting with other content makers. Not all of us have enough energy, financial resources, health, or interest. Personally, I'd rather be writing my next book. My fingers are sore and arthritic and it costs me to type. Knowing I don't have unlimited capability helps me center on what matters most to *me*.

It's not that I'm opting out so much as I'm opting to participate at a level that feels sustainable to me. I did the whole blogging thing in the early 2000s and stressed myself out with regular deadlines and replying to everyone. I don't want to have that kind of pressure around my Insta feed. I get why followers are considered a necessity, though. In an artistic pursuit that often can't be measured, where we can't control who discovers our work or what they think of it, attaining specific numbers on our socials is a concrete goal.

But here's the thing. This idea of *success* is based on a capitalist norm. *Selling* books. *Earning* royalties. Getting enough sales so your next book might sell for a higher advance. And all the bells and whistles that come with that—glossy magazine coverage, book club pickups, reviews in *Slate* and *Electric Literature* and the *Rumpus*, and we may as well hope for the *New York Times* and maybe a mention in *People* while we're at it.

Platform-building advice is meant for a particular kind of book experience, one that harnesses online visibility in an effective way that makes you, the author, look successful. Or helps you, the author, sell your services as an expert. Sometimes a big platform translates to book sales, especially if you are famous, but mostly it doesn't. If you have, say, a memoir about cooking with your grandmother coming out in six months, and people follow your socials because of your dog videos, your fans aren't going to immediately rush out to get your book.

Sonja Thomas, author of *Olive Blackwood Takes Action!*, said it this way at the 2024 Willamette Writers conference: "I don't think you can move the needle, and if that's what you focus on, you'll be miserable. Do what comes naturally. Do what you love."

And here is a nice reminder: just because someone *looks*

successful doesn't mean they are meeting sales goals (theirs or their publisher's). It means they've invested time into building the appearance of success. I often see writers crowing about big achievements—another five gold-medal awards, a billboard in Times Square, product placement in a fancy hotel—and know it's because they paid for access. Most writers, who aren't inside the industry, assume they have earned these accolades. I get why people put cash down for more opportunities; it's how the world works. But I also don't like how this system prioritizes those with expendable income and makes the rest of us feel shame, or like our books aren't as good as those other ones, when really it's all about how much money you're able to pay.

When we hear about platforms that work and customer/client engagement, those of us who aren't trying to become famous can often feel left behind, dejected, or even hopeless about the potential for selling our books. Even when the person isn't bragging but is giving information to help other writers, it can feel a little abrasive. Or like you've fallen behind and you'll never catch up. Capitalism works that way—fueling self-deprecating thoughts of *value*. It's easy to forget we are talking about a deeply personal art: writing.

If you aren't positioning yourself as an expert, if you don't want fame, if you just want to have your book in the world, then you get to choose if you want to play the followers game or not. I choose not to. I make this choice over and over, every hour that I don't participate in social media in the way that follower-focused people do. I don't post at specific times or at a standard frequency. I want to stay genuine, to use my voice, to be me on social media. The moment it feels like work—and this holds true of my newsletter too—I readjust.

I manage two types of accounts on Instagram, Facebook, and X—Forest Avenue and personal pages. I like sharing others' accomplishments. I rarely cross-post photos between my accounts; if I go to sales conference for a Forest Avenue book, I might share a picture of that book in the Publishers Group West office. Then I'll post a separate picture on my personal account of a book I'm reading or a neat reflection in a window. I glaze over when I see the same photo on multiple social channels, and that experience has driven me to post different content in different places.

Poet Armin Tolentino, author of *We Meant to Bring It Home Alive* (Alternating Current), has opted out of the social media game almost entirely, just keeping a presence on one site—currently Bluesky. He's also well loved by the literary community and frequently invited to read his work at events. I know several other writers who have chosen the same path—a toe dipped in one place, letting the rest stream on without them.

I asked Armin about why using a single platform works for him. He said: "I write because writing is fun. Even when I hate writing, I love writing. And I love many of the ancillary things that come with being a writer. For instance, I love talking to other writers about writing. I love going to readings and hearing others share their words. But I don't like trying to boost sales by asking random netizens for follows (sorry to my publisher who is awesome and deserves better)."

He continued: "If I'm being truthful, I also don't like the version of me that would seek virtual attention from strangers. Trust me, I wouldn't turn down a million followers fawning over my book. But the work involved to make me seem interesting online sounds exhausting and fake. I'd rather be writing."

WHAT MATTERS MOST TO YOU may not be the same.

IT FEELS LIKE INDUSTRY "WISDOM" has us asking the wrong question: *How do I increase my follower count?*

What if that's backward? What if we start with what we want?

How do you want to show up in the world? Do you want to build yourself into a brand and publish a book that connects to that brand? Great.

Do you want to write something strange and beautiful? Cool. You should go for it!

What kind of social media presence would you choose? If you could choose? (Because, really, you can!)

How much time do you want to spend sharing content versus actually *writing*?

If you opt out of the race, knowing there's no such thing as a winner anyway, then what? Can you realign your goals? Separate publishing and capitalism?

Eventually, if you sign with a traditional press, you will be urged to promote your book. You might have to adjust these decisions at the request of your publicist.

But on this side of the desk, before the door to *yes* opens, maybe you don't have to worry so much.

THE LITERARY WORLD IS FULL of success stories that hide the whole picture. Just remember that when you start worrying about your image.

I DON'T THINK OF YOU, or *me*, as a product. We're real people with interesting stories to tell. So that's my approach—connecting with community members in a genuine way, with stories and images and conversations in bookstores.

You might have another guiding principle for your platform building, and that's great. Decide what you believe. Try not to brag so much that other people feel bad about their publishing experiences. Or brag away—you deserve to shine!—but also be human about it. Let the hard stuff show too.

MORE QUERY INSIGHTS

If an agent or editor is not open for submissions, don't submit! Unless that person has specifically asked you to submit anyway, or you have a preestablished relationship that included a "when you're ready" invitation, or an author friend offers to reach out to *their* agent or editor on your behalf, or you have been offered a revise and resubmit. Then you can submit, or at least ask if now's a good time.

If Forest Avenue is closed to submissions, it's with good reason. And it takes time for us to write back to the person and say that we're closed. I try to be cheery and personable about it, but I'd rather not have to bother with that extra desk work.

When publishers are hungry for new work, you don't have to trick us or try to get us to pay attention. If a press publishes nonfiction only, and you send them the most incredible cats-in-space trilogy, you are disrespecting a clear boundary. It takes a few minutes to look at a press's catalog and see if they publish anything close to what you've written. Joe Biel of Microcosm addresses how unhealthy behaviors and ignoring boundaries can actually hurt an author's chances. "Shortening the gap between authors and publishers requires understanding more about where publishers are coming from and that they want to say yes," Joe said. "I understand why, but so many authors think that they need to finagle a back door, when behavior like this almost always alienates the publisher in the long run. Just about every publisher I know resents it when an author is duplicitous or attempts to leverage the relationship socially. Again, I understand why. But it's winning the battle to lose the war."

I prefer to respond to everyone who queries, but the sheer volume when we're not open makes that more of a commitment than I want. When people submit projects that are way outside our bounds—like a children's book or an exposé of a famous person—I don't always respond. If they didn't take the time to read our submissions guidelines or if they CC me along with a group of other editors, then I decide my response isn't mandatory. Besides, saying no to people who are way off the mark can encourage them to escalate with anger or insistence. I don't have the emotional bandwidth for that behavior. It's wild to see how many people think that a persuasive letter is going to change our minds about, say, publishing thrillers or biographies or political theory.

If an agent or editor asks for fifty pages, send fifty pages. Forty-six or fifty-two are acceptable, if a scene breaks at a slightly different spot. But if you send fifteen pages, then we'll guess that the whole book falls apart on page sixteen. If you send the whole manuscript, that gaffe can be read as not following directions or possibly arrogance (*this is so freaking good you'll want to read it all*).

Why do some people ask for a certain number of pages instead of the whole manuscript? Sometimes the query letter can be polished to a warm gleam of plotty goodness, and the pages themselves aren't written well, or revised enough, or don't start in the right place. It doesn't take long to diagnose issues of that sort, or to decide that the voice isn't what we were hoping to see, or that the writing isn't ready. I usually know within a page or two if it's a no.

Some of these fall into the obvious category, but we still see them a lot in our submissions pile.

Follow directions

If you're submitting to lots of places at once, it can feel like a maze determining each outlet's protocol, preferred formatting, and page counts, but it's worth double-checking each time. For those of us with neurospicy brains, instructions can get tricky, and I have huge compassion for writers who mostly follow directions but miss a step. If someone forgets to put their manuscript title in the header or footer of their Word doc, I don't take points off or roll my eyes. Those things happen. Still, in trying to avoid the NO pile, the more closely you can adhere to what the agent or editor wants from you, the more likely you'll look professional.

Be honest about what you wrote

Don't try to squeeze your manuscript into a category where it doesn't belong. If it's YA and you submit to an adult press, you'll get passed over in favor of adult manuscripts. If you have written a romance novel, maybe it also fits in contemporary fiction, but don't submit it to a mystery publisher and claim that the "mystery" is whether the characters will get together.

Use referrals

It's great if an author who works with an agent or editor says you can use their name when querying. Put this in the subject line of your email and in the first paragraph. If you don't have that kind of access, use what you can—a personal note about how you read an interview by the person (with a specific line about what you liked), a mention of a book the person repped or published, anything to show you've done your homework.

Keep making that list

Spend time researching the agents and/or presses you might submit to before *and* during the process; you can always do more research! It's a great way to fill the scary time between hitting Send and hearing back. It's also a quick cure for the rejection blues: find more possibilities. Get a one-month subscription to Publishers Marketplace to see who's making deals in your category. Read book listings online and learn how the big five are using their metadata and statistics research to create book descriptions. Does yours look like others in your genre category? If so, that's another checkmark in the "this author is a pro" category, even if you're querying your debut.

Be genuine

Don't try to exaggerate or lie in your query. We look things up. I can't tell you how many "agented" submissions we get from someone who is pretending to be an agent. We suspect it's a friend of the author, wanting to make the author look fancy, but since we don't require agented submissions, the ruse looks all the more foolish. And we know, from the outset, that this author prefers tricking people to being honest, and that's a NOPE.

Tell us why this is your story to tell

Other editors have different opinions about this, but if you have a lived experience that matches the manuscript you are turning in, that's a huge plus in my eyes. That means it's coming from a place of experience and it's automatically more enticing for me as a reader.

Check your word count

What's standard for your genre? Are you close to that? If not, why? You might want to address this head-on in the query if you're way over or under. You don't want your word count to be an excuse to click your project into the NO category, so make it hard for us to do that. If a press requests a specific range of word count, and you're not in that range, maybe take them off the list for now. Chances are you won't change their minds about what they're looking for.

Read the room

The day after Trump's 2024 election, I received an email from a cishet white male saying his book was more relevant than ever. I was grieving; he was gloating about his manuscript's relevance. He may have voted blue, given the postapocalyptic tone of his novel, but still. Wrong time to push yourself forward, buddy.

THE QUERY LETTER IS ONLY the first part of a successful submission; the letter gets you in the door, earns you the attention of the reader. The manuscript itself (and/or the proposal, depending on your genre) is the primary focus when it comes to moving from MAYBE to YES.

We'll get to a similar checklist for the manuscript itself in a few more chapters; there's still more to cover about the query letter itself.

Also, don't pick up the phone and call an agent or editor. If they pick up, you'll likely catch them midproject, completely uninterested in a verbal pitch from a stranger. I recently had a call from someone about his children's book; it came while I was in the yard with my family, and the author tried to argue that some statistic he had read online about Forest Avenue meant *surely* my company was bigger than I was letting on. Nope. Just don't.

WRITE YOUR LETTER

THERE ARE MANY RESOURCES OUT there about query letters—so many that writers can get panicky about whether they've done theirs *right*. Often the advice from one agent or published author or book coach conflicts with other experts' advice, making it harder to judge your draft.

Not just harder but scary.

After all, this is your chance to put your creative talent into the world and not only do you have to take that risk if you want a publisher but you have to sum up *your own work* in a way that makes it appealing to someone you don't know well. And then there's wanting other people to *like* you. Querying can feel like dating; rejections can seem incredibly personal even if they're not intended that way.

(Nobody gets into publishing to reject people and make them feel bad.)

This is how you need to talk about your work. The smartest verbs and most evocative adjectives won't sell your project; your personality, and more specifically, the *why* behind the work, will move your query into the MAYBE or even the YES pile.

Sometimes we get so caught up in tweaking every sentence and playing by the rules, it's hard to see the bigger picture.

Query letters are a place for you to shine. When you approach the task with dread—which is understandable—it's harder to show off, to let your voice ring through, to put your whole self on the line. That's how it feels, anyway: asking for an agent or editor to care about your story.

You can read all the advice essays and books you want and follow the formatting recommendations, but if you don't put yourself on the line—really back up your work with your whole being—you won't get picked out of the pile.

I asked Dan Lazar about what he wished debut authors knew before submitting their novels. He said: "Personality and voice are most important in a query letter, more than nailing an arbitrary query letter format. If you're writing romance or mystery, you probably already know your genre. If not, just call it a 'novel' and if you're targeting the right agents, the agent can help figure out out the genre. Specific, visceral interesting descriptions are better than generic labels. Avoid saying 'quirky' or 'funny'; show those elements with specifics."

That quote is from nearly ten years ago, when I first started reporting for this project, but it still holds true now. Over and over, as a publisher who does acquisitions, I see brittle book descriptions. Ones that are trying so hard to explain a complicated plot in detail. Ones that don't want to spoil the story for a reader and hold back too much information. Ones that introduce all the characters with such care, but there's no sense of *why* they matter to each other or what actually happens to them.

Another way I like to encourage authors to revise their query letters is by talking about the self. Think back to what I said about myself in high school: I learned to lean into my strengths.

How do you do that in your work?

How does your manuscript or book proposal match your lived experience? What themes, stories, and beliefs are core to the work, and how are you, the author, prepared to share those with readers?

Why is this your material and not your friend's?

The more clear you are about the *why* behind your work, the better. That's not something that fits exactly into a query letter mold. Sometimes specific details fit in the bio paragraph—like if you're a doctor writing a physician sleuth mystery. But other times it's more about the approach.

It's more like embodiment. Like walking into high school knowing who you are at that exact moment.

The other thing about querying is that we change—as people and as writers—over the months and years of drafting a manuscript. Being clear with ourselves about our paths helps us tell the story of our work.

Sharing the *why* behind your work is also a great strategy if you don't have many writing credits; sharing your professional or personal experiences can give the reader a sense of your experience and your ability to interview about your book subjects.

Of course actual credits are great too. Author Clarissa Goenawan went searching for an agent after her novel *Rainbirds* had won the 2015 Bath Novel Award (UK), was a finalist for the 2015 Dundee International Book Prize (UK), and was short-listed for the 2015 SFWP Literary Award (US). She had received a development grant from the National Arts Council in Singapore and a talent assistant grant from the Media Development Authority in Singapore. "I believe the competition awards helped my query stand out," she said. "The short story credits gave me something to say in the query letter." Clarissa signed with the Pontas Agency, which then sold *Rainbirds* to Soho Press. It was published in eleven languages and kicked off Clarissa's successful fiction career.

I had almost no credits, aside from being a publisher, until I started getting essays published. That's the thing about writing novels; until you publish your first one, there isn't much to report. I began publishing essays just to have some work out there. Between 2020 and April 2022, when *Singing Lessons for the Stylish Canary* came out, I had work published in the *Rumpus*, Shondaland, *Santa Fe Writers Project*, the *Vincent Brothers Review*, *Passengers Journal*, *Big Other*, *Longridge Review*, *Hippocampus Magazine*, and several print anthologies. My *Rumpus* essay was the second-most read piece on the site in 2020 and was also picked up by Longreads—an incredible honor, especially for someone new to writing essays. I'm not sure whether my credits helped sell my novel—but they didn't hurt! And it was nice, as a long-form author, to have some shorter pieces to fluff up my bio. It showed that people cared about my work and other editors had chosen pieces by me.

A Basic Query Letter

By all means, if an agent or editor requests a certain piece of information in the query or offers a basic format to querying authors, follow those guidelines. If you don't know where to start, though, here's a sample.

First section: introduction (one paragraph)

Why would this agent or editor want your book? This could include genre, comp titles, a pithy tagline, a referral from another agent or publisher, why the book is timely, etc.

Must include basic facts: title, word count, a teaser about the content, whether it's fiction or nonfiction.

Second section: about your book (aim for one to three paragraphs)

What is your story about? Share the arc of the plot without spoiling the ending or oversharing about minor characters. When in doubt, name as few characters as possible.

Describe your manuscript in a way that includes the sound of your story—not necessarily a character's voice, but language that tells a reader what to expect in the coming pages.

Avoid telling the reader how to feel or asking them what-if questions. Look at flap copy for books that are like yours for reference; if you get stuck, you can count the number of sentences in a few examples, consider what is revealed in each sentence, and try to pattern your draft description according to those marketing departments' efforts.

If you don't like your current draft description, start fresh with a new document or a blank notebook page. See if you can come up with sentences that don't repeat anything from previous drafts. This technique gives you fresh eyes.

Third section: bio (one paragraph)

What makes you qualified to write this book? Why are you the best person to tell this story? If it's a memoir, why does your story's appeal reach beyond your family and friends (i.e., what's the bigger picture)? If you don't have publication credits, that's okay. Add professional experience, especially any education or awards that relate to your subject matter. Add any relevant writing degrees or classes too.

Closure: one line

A quick *thanks for your time and consideration* type of phrase is appropriate.

ANOTHER RULE OF THUMB: QUERIES to agents should be short and to the point. Queries to small presses may include bonus material like audience, relationships with booksellers, potential endorsements (especially if you know the authors), and anything else that shows you understand the promotions and publicity side of publishing.

And remember: this is not an exam or something to dread; try to enjoy the process! It's a chance to show off your chops, to share the story that's been brewing in your heart and during your long hours at the keyboard. Have fun with it.

RED (LETTER) FLAGS

In the early days of my publishing career, I often read one hundred pages of submitted novels, even if the opening sequence failed, because I wanted to give the author the benefit of the doubt. I don't regret those lost hours. They taught me so much about story structure, character development, dialogue, making the most of your setting, and so forth.

I also earned my chops as a publisher—becoming, over many years, more confident in my decision-making. It turns out that I can usually tell from the query letter and the first page or two whether a manuscript is ready for publication, if it's the kind of storytelling that appeals to me, and whether it might accomplish the goals we have as a press.

Sometimes all it takes is the query letter to sort a project into the NO pile.

Typos happen; they aren't too concerning unless they are coupled with lots of grammatical mistakes or strange syntax that doesn't seem to be intentional.

But there are other red flags that do matter. Here are a few things we see often that make us worry about establishing a relationship with the writer.

You didn't follow the guidelines

This happens to the best of us—when we rush, when we paste an agent letter into an email to a publisher, or when we grab an old version of our query and send it out by mistake. It happens. We're human! If the agent isn't open for submissions and you send a query anyway, without personal invitation (say, from a conference), then you're pushing against a boundary. If the press doesn't take children's books, don't send a picture book manuscript because the editor won't have any interest—and there you go, triggering sad rejection feelings for no reason.

The omission we see overlooked time and time again—and it's probably the thing that frustrates us the most—is when writers don't give us a description of the story. We've used different language over the years to ask for this—a summary, a paragraph, a description, the plot. We want you to show us the arc of the story. We don't need a full synopsis treatment or for the character names to be all caps (although it's fine if you do that). We don't need a million spoilers. But if you don't tell us what the story is *about*, the first pages don't speak for themselves. They feel like staring at the edge of a jigsaw puzzle. We can hear the sound of the story and imagine that a picture will develop, but we have no idea what that picture might be.

Sometimes this happens because a writer believes their work is so special and so unusual that a) someone might steal the plot, or b) they can't possibly explain its brilliance in a few sentences. Well, the former is not anything a reputable agent or editor would ever do. We have so many manuscripts coming in, why would we ruin our reputation for yours? And the latter tells us you have a really developed sense of your own amazingness, which means you might be hard to work with.

You're aware of the guidelines, but your book is special

We get a lot of these. They usually start out with:

I know you're not open for submissions right now but . . .

Or, *I know you don't usually publish children's books, but you'll love mine . . .*

One submitter, years ago, wrote to us that their project was "against the wishes" of the submissions call, but they sent it along anyway.

When an agent or publisher specifies what they are looking for, it's tempting to send something outside of those parameters. I get it, on some level, because as writers we are filled with hope. With what-ifs. With *maybe if I . . .* It's magical thinking gone awry. But it feels, to those of us on the receiving end, like we're being ignored or misinterpreted.

Like the submitter is thinking, *You think you know what you want, but you're wrong.*

Once we asked for contemporary fiction and we received tons of submissions set in the past. Which is great, ordinarily; I love historical fiction and books set in the seventies and eighties. But that's not what we wanted for our catalog, and *we went to the express effort of saying so to save everyone some time and heartache.*

If an agent or editor shares their dislikes, pay attention and respect those. It's not like those of us on this side of the desk enjoy sending rejections or completely ignoring bad-fit queries, as many overworked acquisitions folx end up having to do.

You don't know you are submitting to a small press

We often get "I'd like you to represent my novel" queries, which tell us the author is really hoping for an agent. Or they *were* looking for an agent and now they're trying a few small presses, which makes us feel like we're a last resort. I know sometimes this is a brain error, a neurodivergent glitch from picking up a query letter from a previous submission and pasting it into a new email, but this particular error makes me pause in ways that typos or other glitches don't. If you want an agent, and are reaching out to an editor, that means you've had rejections, maybe a lot of them. It's also possible that this kind of "represent" language means this is a brand-new writer who doesn't know the industry enough to differentiate between an agent's role (*representing*) and an acquisitions editor's role (*signing a manuscript with intent to publish it*).

Often, too, we hear from overzealous authors promising they'll do everything they can and that they can't wait to be on, say, Jenna Hager's show. It's highly unlikely a small press like Forest Avenue will be able to get you into the hottest book club in the country. I mean—it's possible, I guess? But this kind of language can foreshadow a huge gap between author expectations and publishing reality in the realm of micropresses.

I'm not sure if there's an equivalent that agents get—perhaps authors who think agents can publish them?

Any language asking about how much agents charge should not be in the query; you're not auditioning them. They are considering *you*. If you get an offer, that's when numbers come into play. Traditionally, though, agents take 15 percent of royalties of books they sell and 20 percent for foreign rights, because they're sharing that percentage with their translation agents.

You don't know what you wrote

Often, thanks to the wealth of information on the internet, people submit with a clear understanding of their genre or blend of genres. Sometimes, though, the blend gets complicated and hard to understand.

On a similar note, if you include a book description but it doesn't actually include a plot arc, or if it stalls out in some kind of thematic assessment where we don't get a sense of what's at stake or who's important, chances are we'll read that as you not fully understanding your story.

If you've written a novel, you don't have to say it's a *fiction novel*. That's inherent in the word *novel*. *Autofiction* is a newer term that refers to manuscripts that spring from seeds of truth, and I think there you can skip adding the word *novel*, because it's inherent in the *-fiction*.

Misgendering the editor or agent

I can't tell you how many queries I get that begin with *Dear Sir*. There are plenty of nonbinary and women editors out there—and our reading committee is always female-identifying or nonbinary. To drop an honorific in front of a specific editor or agent's name is only professional if you're sure of their identity.

Dear Lady Publisher is *not okay* in any instance. And yes, when I actually received a query like that, my friends told me I needed to turn it into a T-shirt. So I did.

You don't bother

We sometimes get queries like this:

Dear Editors,
Thanks for reading.

Your letter is a sales tool; it's an opportunity. Use it to market yourself and your manuscript. Please tell us about your book! We want to know! When you decide it's not worth your time to sell yourself, you're telling the acquisitions readers that you aren't very invested in whether we say yes or no.

Most of all, if you don't bother, why should we read on? Or write you back?

You, the reader, will feel . . .

Another common issue we see is writers who tell the agents and editors how to feel about their work.

This is where the author puts on the reader's shoes and imagines how delighted, tickled, titillated, charmed, surprised, and so forth we will be when we read this book. I don't know about you, but I balk at the idea of someone claiming I'm going to feel a certain way when I experience their art.

Sometimes this kind of positioning comes in as a question—*Who wins the big game? Read on to find out!*—but I don't know enough about the people playing the game to care. An alternate history novel, where a certain event never happened or a recession lasts for twice as long, can be talked about in question form if necessary. It's the questions that make the acquisitions team ask themselves about the story that end up pulling us out of the fictive dream before we get started.

For instance: *Who gets the girl?* Not only do I not care because I haven't met the characters yet, but that phrasing is horribly sexist and reductive. Whoever "gets" the girl in this example would be the antagonist in my opinion.

You *can* use adjectives to describe your work, like calling your manuscript *a bittersweet journey*, but keep an eye on how many you use. You want to walk the line of sharing your work without bragging.

Apologies

This, shockingly, happens a lot. Sometimes it's in the form of humorous self-deprecation, and maybe certain editors and agents who like that kind of humor would respond well to it. But we also get a lot of *sorry, but*s and what follows them is usually not at all a fit for our open call.

Once we received a query claiming that the book would be "attacked," and the author would be "mocked." I can guess what prompted the author to self-implode their chances, but it came off as odd and unsettling. We've also gotten a handful of queries that say things like *I know this isn't finished, but . . .* and again, we must then take the time to send a rejection.

On a related note, *I believe I have written . . .* should never, ever appear in your query. It makes it sound like you're doubting yourself! *Did* you write it? Did you *not* write it? If you doubt the genre, and that's what "I believe" is supposed to tell us, then it's too early to be querying. Agents and editors aren't here to confirm or deny what kind of book you have, unless you've signed up for a one-on-one consultation at a conference. Which you should totally do if you want specific answers to these kinds of questions.

Avoid "recently completed"

This isn't a rule people teach, but it's a tic that I see over and over. Every time an author calls a manuscript "recently completed," I feel certain it's not ready for publication. It sounds like the author rushed to meet a submission deadline and didn't pause to get feedback from beta readers, a writing group, or a professional editor. Whether or not that's true, "recently completed" doesn't mark the work as a new, hot property; it is a yellow flag of caution.

Instead, just call your book a 77,000-word memoir or a 100,000-word historical saga. You don't have to say *when* you finished it—and as we all know, many full-length manuscripts get "finished" and then started all over again with editorial feedback in the mix. If you've been working on your project for an impressive amount of time, you could mention the number of years. Some agents and editors counsel against this, but I know if a project has been percolating for ten years, even if the title doesn't work for me or the opening pages are slow, it's worth reading a bit more. That's my lived experience, and my long gestation process for books, showing as a bias. Which is another reminder: editors and agents and publishers are human. A detail that might make someone look away could be a delicious carrot for a different reader.

Leave cover designs to the pros

Even if your best friend made you a cover for your book, and you love it, don't submit your manuscript with a draft cover. Please. That'll tell us you're going to be hard to work with, that you don't understand publishing, or a combination of the two. Same with cover ideas: don't tell us! Eventually, if you get representation and/or a contract, there will be time for sharing. At this stage it'll just look unprofessional. Related: critiquing covers released by the press you're submitting to doesn't make you sound intelligent. It makes you sound hard to work with.

Don't lie

I've said this before, but it's one of my pet peeves. Sometimes submitters are trying so hard to get our attention that they claim to have read a book that they haven't read. Or they embellish their bios. Believe me, we can tell when people lie.

Don't write in blood—yours or anyone else's

Yes, we've received a manuscript partially written in the author's own blood. On that same note, any gimmicks like weird fonts, colored fonts, perfumed paper (on the rare chance that it's a physical submission), and so forth are bound to be more annoying than interesting. You might think it's clever, but we've seen it before. Let your work stand out, not your method of presenting it.

VERBAL PITCHES

UNLESS YOU'RE A FREQUENT CONFERENCE attendee, chances are you won't be pitching out loud very often (or at all). Most of these opportunities occur at events. It usually costs extra to meet with a publisher, editor, film scout, or agent; once you sign up, you can work on a pitch and then practice, practice, practice. All the work you've done on your query letter should help you out.

You can start planning for this anytime, mentioning to friends or coworkers that you're a writer and answering, "What's your book about?" with your best attempt. See what language makes your listener ask more questions, see what makes them laugh. That'll be great practice for your five- or ten-minute slot at a future conference. It's also a helpful exercise when you're middraft, because it can help you hone in on what you're really trying to convey.

The great thing about pitching in person is that you are just two people sitting in a room together (virtually or physically). You get to be yourself and you don't have to have a formal memorized speech. Chances are the agent or editor might interrupt you for more clarification, or they might ask you a question. That's great! The more comfortable and conversational it is, the better the interaction feels. The less awkward and transactional it seems. Your job here is to get enough of the story across for the person to ask for pages. That includes not chastising them for ignoring a written pitch you sent two years ago for a different project.

Writing conferences can be magical because they can offer that chance to meet in person (whether that's in the same room or via Zoom). So can MFA programs, book festivals, and community workshops. Some fabulous programs that are not university affiliated include Sackett Street in New York, GrubStreet in Boston, Ariel Gore's School for Wayward Writers in New Mexico, and The Attic Institute in Portland, Oregon. Many states have literary nonprofits that offer classes on writing and submitting.

I think of these conference experiences as having value not just for formal learning but also for the potential of connecting with the writers around you. My closest writing friends came from the Pinewood Table and having Steve Arndt introduce me to some of the writers he knew through Tom Spanbauer's Dangerous Writing. Besides, talking about the craft and your particular project often leads to new insights. Most of all, hanging out with writers is fun. You already have something in common!

That being said, you shouldn't pitch an editor or agent if they sit at your table for lunch. Talk to them like a normal person. Make everyday conversation; comment on the food or the keynote that you both just listened to.

Same with the elevator! The elevator pitch shouldn't *actually* be delivered in an elevator unless the agent or editor asks for it. (And honestly, I've never asked to be pitched while in an elevator and have no intention of doing so.) Find yourself sharing elevator space with an agent or editor? Great. Share a compliment or an observation or just ask, "What floor?" This is not the time to whip out a prepared speech. Chances are the editor or agent is heading back to their room for a bathroom break, a snack, or a nap. Maybe they have a headache.

They are not in the public domain in the elevator (or the bathroom). They are taking care of themselves. Respect that, and later you can always query by saying, "I saw you speak at XYZ conference, and I'd love for you to consider my manuscript." That will go over way better than an awkward description of your plotline in response to, "Can you please pass the bread basket?"

Conference Etiquette

- Applaud with generosity when each session ends.
- Say thank you to panelists and speakers on your way out the door, if they aren't deep in conversation with someone.
- Take notes; when querying an agent months later, if you can say something specific about their perspective or what in particular impressed you about their speech, that is a really nice way to show yourself as professional and curious.
- Don't raise your hand to ask one long-winded question that really shows off how much you know; keep your questions succinct and ask what might be relevant to the other people in the room.

- Bring business cards; if you don't have a published book yet, no worries. Your name and email address will do. A phone number is fine, too, if you are okay with people calling you out of the blue.
- Be prepared to meet writers who are in a similar place with their careers as you, or who write similar genres. You might find your new favorite writing pal if you are relaxed enough to listen and ask questions.
- Don't put your pitching paperwork on the floor of the bathroom and then put it on the table where people are going to eat lunch. Because ew. (True story.)
- Related: don't pitch agents or editors in the bathroom. Let them wash their hands in peace!
- Choose your attire with purpose. I used to dress to blend in at these events; now I wear bright colors and prints to give anxious people a reason to say hello to a publisher. No matter what your choice of wardrobe, think of it in terms of approachability. If you feel up to it, carry a special notebook or wear a book-related pin or tie—anything that could invite a conversation with a stranger.
- Don't bring printed pitches about your manuscript and try to make guest speakers take them. Unless, of course, you're at a conference that recommends bringing printed materials. Usually though, especially if an agent flies in from New York or California, they will feel burdened by your neediness. It's awkward to

have to say no to a handout, but equally awkward to take it and then have to either recycle it when you might be watching or have to tote it around for the rest of the day.

- Don't grill an expert over lunch; let them eat. By all means converse, but keep it light and friendly, not needy.
- If you're anxious, take deep breaths; maybe bring some mints or a piece of gum that will help ground you in familiar tastes. All the "experts" are real people, too, and they learned what they know from practice and failure and trying again. If you treat them as real people and not as targets, you'll be a step ahead of some of your peers.
- Use the outfit/accessory tip, but reverse it. Comment on someone else's book dress or clever laptop sticker. Or give them a compliment about a question they asked at an earlier session.

PROPOSALS

NONFICTION IS OFTEN SOLD ON *proposal*—a packet that includes a detailed description of the project, a table of contents, comp titles, sample chapters, and possible blurbs (or actual ones, if you have some already). The process is similar to submitting a grant proposal. You want to shine a light on the importance of the work, whom it will benefit, and why the reader should finance the project. Include as many specifics as possible. The document should highlight your talent as a writer (and/or researcher or journalist), and it also needs to address sales expectations.

Memoirs and essay collections are, more often than not, sold only when the manuscript is complete. But sometimes proposals are requested for those too. It doesn't hurt to have one you're working on even if you never turn it in. Working on a proposal can help you see where you need to revise and help you create a better book description.

If you sell your project on proposal, you will get an advance that you can put toward expenses as you actually write the full manuscript. The math may not work out if it's a small press—a definite plus for going the agent route and having your agent try to sell your project to a big five or a larger independent press.

A lot of the requirements for querying also are true for proposals. Be kind and genuine, proofread carefully, and follow the guidelines. Editors and agents are often specific about what they like to see in proposals. It's worth the extra time and effort to adjust your document to match their specifics, otherwise you're giving them an easy reason for a no. So *follow the directions* applies once again. If you're working on a proposal before homing in on who to send it to, that's okay. Read about the format options, choose what works for you, and then later you can tweak it for individual submissions.

If you have an agent already, ask for successful client samples so you can build your proposal according to your agent's taste.

An earlier version of this project, in proposal form, looked like this:

I. Overview
II. Introduction
III. Target Audience
IV. About the Author
V. Testimonials
VI. Previous Works
VII. Comparable Works
VIII. Marketing and Promotion
IX. Detailed Table of Contents
X. Sample Chapters

Right up front, you need to explain the concept behind your project, why it's relevant and needed, and why you're submitting to this person or press. I opted to separate this information into an overview—about the project as a whole—and an introduction, a personal message from me, the author, about why I was writing this book. The rest of the package was outwardly focused—toward audience and how to reach those readers.

I added testimonials to my proposal because I'm a public speaker and teacher, and I have great quotes about how I present information. Maybe that's not necessary, and it might rub some people the wrong way, but I felt like it might help address why I'm the person to write this book. I also figured that would prove the points I'm making about building community for the sake of relationships and not because of what people might do for you someday.

The table of contents (showing the scope of the project) and the sample chapters (your writing and stance) hold a lot of weight in the proposal. Everything around those two components should show an understanding of the market: how your work will be different from what's available already, who will buy your book, and why it matters *now*.

OFTEN ANTHOLOGIES ARE SOLD ON proposal, before or after all the contributors have been chosen, depending on the project. Susan DeFreitas, editor of *Dispatches from Anarres: Tales in Tribute to Ursula K. Le Guin* came to us with a full proposal and attached contributors, because she had done all the legwork herself. That was an outlier project, though. I've mostly accepted anthology ideas based on the editor pitching a concept in conversation with me, or over a series of emails. In this model I can help oversee and financially support the submissions process; putting out an open call can cost money for the submission platform (i.e., Submittable) and advertising to get the word out. While our advances are small, I try to give bigger ones to anthology editors so they can use those funds to pay the contributors.

Gigi Little's *City of Weird: 30 Otherworldly Portland Tales,* which came out in 2016, is still our best-selling book in part because of its regional appeal and the support of Powell's. She pitched a few regional ideas before we settled on this one, riffing off the Keep Portland Weird slogan. Annie Carl, editor of *Soul Jar: 31 Fantastical Tales by Disabled Authors,* pitched in conversation, and I said yes immediately because of our success with *City of Weird* and *Dispatches,* and because I agreed with Annie that there isn't enough disability representation in genre fiction.

FIRST PAGES

If you have an excellent query and/or proposal, but nothing happens in the opening pages of your manuscript, you are doing yourself a disservice if you submit anyway.

In my cub reporter years in a newsroom in the Washington, DC, area the editor in chief of our community paper chain, Mary Kimm, used to copy examples from the papers to talk about in our weekly staff meetings. This was part of her campaign to have us write strong ledes—meaning the opening sentences to an article. (You pronounce it like *leed*.)

If you wrote a boring lede (i.e., "The Loudoun County Board of Supervisors Met on XYZ Date"), your work might end up on the shame page. Not that Mary called it that! But she always circulated a two-sided batch of copies. One side was a don't-do-this page; the other side featured a bounty of good lede examples that she wanted the rest of us to emulate.

I was terrified of landing on the don't page. Maybe I did in my first weeks and that scared me into always making the most of that opening paragraph so I wouldn't get called out again. Same with sources. Three sources minimum: I wouldn't run an article until I could get that third one on the record.

Her training about openings stuck and has continued to influence me. Whatever you write, the first few sentences matter. First paragraph of your query letter: it matters. First pages of your manuscript: these really, really matter. You might, if you're lucky, earn a few minutes of attention, but it might be more like a few seconds if there are lots of waiting submissions.

I often meet writers who say, *Oh, but then it really gets good on page four*, or, *Wait until you see what happens in the seventh chapter.* Have you said this kind of thing to your friends? These are great signs that your story isn't beginning where it ought to. When I see that kind of language, I realize the author *knows* the beginning doesn't work (yet), but they don't know how to fix it (yet). Sometimes I see this kind of language and the story carries itself enough—gives me enough of a jolt of excitement—that I read more anyway, looking for the real beginning. But in competitive open submissions periods, it's more likely that I'll use this issue as a reason to pass.

Here are some common first-page issues you can find and fix in your work.

Formatting and grammar

Use a standard, twelve-point font and double-space the manuscript. Some folx have specific requests—a preferred font, like Times New Roman, or asking for page numbers in a certain place on the page. For those of us with older eyes, double-spacing is mandatory for us to spend time with your characters.

If you write experimental work, or poetry, then punctuation becomes its own language, and you have some freedom to play. If you are writing a more standard narrative, though, you'll want to standardize your punctuation usage and be as professional as possible.

If you know Chicago style or can borrow a copy of the latest manual from the library, that can help your manuscript look professional—and it also whispers to the agent or editor, *Hey, this person knows what we like*—although presses and magazines often have in-house style guides and some do use other forms.

Being consistent throughout your manuscript matters more to me, though, than a mastery of Chicago style. Our Forest Avenue style is having zero spaces on either side of an em dash, as per Chicago, but I don't care if an author uses spaces. If they're consistent I can just take them out with the find-and-replace function. If some have spaces and some don't, I know I'll spend extra time fixing that (and likely other small inconsistencies). Here's another example. *Gray* is the preferred US way to spell the color, but British English and some science fiction and fantasy authors prefer *grey*. If a manuscript used both interchangeably, I would worry the author had been sloppy and that more difficult errors and inconsistencies were lurking.

Long nature scenes

Successful openings can have incredible descriptions of place, where the reader feels swept into the story. But a lot of times these nature scenes go wrong because there's not enough sense of the character's relationship to the place or the stakes.

I love nature writing, and it can make a great opening when done well. But we need a sense of character development and what's at stake; we need to *connect* to the human (or the alien, or the protagonist deer, whoever the characters are) for the landscape to do its work.

Unpleasant content

We had a ton of naked male scenes show up in one submissions period. They were (not surprisingly) all written by men. And they heavily featured male characters' penises. I personally had *no interest at all* in these shower and bathroom scenes. I'm a pretty G-rated editor with some exceptions—gritty, realistic themes shared with a lot of poetry and whimsy, balancing the horrors with resilience and playfulness, work well for me.

I say no to misogyny from the point of view of a misogynist. Even if it's the story of a misogynist growing up and changing, there's enough of that in the world already. In real life and in stories. I have no interest in amplifying another narrative from that perspective. Even if there's a redemptive arc, nope. Not for me.

Dialogue that explains

One of the biggest mistakes writers make with their first pages is setting up the story with a lot of dialogue. I understand the impetus—bringing characters into a room together, doing things and saying things. That makes for a dynamic scene, especially if they are arguing. But this can go very wrong.

Often in these openings, the characters tell each other the story (i.e., *Oh, like that time we got matching butterfly tattoos, do you remember?*). That technique of sharing information can feel false and wooden. Like the author pulling the puppet strings. Especially when a character asks another character if they remember something. But even without a question, dialogue can feel wooden and false anytime a character tells another character something they both already know. I used to read beyond dialogue-heavy openings, knowing these kinds of things can be fixed, but as our submissions volume has increased, I need reasons to let go of projects, and this is an easy no. Remember, you're trying for the MAYBE pile, and this is a tic that definitely impacts your chances of staying in the running.

Without knowing anything about the story (yet), even the cleverest of dialogue will feel flat without some internal thought on the page and without the author pulling us in with a particular point of view. If we jump into dialogue and we are inside one character's head, seeing the world through her eyes, that can work really well. Dialogue does wonders for pacing and increasing tension. If you want to pull off a dialogue-heavy opening because you're dead set against doing a long nature opening, then slow it down. Bring us into the scene, linger with your characters' discomfort or frustration, so we understand who's in the room and what's at stake. Prioritize letting the reader *be* in the scene with you over delivering a lot of information. It's a balance; we want to know who these people are and what's wrong, what's brought them here, but we need only *enough* to get us hooked.

Is this your story to tell?

I always ask myself: If I had to choose between a book about XYZ written by someone who has that specific identity and a book about XYZ written by someone who is outside that identity, which would I want to stand behind? There's no question. I'd choose the narrative informed by lived experience. You can add characters who aren't like you to the work, of course, and that's where sensitivity readers can be helpful. But if the central story connects to your passions, experiences, or identity, then that's great information to share with a potential agent or editor.

I like to see query bios include a sentence or two about what motivated the author to write this particular tale—the why behind your work. My novel is set in nineteenth-century France, where I never lived, but it's about a family of music box makers, and I grew up with mechanical music and a father who always tinkered with cylinder boxes, automatons, jukeboxes, and pinball games. The questions I explored in the novel stemmed from my lived experience, even though the circumstances I put on the page are fiction. While we don't ask people to directly disclose their race, gender, or disabilities—because that's none of our business—you might consider an identity statement especially if your work is related to that identity.

I still feel absolutely horrible for passing on a manuscript by an indigenous author who didn't disclose her identity; at that time, we had been getting lots of white authors submitting projects about BIPOC characters, specifically multiple subs from white people submitting first-person indigenous content, trying to imagine from a Native perspective through the lens of their white privilege. Those are destined for the NOPE pile at my press. I rejected this one author with a note about wanting to hear indigenous perspectives, and she rightly wrote back with anger, self-identifying. I still feel horrible. I carry that shame. I did try to look her up, but she didn't identify as Native in any of her online bios, so I assumed wrongly that she didn't identify.

We adjusted our submissions policy in the following year to help navigate that terrain a bit better. Checkboxes feel reductive; we did try those but then opted against them. Now we lean on the language of lived experience, urging people to confirm their fiction is based on their lived experience even if they are uncomfortable with putting themselves into a category (like self-identifying by race or gender or sexuality) or sharing their specific identities or traumas. We don't want to come across as entitled to personal information but we do want to offer an invitation to share the *why* behind the work. Identity is complicated; asking about it without asking someone to perform their trauma or reveal too much personal information is complicated, too.

For our disability anthology *Soul Jar*, edited by Annie Carl, we put a yes-or-no box in the submissions form. Do you identify as disabled? *Yes* was all we needed to consider the story. A number of the authors did disclose ttheir diagnoses o us or in their bios, but a number of them chose not to. Some took a middle route of sharing their disability identity language but using a pseudonym. I didn't want authors to feel obligated to relate personal details—*medical* ones!—publicly to readers or even privately to our team if they didn't feel comfortable. I really didn't want anyone to feel like they needed to prove that they belonged in the category. After all, I've struggled and still struggle with using the word *disabled* to apply to myself, even though I'm here typing with a brain injury and snapping thumb ligaments and early-onset arthritis and so forth. I think that was the right choice—privacy, respect, and autonomy—but we received at least one review that said the authors weren't disabled enough, that their stories weren't disabled enough. That's a common misperception that's extremely hurtful; people with disabilities can and do exist in the world as people (of course they / we do). A story by a disabled person about a dragon is disabled representation, end stop. No disabled writer ought to feel obligated to perform disability on the page for it to count as disabled representation.

Write Your Yes

WHAT WOULD YOU WANT AN acceptance letter to say about your work? This is a great exercise for when you're in the middle of querying and feeling bummed or worried or tired of waiting.

What do you love about your story?

What are you proud of getting on the page?

Are there hard parts, parts you struggled with or rewrote, that you're especially proud of?

What makes your book special?

What have you given *yourself* by writing it?

Now turn these into your own acceptance letter!

HOPES IN A PILE

I OPEN OUR SUBMISSIONS QUEUE and feel the weight of wishes.

The candles lit.

The hopes written in text messages to another writer.

The dreams spoken in writing group.

The coins flipped into fountains: *I want to be an author.*

The *please* of this process. It's so loud.

Every single sentence a sigh, a cry, a raised fist. From the writer—the artist, the creator, the talent—to the maker who might choose this assemblage of words. Or not.

Mostly not.

On this side, the deciding side of the desk, it's about the numbers.

How many submissions come in during an open period, that's the denominator.

The numerator is one. Or two. Or three. How many novels I want. How many I can afford to love.

This time, our most recent open period, netted more than three hundred manuscripts. We expected to pick 1 percent. Maybe fewer.

From the writer's side, which is not just one desk but everywhere outside the queue, it seems obvious to hope.

If you nailed those first five pages.

If your query letter includes a snappy description of the novel.

If the bio you've painstakingly added to, one writing credit after another, is enough of a platform.

If the rest of your manuscript matches the potential of the first pages. *If*, in all these years of writing and revising, you got down on the page, in the get-down way you have, exactly what you intended.

If, then: What?

It's supposed to be enough.

That's what all the books say.

That's what all the writing coaches and workshop teachers say.

That's what everyone, everywhere, tells you about selling your first novel.

If you can do all the things the people say to do—on social media, in books, in interviews—an offer should follow. A contract that may or may not come with cash, as small presses often can't or won't pay advances.

And then it's your choice, your decision:

To say yes to the yes.

To say no and keep looking.

But here's the thing.

You could have crafted those opening pages exactly the way

you intended according to the teachers you've had, your vision of a perfect manuscript, and in relationship to some of the books you love to read. Let's say you achieved exactly what you wanted to achieve. Maybe even what your mentors or teachers or writing partners wanted you to get on the page.

Then let's say you wrote the most perfect query, revised and edited it until nobody could argue with its greatness and how evocative it is of your plot.

You could have a bio brimming with accomplishments. Perhaps even that illusive thing big five editors call a *platform*.

Even *if* all those things are true, I might not care.

I MEAN, I DO CARE about you. Your wishes and hopes and goals. Those candles you lit. I'm a novelist too. I've done my share of wishing. If I had to choose—representing the industry or sitting with the pack of writers, I'd claim the author identity first. I publish and share views from inside the process *for* people who write and don't have the privilege of access to what goes on in publishing.

But when the denominator is two hundred of you, three hundred of you, I have to let go of wanting to protect your hearts. Of worrying about each of you. After all, this is a business, an industry, and I can only pick what I know how to sell.

It's a matter of sorting.

And it's a matter of pleasure.

IMAGINE, IF YOU WILL, PLANNING for tonight's dinner.

What interests or excites you?

What ingredients do you have on hand?

What do you *feel* like having?

When I pick a manuscript, it's a lifelong relationship—intense and deeply connected for the first two years, and then less so as the next crop of authors moves into focus. I definitely think about the books that have come before. What I want to add to that list. What we're missing.

Sometimes I read a query and think, *Not interested.*

Other times, I think, *I have seen too many manuscripts with a similar premise*, or, *We just published a book about XYZ.*

Always, I ask myself, *Does this feel like it could be one of our books?*

YOU CAN'T CONTROL WHAT I want for dinner.

What kind of ice cream I like.

Which novel in my queue draws me in.

Maybe your novel is the literary equivalent of sushi, but in reading the opening pages, I recall the humiliation of my first time trying it, out to lunch with my first newspaper editor. The hot burn of her laughter. I had been too scared—fresh out of college—to tell her I didn't know if I liked raw fish. She couldn't understand my holding back that information. Why I'd be afraid to say, *Let's go to a different restaurant.*

Maybe you wrote a butter pecan sundae of a novel, and I don't like the texture or understand why anyone would purposefully want nuts in their desserts. No amount of hot fudge, or deliciousness of language, will change my mind.

Maybe you wrote a character with Alzheimer's, and this is important material to me because of my dad, but I don't want to spend two years on that specific kind of fictional suffering when I am living the worry, when my father says he's had enough birthdays, when he tries to fix something that used to be easy for him and now all he can do is break it more.

THE NEXT TIME YOU GET a rejection, instead of devaluing your work, berating yourself for submitting that version instead of revising one more time, or getting mad at the editor, say this:

My work matters.

I wouldn't want them to say yes to this novel (story, essay, poem, memoir, screenplay, ________) unless they really loved it.

This person is not besotted with my work. That's okay.

I love my work. I'm not going to let this stop me from making more work.

THEN GO MAKE MORE WORK.

Lose yourself.

Play.

Don't try to write for the market, a particular agent, a small press you love. When rejections hurt most, we can feel crushed by that outside pressure. So let it go—release it.

Write for fun.

Write for you.

JUST BECAUSE YOU FINISHED YOUR MANUSCRIPT . . .

DOESN'T MEAN IT'S GOING TO sell.

Doesn't mean it's *ready* to sell.

Doesn't mean you should send it out to be judged by an agent or editor yet.

Especially if you finished the first draft yesterday.

Especially if you aren't sure *who* your audience is.

I know it's hard to hear this—years ago, I might have given up if I believed this—but sometimes your first (or second, or third, or fourth) finished manuscript isn't the one that's due to go out in the world.

I think of them as training novels or under-the-bed books or unsold projects or reams of paper that live in my desk drawer or my basement crawl space.

As alarming as it is to think about a full-length work you've labored over for a few years going unrecognized, moldering in the dark or on an outdated floppy disk, these set-aside projects are deeply important.

They matter, as much or perhaps even more so than the first manuscript you sell, because of what they teach you.

Because of the craft lessons, for sure.

But also because they teach us to let go.

After all, when your book is in the world, you can't change it.

You can't argue with readers about what you *really* meant. You have to separate its existence from your personal worth or else feel every piece of criticism as a brutal one.

AT FOREST AVENUE WE LOVE working with debut authors, but we also see a lot of work by writers who aren't ready. It's too bad because often the concepts or characters are intriguing, but the craft is not polished. Or the writing is gorgeous but there's not enough plot. Or the plot and writing are top-notch, but it's not enough of a match with Forest Avenue's taste as a press.

Or—and this is rare but does happen—we love the work, but we love a different manuscript even *more*. In that case we share what we appreciated most and try to suggest other presses to try.

Our committee of readers uses metaphors when we flag books that aren't ready. We call these stories interesting but *undercooked*.

Or we say the pages need some work before *prime time*.

Other specific reasons for rejections include:

- The work needs another revision or two; it has potential but it's not holding together.
- The author can't describe the story in the query letter—a telltale sign that it's not working yet.
- It's too long—for the market, for our budget, and / or for

the story the writer wants to tell. Or it's too short. But since pages cost money, too long comes up a lot.

- The author drops action onto the page and then describes the action and/or how readers should feel about it. The balance between characters having agency to make mistakes and the narrative voice's ability to offer commentary takes practice.
- Exposition in dialogue. So often writers are asked to put something into a scene, which generally includes dialogue, but often we see characters droning on (and on) telling each other something they should already know. This results in awkward prose and questions like, *Hey, Piper, remember when your brother died in that car crash?* What's Piper going to say? *Gee, how could I forget?*

FOR MY COLLEGE HONORS THESIS, I wrote about F. Scott Fitzgerald's debut novel, *This Side of Paradise,* and compared it to what many consider his masterpiece: *The Great Gatsby*. I delved into the writing itself and the social pressures he wrote about in both books, categorizing where these ideas fell short, execution-wise, in the former and how those same themes and techniques became much lauded in the latter.

Publishing in the 2020s is vastly different than in the 1920s, when Fitzgerald got his break. Technology has changed so much about how we read, accessibility accommodations, and how books get printed. I had read lots about Fitzgerald's relationship with his editor, Maxwell Perkins—their friendship plus how they worked together as an editor and an author. That kind of relationship mirrors the agent-author relationship more today, as agents have taken on a lot of the editorial work that used to be done in-house at big publishing companies.

While I believed in my early novels and felt sure they would sell, my wishes weren't enough. I read some pieces in public and shared the arcs in writing group, but besides that they mostly existed in my head and heart. Because of the hours I spent with myself working on chapters and revising character arcs. I might have stopped if I knew ahead of time that they wouldn't get picked up. I loved them too much to think about anything other than a cover, a release date, signing copies in a bookstore.

But I didn't give up, and that's important, because I found my voice in those pages. I learned the components of a scene. I practiced fancy tricks—multiple points of view and flashbacks. I *even* started figuring out my material, the themes and issues I wanted to write about. I started to understand where a story starts and how to create characters who seem to breathe on the page.

I had heard this advice about first books almost never being picked up and published when I was writing those early novels, but I wanted to be an exception. I expected to be. After all, I had been told I was a good writer since elementary school—and my mom saved the report cards and teacher comments on my essays to prove it.

"If there were a convention of English teachers," wrote teacher George Berry after my first term of sophomore English, "getting a student like Laura could be the door prize."

No way would *my book* fall into that not-for-us, no-thanks camp of rejections. I needed to prove to Mr. Berry—and all the other mentors who believed in me—that I could do it. I wished on every fountain penny. On every birthday candle.

I *couldn't* fail because I've always had a narrow skill set, and writing is at the core of it.

But it turns out, however many books you devour, however many bookstore events you attend, however many printed author interviews you highlight, however many pieces of advice you jot down in your writing journal—none of that preparation can substitute for writing a full manuscript, finishing it, revising it a few times, and then writing the next one.

I wrote several partial novels and a jazz band biography for hire before I wrote my "first" two novels that didn't sell. I see glimmers and gleams of the writer I wanted to be in all those discarded pages.

Allow for Your Worries

WHEN WE'RE LOOKING FOR AN agent or editor, sometimes we tie our self-worth to the process. In waiting and wishing for a positive response we often create a false dichotomy:

> Acceptance = my work is good.
> Rejection = my work is bad.

First, remind yourself to uncouple those things. There are so many reasons why a manuscript or a short story or a poem isn't chosen by an editor.

Then dig in to where the fear and judgment are coming from—where you're holding yourself back.

What part of the author journey scares you?

Are you worried about standing in front of the mic? See if you can get an invitation to a reading series to practice.

Are you worried about bad reviews? Read reviews of friends' books and best-selling books. Remember that the better the book does in the marketplace, the more likely the book will get panned by readers. A book with only five-star reviews hasn't reached beyond its author's personal circle of friends and family. Repeat as needed: My book isn't for everyone in the world.

Are you scared of sales numbers? You cannot control who buys your book. Or who reviews it. You can set yourself up for success by investing time and energy in promotion, but there are no guarantees.

Ask yourself all the questions and come up with reasonable answers. You might even chat about your fears with some of your local or online writer friends. I guarantee that kind of conversation will help you feel less alone and more equipped to make that transition from private to public.

REJECTION RESILIENCE

When my youngest was in kindergarten, her teacher invited her to present at an all-school morning assembly about perseverance.

"I won't give up on myself!" she proclaimed into the microphone.

I didn't know, until the teacher told me, how often she reminded her peers to keep trying. To not give up on themselves. Or that she regularly gave herself this pep talk.

A few years later my business strategist Nikole Potulsky introduced me to the idea of rejection resilience. I understood it first in relation to my writing career. You put work into the world; someone says no. You need to shake that rejection off. Keep going. Nikole told me to remind myself with every rejection, *I still matter. My work matters.*

I realized I lived with someone who innately grasped this concept: my child. In her single-digit years, she often set up lemonade stands on Saturdays, even though our neighborhood has a high percentage of observant Jewish families. The adults and kids walking by our house on the way to and from synagogue said no, weekend after weekend, explaining to her that they couldn't handle money. And she *understood*, but she kept standing out there, offering lemonade for free when money was an issue. After all, she had purchased a boxed kosher kind at the grocery store because she knew the neighbors. She intended to share. If they couldn't pay, and they wanted lemonade, she'd make it work.

She never doubted herself when they said no.

Rejections are bound to happen when you query your proposal or finished project unless you get a yes right away from your dream agent. No response at all means your material isn't working *or* you've approached someone so busy they can't possibly look at your work. It's a frustrating in-between of a no, necessary for editors and agents who are swamped constantly with projects that aren't right for them.

That kind of nonfeedback could mean stepping back to rearrange and rethink your approach—who you're submitting to and how you're querying. It could also mean you're reaching out to agents or editors who are so well established they have their hands full with existing authors.

Rosanne Parry, *New York Times* best-selling children's author, told me "Over the years I've learned that the game is almost entirely the art of persistence. I wrote *A Wolf Called Wander* in the middle of an eight-year dry spell in which I could not get a new book contract, even as my third and fourth middle grade novels from prior contracts were being released to critical acclaim. It was clearly time to try something different."

Rosanne decided to create a novel based on the real-life journey of the wolf OR-7.

> Nobody was asking for an animal-narrated novel. And when it was finished, no American publisher would touch it. My agent and I liked the book and had confidence that kids would too, so after some soul-searching we persisted,

> giving other English-speaking countries a try. We found a British publisher, Andersen Press, who had a vision for the story, adding more than 100 gorgeous black-and-white illustrations to the book. That was a huge risk for a small publisher to take. And it paid off brilliantly. The book has been translated into fourteen languages and has been on the *New York Times* and indie bestseller lists for most of its first three years in print.

She brings it all back to rejection and perseverance here: "If we had given up on our intrepid little wolf after forty-two rejections in the US, none of this would have happened. If we had turned up our noses at smaller presses and international publishers (where all the great innovation is happening) we wouldn't have even considered Andersen Press. If we had decided to tone down the voice of the wolf or added a human character, the story would not have been universal enough to appeal globally."

Most of all, Rosanne reminded me that we, as writers, can't know in advance which pieces of our work are going to resonate most with readers. Which means—and this can be really hard, but it's important—we have to trust ourselves and our vision for our work. "I had a story idea that sparked my curiosity," Rosanne said. "I stuck with it in spite of discouragement and I ended up with a story I genuinely liked. I've learned to trust that in myself. Just as a musician knows when they are on tempo and in the right key, a writer knows when the story works. And the secret to sanity is to prize your own satisfaction and write toward it with all the heart and skill you have."

REACTING TO FEEDBACK

FEEDBACK ON THE SUBMISSIONS JOURNEY is gold. That means the person evaluating your query thinks it has potential. Sure, you wanted a yes, or to hang out in the maybe pile a while longer, but a rejection with information means you're being taken seriously. And that's huge! Someone else sees the possibility in your project, even if it's not ready for prime time.

So first: celebrate when you get personalized rejections, especially if there's advice in there that resonates with you.

Don't try to revise the next day. Sit with the agent or editor's words for a while. Consider going back to the "What's Your Why?" sidebar on page 50 or to page 356, the self-inventory chapter. Who do you want to be in the world as an author? Then flip forward again to the start of this section and do the "Ready? Set?" exercises from this perspective.

Are you on the right path?

How does the advice you received match up with—or conflict with—your reasons for writing your book? Do you think implementing the suggestion(s) will make your book better? Are you willing to commit the time? If you're willing, imagine doing the work and getting a no from the agent or editor who encouraged you. Would you regret that journey? Or does the information in their response feel alive to you, alive and useful?

You have to revise, first and foremost, for you. Even if you receive a revise and resubmit, the gold standard of rejections, and you change everything according to the editorial requests, there's no telling if you'll get an acceptance.

With *Singing Lessons* I got a number of R&Rs from agents, and I followed the recommendations dutifully. I felt sure I could turn those *no thanks*es into *yes*es; after all, the agents had taken the time to give me valuable advice! And I was an editor, you know, the kind of person who knows how to edit? How hard could it be?

One agent early on, in 2014, questioned aloud whether I could take such an intricate idea and make it commercially viable. She didn't think she could sell it as written, but she wasn't sure she wanted me to squeeze it into a commercial box either, because that would change some of the things she liked most about it.

Turns out she was right; I tried making it into something taut and faster paced, but it didn't work for her. Other R&R attempts had similar responses—along the lines of *well, you did what I asked but it didn't turn out like I expected.*

Eventually I rewrote for Laurie Fox based on her initial interest, and we had a fabulous conversation about what still needed fixing. In that chat she said yes to being my agent. I finally had representation with someone who understood my work and wanted to invest her energy in my career. Revising for her was different than the stabs in the dark at deciphering quick feedback from less interested agents. We were doing it together.

When I started Forest Avenue, I used to write personal notes to every author who submitted a book that vaguely matched our submissions criteria. We wanted to give those authors hope, to let them know *we saw them*. To suggest another press, if we had an idea of a taste match. Over the years, as the quantity and quality of submissions increased, it became harder to offer significant feedback not because we don't care but because the volume is high. And sometimes when we do take that extra time writers are mean in response, and that's not anything we have energy for either.

There were two vociferously angry men in our most recent submission period—one who blocked us on Twitter, and one who sent outraged emails, spitfire-style, one after the other, until his rage subsided. Not only did he send them via our Submittable platform, but he found our business email and sent more complaints there.

In those cases we felt relieved that we hadn't opted in to a business relationship with someone who was so quick to tantrum on a public forum. I can imagine that these authors are taking out their frustration about the industry—feeling like their work is being kept out by people like me and my reading committee—but that's part of why I've been trying to pull this book together for years.

It's not you; it's how popular streaming shows are right now.

It's not you; it's social media.

It's not you; it's that what you wrote isn't a match for us.

And the dreaded it's not you; it's the market.

Which is how we get into this place of shaking our fists at capitalism, or telling ourselves stories about the worth of our words based on a system we don't have access to.

We still try to share insights when we can, especially when the author has taken the time to research our press and point out a title of ours that they have read. Still, we have to pay attention to our existing authors, and we're a tiny team—I'm the one full-time person. To solve this dilemma, some presses add feedback to their financial model. Authors who want a response can pay.

But I haven't wanted to charge for feedback; it's not right for Forest Avenue. The one time I tried a tip jar on Submittable, it felt awkward and wrong, and my cheeks burned every time I saw a tip come in. I felt like people wanted to buy my attention even though we were ethically clear that the tips didn't have anything to do with submissions.

NOT ALL ADVICE THAT COMES from editors and agents is worth taking; some advice is intended to cut or wound. I received a condescending rejection for my new novel while working on final edits for this book. It read, in part: "We do tend to keep the bar higher for fiction occurring in a historical way, maybe because a faraway time or faraway place adds something inscrutable to the novel's dimensions. Few authors ever try to offset this by being more intentionally scrutable in other ways."

For me, the phrase *fiction occurring in a historical way* confirms this being an editor's ego trip, making fun of me. It's clear the editor had no intent on offering advice. He just wanted to hurt me. Maybe because my press is bigger than his? Maybe because I rejected his novel and he's held a grudge? Or maybe, as a male editor, he believes a story about a childless spinster woman who isn't looking for male companionship is *inscrutable*? I can imagine him smirking at his own word usage here, his cleverness. He probably spent the rest of the day feeling good about his intellect.

If you find yourself earning a dig like this, shrug it off. Share it with friends who will roll their eyes and tell you that the editor is on a power trip.

For feedback that actually means well, and intends to support your work, you have to measure your view of the manuscript against what the professionals have to say. I'm not the only author who has broken a book by bending it toward other people's preferences.

I asked journalist Lori Tobias, author of the novel *Wander* (Red Hen), about researching and revising her second book, a memoir, *Storm Beat*, which came out in 2020 from Oregon State Press. Before she started writing, she went through all her reporters' notebooks, former articles, and computer notes to gather information. She cross-checked the material during revisions, "making sure I hadn't edited in errors or moved something out of order," she said. "It was tedious, but there really was no other way. I don't know that I'd do anything differently."

What would she have done differently, though? "Trust my instincts," Lori said.

> *Storm Beat* is not merely a record of the big stories I covered, but what was going on in my life at the time, and how personal events impacted my work and vice versa. One of the stories I included was the loss of my beloved dog from uncontrollable seizures. It utterly gutted me, but it was an important part of my life, especially as I was also generally writing about tragedies and the toll on my psyche was great. I'd sent the manuscript out to a university press (not OSU) and when it came back, one of the student editors had made comments trivializing the loss of my dog compared to what others suffered in human loss. Of course, I was making no such comparison, merely sharing a loss and attempting to make clear that journalists suffer loss like anyone else, but when that loss is coupled with tragedy on the job, the burden can be overwhelming. In any case, I cut the story. And I regret it. The lesson learned, trust your gut and remember that just because someone is an editor, it doesn't mean they are right.

IF YOU GET AN R&R, it may feel like a ticking clock, but unless you are given a timeline (like for a political project that will be outdated if you take too long), you should sit with the advice for a while before deciding which parts to take.

When I offer one, I want at least a few months of work to go by before I see it again, but I've also had authors take a year or two or three before they come back. When a piece comes back fairly quickly, it usually has been revised on a cosmetic level more than on the deeper, foundational level that I had hoped to see.

The revised manuscript doesn't have to be *perfect;* it just has to be closer to what the requester would like to see. If you don't go deep enough, which generally happens when a project comes back "fully revised" after only a handful of weeks, that's a reason to pass.

Writing takes a long time. Good writing especially.

WHEN CRAFT GETS IN THE WAY

SOMETIMES, AS WE MAKE LISTS and notes on who and how to query, we forget that the process can be distilled into one question:

> Is my project
> something that
> this particular person will want
> to put into the world?

There are several variables at work here, including the tastes and schedule of the editor or agent receiving the query. In asking a professional to consider taking you on as a client or as an author, their response will have a lot to do with what they like to read, what they think they can sell, whether your manuscript matches these variables, and whether the draft is in good shape.

If we could simplify publishing into a multiple-choice exam, the possible answers might be:

Yes
No
Maybe but . . .
Unclear

Yes and *no* are obvious.

Maybe but speaks to problems of craft. You might have a pitch, a proposal, or an idea that sparks interest, but there's something off. The query might not show a clear enough story arc. The first pages might be flat or flawed. Your dialogue might feel stilted.

In other words, the reader might really like the concept, but something is wrong in the execution of that concept. Or your craft decisions fall so far outside the usual, the reader isn't sure what to make of them.

Maybe but can also happen when a book is way too short or way too long for our preferred word count. Sometimes we read pages anyway, but other times we use the length as a reason to weed it out. In recent years I've been more inclined to consider manuscripts in the 40,000-word range because they can be produced much less expensively than longer novels, and because novella-length works have been having a heyday. Especially when I'm working on a book that's at the top of our range, 100,000 words or even more, a lower count looks pretty attractive.

Unclear generally needs more pages read, more thinking done. This "um, I have no idea" category is usually reserved for those submissions that take chances or fall slightly outside the boundaries of our intent, or rather push us to imagine those boundaries a bit further out than we intended. Sometimes these get dropped quickly, but other times they soar to the top of the pile because we love strange and unexpected manuscripts.

We don't actually use these categories internally; when we

are using the Submittable platform, working as a team to decide which manuscripts to move forward and which to let go, we flag submissions as *total contender* or *personal rejection* and a series of other labels we've found helpful. We use the platform's thumbs-up, thumbs-down, and thumb-in-the-middle buttons as a way to communicate our preferences with each other.

But as an author, imagining a response falling into one of these four categories can help you take the answer less personally and examine your results in a more mathematical way.

I'd say that most or even all of Forest Avenue's yeses—the sifting of submissions by our reading committee—start out in the *maybe but* category and occasionally in the *unclear* category.

If the plot holds together, this could be the one.

If we like this one more than the others in the top ten.

If the characters show real growth.

If we understand this book's audience and know how to reach those readers.

CASE STUDY #13: Neil Cochrane's *The Story of the Hundred Promises*

ONE OF THE INITIALLY UNCLEAR submissions we received—and I'm calling it that now, looking back—turned into a book that was named a *Washington Post* Best Book of 2022: *The Story of the Hundred Promises.*

Neil Cochrane submitted a fantasy novel, which is a step beyond the literary-with-fabulist-components projects we had published at the time. I saw Neil's name in the submissions queue and immediately flagged it for other readers, since I knew him from his time at Another Read Through, a local bookstore. I leave first-read responses for people who don't know the author (if at all possible).

Neil's manuscript stayed in the running as we weeded other books out, in part because we had no idea what to do with it and in part because the original title didn't really speak to me. But at the same time I was completely intrigued by Neil's decision to create a loosely reimagined "Beauty and the Beast" with a trans protagonist and featuring lots of queer representation. Those things made his book feel awesome and like it could be a great fit with our existing catalog.

One of our readers finished the full manuscript before me and put it at the top of her list. She made a great report and cited multiple reasons that Neil's book could be a great Forest Avenue title. I reprioritized to finish it right away—not because I knew the author but because an objective reader made a great case for the project. Sure enough, the writing was incredible. The world-building felt so satisfying and—I didn't have the word for it then—deliciously cozy. I hadn't read Becky Chambers's Monk and Robot books at that time, but I knew as I read deeper into the manuscript that surely there was a market for a warm, generous, epic fantasy, with a quest and low-lit taverns and magical forests, but also with characters who had formal language and tattoos to announce their pronouns, identities, and choice of partners.

Later, after we acquired the novel and got into promotion and publicity, Neil told me he writes all his books from a perspective of queer optimism. Again, I didn't have the language for it at the time, but *that* perspective is part of why we fell in love with *The Story of the Hundred Promises*.

I asked Neil to tell me more about his process. He said:

> To me, speculative fiction is a playground of alternatives—a space ready-made for thought experiments, for radical what-ifs, where questions and ideas can be pursued to their logical ends. That's why the best of science fiction and fantasy has pushed hard at our ideas of society and human nature; and why I, growing up in traditional small towns and chafing at the sameness of it all, was drawn to it from an early age. It was only natural that when I began to write fiction myself, it was fantasy through which I tried to make sense of my inner world.
>
> Writing from a place of queer optimism (i.e., imagining positive alternatives to binary and cissexist systems) can take many forms. In *The Story of the Hundred Promises*, one of my major questions, as a newly out trans-masculine person, was what it would look and feel like to embody a masculinity not dependent on power over others. In various other works, I have considered what would change in a society that did not couple gender and reproduction—how would the physical mechanics of reproduction be discussed? If gender as a set of social categories even existed, how would it be described?

Neil added that speculative fiction is a place where innovation and collaboration can come together. "Such fiction is, in a meaningful way, a collaborative effort of future-building by way of introducing possibilities to wide audiences and playing out the results. My commitment to queer optimism is a contribution to the effort to reframe our societal understandings of identity, relationship, and community, in the hope of achieving change in our real lives."

In Neil's case the fabric of what he wrote and the intent behind it matched the kind of storytelling Forest Avenue wants to put into the world, even though the genre was more of an outlier. I couldn't have predicted that would be our book, but it seemed obvious once I got into reading it. While there are dramatic and difficult moments in the novel, there are also so many moments of kindness and courtesy. It's hopeful. I had no doubt by the time I read the final section of the novel that I wanted to make an offer, and I'm so glad Neil accepted.

THE NO-RESPONSE NO

AREN'T WE DONE TALKING ABOUT rejections yet? Almost. Sometimes you, as the writer, have to decide a submission is no longer active; many agents and some small presses leave the door open for author interpretation. They say hearing nothing is the same as a rejection. But when do you decide there's no hope? It's so much easier to keep hoping.

As an author, I hate not knowing. The uncertainty of hearing nothing. It's easy to obsess over a long wait period.

Maybe good news is coming!

Have they read it yet? Are they deciding?

Maybe they need to get the next issue (or novel) to press and then I'll hear.

If the agent or editor doesn't expressly say, "Do not contact us to follow up," you can send a gently worded nudge. Maybe your manuscript got caught in a spam filter or never made it into the active reading stack. It helps if you nudge with a cheery tone and with a piece of new information—like you just had an essay published in a journal, or you were accepted to a residency program. If you don't have any updates, just ask quickly and politely. And don't be surprised if you get no response to your query. Agents and editors are so busy that this lack of answer has come to stand in for no.

Depending on the guidelines, you may be able to pinpoint when that possibility window closes. Some submissions instructions offer timelines. *If you don't hear from us in three months, consider it a no.* But if there's no instruction like that, then you should set your own timeline to circle back and cross it off your list. That could be a month later, three months later, six months later. Even a year later.

What's the worst that happens if you cross off a submission too soon? You get a positive response when you're not expecting one, and then you can celebrate that!

Marking a submission complete in your note-taking system helps to offer closure that a no-response no doesn't give. Here are a few other suggestions of ways you can create some closure that feels good:

Perform a ritual or ceremony

Light a candle or hold a solo dance party. Bake cookies. Anything that gets you engaged in the world, using your senses, and feeling good about yourself. You might also say aloud a phrase that feels right. *My work matters*, perhaps, or, *I am a writer and rejections are part of the business.*

Give yourself a small gift

You are doing the hard work of getting your work into the world, and there's no reason you can't celebrate a no-response no. Bonus points if your gift makes writing more fun (a cat pen) or comfortable (fuzzy socks) or fast (caffeine).

Make art with everyday objects

Cut a piece of paper into a snowflake. Doodle a poodle. The point is to create something that isn't commercial, salable, or even Instagrammable. Don't think too hard, don't try to achieve specific results, just play. For you.

Or my go-to: submit to another venue

Boom! You're replacing the submission that's no longer active with a new, exciting possibility. You're looking forward and keeping hope on the table.

CALLING IT

THIS IS THE HARDEST STAGE for me.

Deciding when to let a full-length manuscript go.

To stop fiddling with individual sentences.

To stop revising big swaths. To stop sending it out.

To say *enough.*

At a certain point, to acknowledge *the industry has spoken.*

IF I HADN'T LET GO of my first two novels, with all kinds of hand-wringing and tears and negative self-talk, I wouldn't have matured into the writer I am now.

I MEAN, OKAY, IT WOULD have been great to have those books in the world too. Authors grow into their styles, and I maybe would have grown into the writer I am now even if I had a bit of success along the way.

So often, though, we get marooned trying to *fix* something we believe in, and instead of moving on to the next project, we just keep circling. And circling. And sometimes this pays off in a deal—we unlock that special combination of a new opening sequence, perhaps, or an even better query letter. Other times, though, we become increasingly skittish or despondent. We stop writing for joy. We stop imagining the door, letting ourselves play and wonder on the page. Because we're too focused on the existing work. The structure of it. The story we have told.

If Rosanne Parry and her agent had given up after querying forty-two US editors, *A Wolf Called Wander* might have disappeared. Instead, they kept going and Rosanne got her first *New York Times* best-selling book, which kicked off a series of animal-centric middle grade novels. Go Rosanne!

If you've landed here, in this hopeless place, or a place of bemoaning the industry, there are a few things you can do.

You can find another avenue for publishing. Maybe what you chose—what you thought you wanted at the beginning of the process—isn't right for you at this time in your career.

Give up on agents? Try small presses.

Give up on small presses? Try hybrid or do it yourself.

Give up on self-publishing? Look for an agent.

Try an agent or publisher in another country.

Try someone you haven't put on any of your lists before.

Try printing your whole manuscript out and pulling chapters out at random to revise.

This is not the end of the road for your project. There's no way to know if it's just another mountain to climb or just a small speed bump. It's okay to feel bad, though. Maybe as you're wallowing, turn off social media for a while so you don't see other writers trying to look special and important, because chances are that'll sting.

If you feel up to it, write something new. It can be a different genre—it can be short-form work—it can be anything. A new project, even if it's for yourself and especially if it's not a noodle you intend to throw against the wall of publishing (*is it done?*). Writing for a noncommercial, nonpublication reason can get you feeling great again.

Or maybe writing isn't possible right now. Pick another creative pursuit that will delight you. Try watercolors. Cook a new recipe. Learn to crochet. This is a way to tend your artist heart through the grief of moving on from your beloved manuscript.

You can take a pause in submitting and restart at any time. Or you can move on fully to a new project and circle back months or years later. There are all kinds of examples of authors who put away their earliest work, write new books, learn new ways of storytelling, and then when they come back to those initial manuscripts, they know how to fix them. That distance—time, experience reading others' work, and crafting a new narrative—helps them (us) see what's wrong. I know now how to fix my journalism novel. My protagonist Megan is autistic, undiagnosed but constantly seeking cues and clues from her roommates on how to behave in different social situations. It wouldn't take much to put that on the page—whether she's diagnosed during the story or if I just let the reader in on her neurodivergence, which is already splashed around everywhere. I didn't know *why* she was different or how to explain it to an audience before, and now I do.

Will I go back? I don't feel the energy there anymore. But

maybe someday. There are scenes in that book that I still love.

Right now, though, my energy is all forward momentum. All I want is to write more books. I've spent decades working on projects that didn't sell. They still exist in my brain—not all the twists and turns of the plots but the craft lessons, the wrong turns and rewrites, and the insights about my characters and myself. I can pour all of that into whatever comes next.

Besides, it's pretty great to have spent all these hours writing instead of watching media. Making instead of consuming. I wouldn't trade those hours or wish them away.

Sometimes we get so wrapped up in the product, the *results,* that we forget to value the journey.

ACCEPTED!

I WISH THIS FOR YOU. In fact, I wish it right away! Especially if this book has helped you decide who and how to query and what your goal is for your writing.

Apply to get an MFA? Accepted.

Send a story to the *New Yorker*? Accepted.

How about an essay to the *Sun*? Accepted.

Your debut novel? Accepted! Huzzah!

A memoir? Accepted! Go you!

There's no reason to wish for anything other than a happily-ever-after publishing journey, but the truth is we can only do the best work we can and then be brave and send it out. And we can cheer for each other in community. There are so many amazing dream publications and presses that seem nearly impossible to crack, and yet it does happen. If you keep writing and believing in yourself, and then you start submitting your work, you're on the path to . . . well, who knows? We can only open the door and start the journey and see where it leads. Publishing is a business, and like I've said, there are a million things we can't control.

When you get a full-length manuscript accepted, it's time to start celebrating all over again. Read and make sure you understand the contract; ask the Authors Guild for help if you don't have an agent. Sign the contract: woo-hoo! Finish your first editorial pass: time for cupcakes! Find some other writers whose books are coming out in the same season: friends! Have a first meeting with your publicist: yes! Wait for advance reader copies to roll out: here we go! Read your first review: uh-oh.

It's all good stuff, even your first bad review, because this process is about reaching people with your words. The passage of your work from a query into a finished object is as terrifying as submitting your work, only this time you don't get to control who sees it, who reads it, who *judges* it. After all, you want people to read your book, right? Not everyone is going to like it, and that comes with the territory of making a piece of art public. Of handing it to the world and saying, *Here.* And the sales numbers! And *bad* reviews! What about *no* reviews? That can feel worse.

It's a whole other journey, one that's explored in many blogs, websites, and books, but you can use a lot of the same techniques in handling the emotions of it.

Be clear with yourself.

Communicate with your agent and/or editor in a professional and timely manner.

Complain to your trusted friends, who can offer perspective and help you ride out any prepublication bumps.

When in doubt, center yourself on why you wrote this book and why it deserves to be in the world; who is going to be helped, entertained, or healed by your words; and the fact that you are accomplishing your wish. You are getting published!

All the dips and bumps, the speed zones and yellow lights, the stop signs that feel like they're everywhere in the first months (all that waiting), and even the fast, flashy drivers who speed by you—they're part of the journey, but they can't touch your purpose or erode your accomplishment.

A book! It's happening! You imagined the door and then found your way through it, unlocking your own success. What's on the other side might not be what you *thought* you were traveling toward, especially when you first started out, but that's the case with any creative journey.

Before I found my first publisher, I read all the books about the publishing journey, feeling left behind, unable to get to that first step. I felt so frustrated and left out because I wasn't *there* yet as a writer. I learned all I could, gobbling up details so I'd know for when my lucky day came, but then I'd open my laptop and find another rejection in my inbox.

This part, the first part of the journey, matters too. And I wanted this book to honor that part in all its messy hopefulness. Maybe I'll write a sequel to this book for those of us who step over the transom, from unpublished to about to be published. A guide to that liminal time between acceptance and having your book in the world. There's so much more to share.

But this is a liminal time, too, where you're believing in yourself enough to ask others to believe in you, to take a chance on you. To say yes.

It's a big deal to write a book and start querying. I hope you can hold that in your heart and appreciate how far you've come.

BEGIN AGAIN

WHETHER YOU FIND A HOME for your work or not, at some point if you want to write more books, the blank page awaits.

It's really hard to start again after you've poured your heart and hours of your precious time into a piece of work that doesn't find a home. There's a whole path you can take: the self-rejecting path. By not starting something new. By giving up your dream of a writing career. Or a published book. You can walk away. Or you can tiptoe into a new project. A comely phrase, a strange idea, a scent that unlocks a story.

As I've shared, starting *Singing Lessons for the Stylish Canary* as a newly unagented writer felt terrifying—but it also allowed me the freedom to play. I couldn't have written that book if I had tried writing it *for* a particular agent or audience. I wrote and revised a whole new novel before *Singing Lessons* found a home. My agent had other clients turning in manuscripts, plus my manuscript on submission, so I didn't feel pressured by her.

Once *Singing Lessons* came out and I circled back to this writers' mental health project I started in 2016, revision was a different kind of scary, with lots of stops and starts.

Am I allowed to say this?

Am I enough of an expert?

What if people disagree?

What if the Regional Arts and Culture Council, which kindly granted me $5,000, wishes they hadn't bothered?

Even after I had a full draft and received excellent developmental edit notes, helping me see a clear road map for revising, panic still got in the way of my process.

What's taking you so long?

People are waiting for this book!

You're switching genres—is that even okay?

You can't explore mental health; you're not that kind of expert!

Maybe you should work on the novel revision instead.

Or the new, new novel idea you keep thinking about. Because nobody's waiting for it. It's third in line!

I procrastinated revising based on the second developmental edit of the second half of this project for five months. Prioritizing everything *but* finishing. Feeling sure it wasn't good enough. I only finished, finally, because I needed to prepare metadata for my distributor. I had to either find the courage to finish or push the pub date back.

At some point I realized that my reluctance to call this manuscript done might be second-book syndrome. There's so much pressure, especially after your first title is well received (whether that's critically, in terms of sales, or hearing lovely words from friends and strangers), to repeat that effort. I asked Omar El Akkad, author of *American War* and the Giller Prize–winning *What Strange Paradise,* to share his thoughts on second books. He admitted feeling claustrophobic working on his sophomore novel. "For the previous four books (three unpublishable ones, then my first published novel), I had no book deal, no agent, no expectation anyone would read any of it. With that absence of expectation comes a kind of freedom that I've never been able to regain. With my second published novel, I spent so much time worrying about what readers of the first one might think, how I might be doing a disservice to my (admittedly tiny) readership by switching modes and theme and genre."

Aha! I thought when Omar told me this. *Maybe that's why I'm dragging my feet on these revisions. And maybe that's why my new novel is buried in my closet, even though I have great feedback from my agent, and it shouldn't take too long to revise. And maybe that's also why I'm leaning into a newer new book, one that nobody is waiting for.*

People expect things of me now. My career is launched, admittedly in a small way that doesn't put me on the commercial author map. Still, there are stakes. There's pressure. Omar continued:

> In hindsight, all that worrying was worse than useless—I wish I'd spent all that mental horsepower on the work instead. In my limited experience, there's really nothing as daunting as a blank page, which makes the beginning of every project an anxiety nightmare, sometimes so much so that it's oddly comforting to worry about something as concrete as whether the next story will live up to the last one. But it never helps. I try now not to think about the future or the past work, only the new world that can be dreamed into existence on that blank page, which in the end is the reason we write in the first place.

AT ROLLER DERBY PRACTICE ONE day, a younger sibling of one of my daughter's teammates saw me with my notebook out.

"What are you working on?" the girl asked me.

We hadn't ever had a conversation. I didn't know her name. How did she know I was *working* on something? I had woken up early that morning thinking about new material for *Imagine a Door*. So I told her: "I'm writing a book about how to publish a book. Would you like to see how far I've gotten today?"

She nodded yes.

I showed her a blank page in my spiral notebook. "This is how far."

She proceeded to tell me I should write down my title in bubble letters: HOW TO PUBLISH A BOOK. That could be the cover. Then I should turn the page and make a numbered, bulleted list about the steps it would take. We spent more than an hour writing together, taking turns with the pen, her adding some words and illustrations and dictating what I should write at other times. When scrimmage finished, I had three handwritten pages, including some charming sentences about using cardboard, felt, glue, and scissors to publish your book.

I had gotten so wrapped up in the worries that I had forgotten how to make any sort of progress.

All it takes is paper.

All it takes is a pencil or a pen and cardboard and felt and a sharp pair of scissors.

All it takes is time and imagination.

There are all kinds of ways to publish, to get your work into the world.

We were both so pleased with our efforts by the end of the scrimmage. I wanted her to keep our work, but she insisted I keep it. She also told me to go home and work on it more before we saw each other again next week. She could tell I needed the support.

And there I was, the very next morning, rearranging chapters and adding new content. Believing, like I always do when I'm working on a book, that I have something worth exploring.

IT FEELS LIKE THERE'S A huge gulf between the two paths for a manuscript:

You get your book published.

You *don't* get your book published.

But really, they lead you to the same place: starting over. Whether your book finds a home and readers or whether you give up, the best next thing is to find a new project.

To imagine a door.

To consider which stories are waiting to be told.

Which ones are yours for the telling.

What creatures and characters and emotions you might conjure with your imagination.

Where your brain might pull you.

There's always more to learn, no matter how many books, stories, plays, poems, or essays you've finished. Every project makes writing fresh and new. Sometimes that feels terribly daunting. But it's also pretty great. To start again. To slough off the rejections and the one-star reviews and that guy who compared your work to cheesecake, saying a few bites are delicious but a whole book of cheesecake sentences would make him sick. (I don't remember his name, just that one remark. Here, I place it on the page so I can let it go.)

There's so much room for wonder when you can let go of the last project and where it landed and all the feelings that erupted during that process.

One of my favorite writers, Joanna Rose, has been a mentor to me as a teacher at the Pinewood Table and as a Forest Avenue author. I learned so much from editing *A Small Crowd of Strangers*, which came out in 2020 from my press; in 1997, her debut novel, *Little Miss Strange*, was published by Algonquin.

Joanna has never been content to write one kind of work.

Or teach one particular topic. She's constantly exploring in her practice. Expanding her craft. I love how her curiosity propels her creativity. Not the commercial market. Not others' expectations. Her own wonder fuels her work. I asked Joanna about what keeps her going. She said:

> High school writers are my great source of inspiration and courage. I've had the privilege of working in youth language arts settings for over twenty-five years, and they never fail me.
>
> Young writers have an affinity for story (even when they claim to hate writing!). They tend to use language in surprising ways that leave me feeling in the presence of pure poetry with their tenderly awkward syntax, and their misuse of grammar and strange new words.
>
> They always write about what is important, often not realizing how revealing they are being. I want to be that angry, that in love, that sure of my right to speak.
>
> Once I passed out a list of about fifty words and told the students to write a sentence using a few of the words. This sentence happened that day: *The children found a top hat in the thicket*. The writer later asked me what a thicket is.
>
> That sentence stays in my head, sometimes appearing like a song refrain that refuses to go away.
>
> It's a mantra for me.
>
> Writing is hard. Publication is distracting. Bad reviews are forever. In my low periods I try to remember to search for top hats in thickets.

Wherever your journey as a writer is taking you, I wish you creative courage.

I wish you luck.

I wish you top hats in thickets.

ACKNOWLEDGMENTS

I’M GRATEFUL TO ALL THE authors, publishers, editors, and agents who took the time to answer my interview questions from 2012 to 2024. Their wisdom and insights add so much to these pages. I felt a great responsibility to create a narrative that would hold and honor your words. Any mistakes are mine.

In 2023 the Regional Arts and Culture Council gave me a $5,000 grant to support the editing and printing of this project; that external approval lit a fire under me. Thank you, RACC.

Liz Prato, so much of this book has developed in conversation with you over the years—about publishing, about redefining success, and about genuine community. If *Imagine a Door* were a dining room table where all writers are welcome, you’d be the chandelier: blazing, bright, beautiful, and true. Thanks for being my developmental editor on this project, Forest Avenue’s editor at large, a guidepost on my disability journey, and my friend.

Suzy Vitello, your edits and guidance continue to be a shining beacon for me. I couldn’t have pulled this project into publishable form or found the courage to get it out there without your firm editorial hand and huge heart.

To the writers who endorsed this project—Christina Vega, Joe Biel, and Judy Reeves—thank you.

For my childhood essay on Chopin, I used two biographies—*Chopin* by Henry Coates (1939) and *The Life and Death of Chopin* by Casimir Wierzynski (1949). I am grateful to my teachers at Montclair Kimberley Academy who taught me to document sources and to my parents for keeping obscure Chopin tomes on those low shelves in the den, so I could reach them and wonder.

Gigi Little, thank you for wrapping my thoughts in lovely blue and handing them a bouquet of wildflowers.

Gina Walter, for your copyediting and your sharp eye.

Alyssa Graybeal, for your deep care and attention in indexing this beast of a project. Thank you.

Beth Kephart, I wish I knew you then, but I am glad we have each other now. Thank you for your beautiful foreword and for inspiring me with your art, in all its forms, and your passionate curiosity.

Edee Lemonier and Desiree Wright, years ago we talked about an early iteration of this project over endless cups of diner coffee. You encouraged me to try.

To Nancy Townsley and Dian Greenwood, your debut novel journeys helped me understand what I wanted to share with other writers.

To the inaugural DIY Book Publicity group, thanks for believing in me and joining this experiment! I'm excited to see how we grow.

Lillian Feldman, your hilarious storytelling and your questions about craft helped me tap into my playfulness and love of writing while I was revising this book. Your short story collection, published with staples in a limited-run edition, is one of my all-time favorite story collections.

To Joanna Rose and Stevan Allred, for being my teachers.

Nikole Potulsky, always.

Thank you so much to my once-upon-a-time agent, Laurie Fox, for believing in me and for agreeing that this particular project ought to be a Forest Avenue title.

Forest Avenue editors, reading committee, and advisors, you have steered me and raised my spirits countless times.

My authors: I love you all. Getting to edit, art direct, and promote your work challenged and changed me. It's been a huge gift to get to publish your incredibly powerful words.

And I miss you, Ramiza Shamoun Koya and Robert Hill. I'll always search for you in townhouse windows and on the way to birthday tea.

ABOUT THE AUTHOR

LAURA STANFILL IS THE AUTHOR of *Singing Lessons for the Stylish Canary,* an editor and publishing consultant, and the publisher of Forest Avenue Press, which she founded in 2012. She graduated from the Yale Publishing Course and Vassar College. When she's not perusing bookstore shelves in Portland, Oregon, you can find her wearing a sparkly top hat while walking her dog.

YOUR TURN

CONGRATULATIONS! YOU MADE IT TO the end of *Imagine a Door.* On the following pages, you'll find a series of prompts and space to respond to them.

List a few writing-related milestones you can choose to celebrate. Think meeting a deadline, submitting, earning a rejection. What else might you celebrate?

What are some ways you can celebrate writing-related milestones? Try to come up with ideas that are free, ideas that cost $10 or less, and some big-dream ones.

Use this page for a pro/con list of your choice.

Trying to decide if you want to attend a literary conference? Figuring out whether to join a writing group? What about hiring a publicist to help with your debut? A good pro / con list can help make the decision clearer.

PROS	**CONS**

There are always new books on writing and publishing, each one adding to the conversation. Here are several I like to recommend:

Before and After the Book Deal by Courtney Maum
The People's Guide to Publishing by Joe Biel
Handling the Truth by Beth Kephart
The Business of Being a Writer by Jane Friedman

Add your favorite writing books, suggestions writer friends have shared with you, and books you haven't read yet but hope to someday.

Go ahead and imagine a door. What's behind it? Or *who* is behind it? In your response, please use scents, time of day, and at least one zany metaphor or simile. If you get stuck, consider the motivation of the person (or creature) hoping to be let inside.

You're welcome to write or draw your answer!

Use this page as you wish. Grocery list? Ideas of presses you might submit to? Words you've always loved that you haven't (yet) added to your current project? Wishes you want to manifest in the next eighteen months? Go for it!

Index

Note: Definitions are indicated by page numbers in **bold**.

G